The State, the Family and Education

Miriam E. David

Lecturer in Social Administration
University of Bristol

Routledge & Kegan Paul
London, Boston and Henley

206886
LC 71

For my father, whose untimely death deprived me of the chance to argue about patriarchy with him

First published in 1980
by Routledge & Kegan Paul Ltd
39 Store Street, London WC1E 7DD,
9 Park Street, Boston, Mass. 02108, USA and
Broadway House, Newtown Road,
Henley-on-Thames, Oxon RG9 1EN
Set in IBM Press Roman 10 pt
by Columns of Reading
and printed in Great Britain by
Billing & Sons Limited
Guildford, London and Worcester
© Miriam E. David 1980

No part of this book may be reproduced in any form without permission from the publisher, except for the quotation of brief passages in criticism

British Library Cataloguing in Publication Data

David, Miriam E

The state, the family and education.
– (Radical social policy)
1. Teacher-student relationships – Great Britain
2. Parent and child – Great Britain
I. Title II. Series
371.1'02 LB1033 80-40713

ISBN 0 7100 0601 2

Contents

Acknowledgments

This book is about the relationships between the family and education. It focuses upon the way the State, through educational policies, has regulated both parental (or rather paternal and maternal) relations with children in school and familial relations within school, that is, the role of the teacher *in loco parentis* and the way the curriculum teaches about parenting in adulthood. The origins of this concern are both academic and political. Specifically, the book is based upon a series of lectures that I have been giving since 1974 in the Department of Social Administration at the University of Bristol, to both undergraduates and postgraduates, within an optional course on The Family and Social Policy. The course itself arose out of my research interests in the politics of education and my involvement in the Women's Movement. I became concerned to understand women's position in education. The theoretical tendency which was prevalent at that time was that to understand women's position in capitalism one had to grasp women's position in the family. To analyse this latter, it was useful and instructive to look at how the State operated with respect to the family. In its early years, the course – which was taught jointly with two other feminists, Hilary Land and Jackie West – was an attempt to develop a theoretical perspective on the family and its regulation under capitalism. Over the years, it has become less theoretical and more oriented to elucidating the precise ways in which the State orders family relationships within a number of social policies. The course has changed partly as a result of my students' interests. I owe them all a great debt of gratitude. It has also altered because of the changes in those who have been involved in teaching.

Latterly, Linda Ward, Noelle Whiteside and David Bull have been my colleagues.

My involvement in teaching women's studies has also affected the focus of my interests. My main mentors here have been the Bristol Women's Studies Group and the British Sociological Association's women's caucus. For all their support and stimulation, I would particularly like to thank Sandy Acker, Liz Bird, Mary Fuller, Hilary Land, Ellen Malos, Marilyn Porter, Helen Taylor, Linda Ward, Helen Weinreich-Haste and Jackie West. I would also like to thank the students who have attended these courses and provided invaluable ideas. I have been helped by other feminists, through my involvement in other women's groups. An Anglo-French seminar, organized initially by Diana Leonard Barker and Christine Delphy, was useful for its critical appraisal of my early ideas. Jenny Shaw has been a kind, supportive colleague and fellow researcher throughout. Caroline Freeman has been a constant sympathetic ear.

My colleagues in the Department of Social Administration – Roy Parker, David Bull, Paddy Hillyard, Ken Judge, Noelle Whiteside and Mike Winwood – have also been invaluable and unfailing in their stimulating criticism. Tessa Blackstone gave useful comments on parts of the manuscript. Kieran Flanagan provided help with literature on the history of education. Sonia Jackson discussed day-care with me. Fred Inglis and Theo Nichols initially made useful and supportive comments.

There are many others who have provided sympathy and who have suffered through the tortuous writing of the book. I owe special thanks to my husband, Robert Reiner, and to Netta Salmon, who bore the burden of looking after my son Toby when the book was in its final stages of completion.* The editor of the series, Vic George, has been a constant support and excellent critic. Finally, I must thank Kathleen Brookes for her tireless typing of my seemingly endless drafts of manuscript. The book, nevertheless, is not a finished product but should be seen as a contribution to the continuing debate on the nature of the family and schooling in late capitalism, and, in particular, the part that women should and can play in transforming the links between the State and schooling.

* In fact the process of publication was more protracted than I anticipated. I also must thank Judith Pliatzky for caring for Toby and my new baby, Charlotte. Both Judith and Charlotte gave me inspiration to continue when my spirits were low: Judith being a former student and Charlotte my hope for feminist educational reform.

1

The family–education couple

What schools should do for boys and girls, how teachers should be controlled and what parents should do for their schoolchildren are all major items on the contemporary political agenda in England. But political rhetoric is not based upon sound scholarship: there is, in fact, very little evidence about the relations between families and schools and the ways in which the State orders these relations. Studies of how schools work and of how families work abound. Descriptions of State policies, especially educational policies, are legion. But the links have not been made between the State, the family and education. This book examines these relationships and looks at how the State has developed parental, and especially maternal, responsibilities for schoolchildren, teachers' duties for schooling, and curricula for boys and girls, both together and separately. The reasons that have been advanced for schooling, its relations with the family and its familial ambiance are also explored. My central argument is that the family and the education system are used in concert to sustain and reproduce the social and economic *status quo*. Specifically, they maintain existing relations within the family and social relations within the economy – what has sometimes been called the sexual and social division of labour. The argument about the role of education within the economy of advanced capitalist societies is not at all new. Indeed, there is a growing body of literature that presents concrete analyses of the contribution of education in a variety of spheres. But the 'family-education couple'* has rarely been seen as an important system in

* Althusser (1971) coined this phrase. In a seminal article he argued that the

the way it is used by the State.

There are many dimensions to the 'family-education couple'. The first one explored here is the growth and specification of parental responsibilities, and latterly rights, in the education system and how these connect with the development of compulsory mass education. Indeed, the origins of universal working-class education were seen as 'a revolutionary invasion of parental rights'. To what extent this has been the case is examined, together with a study of the sexual division of parental rights and duties. The ideologies about what schools are for are also investigated. The second dimension explored is how schools and teachers are expected to put into practice both the political aims of education and their legal responsibility to act *in loco parentis.* This has come to mean that teachers should not only replace parents but be *like* parents. Just over 100 years ago, an advertisement for a private school for girls claimed that: 'The arrangements of the school are as much as possible like those of a private family and homelike habits and ways are carefully maintained.' It has been argued, too, that schoolmistresses had to have the attributes of motherliness and that the authority of schoolmasters derives from paternalism. On the other hand, mothers were deliberately excluded from the teaching profession until recently and women teachers were not afforded equal pay or status with men. Yet the school curriculum has, for the past 100 years, required in varying degrees that girls be taught the attributes of wifehood and motherhood. These contradictions, and their political rationales, are a major theme of the book.

These themes are illustrated through historical and documentary evidence for England, as an example of a capitalist society. A specific theoretical framework informs the choice of evidence and example. I have drawn upon two 'schools of thought' which are now frequently used to analyse State policies and to explain the relation of the family to the economy. The first is a Marxist framework, which provides an analysis of the role of the State in capitalist societies and of the role of education in particular. This analysis regards the State as vital because it is the source of control

*(cont.) 'family-education couple' had replaced the 'family-church couple' as the dominant ideological apparatus in advanced capitalist societies. His analysis provided an important development in Marxist thinking on the role of the State. He argued that the State was composed of both repressive and ideological apparatuses (ISAs). He also specified a research programme which has provided the impetus for this study – that the workings of ISAs 'must be studied in detail if we are to go further than this mere observation'. I have not, however, stuck rigidly to his schema and hold a narrower, more specific view of the State.

in capitalism and because, in order to effect fundamental changes in the capitalist system, State power must be seized and transformed. The nature of the State, however, is a controversial point in contemporary Marxist analysis. Some see it as central government, the judiciary and the army – the political institutions that supposedly guarantee an equal citizenry but, in fact, often function repressively (Miliband, 1973; Thompson, 1978a and b). Others regard the State as composed of several apparatuses that guarantee ruling-class hegemony through both repressive and ideological modes of operation (Althusser, 1971; Poulantzas, 1975). In this latter schema, education is part of the State and can be considered an ideological state apparatus. Most contemporary Marxist studies of education adopt the first approach, although concerned to explicate the ideologies both of and in education (Young and Whitty, 1977; Finn *et al.*, 1977). Education here reproduces capitalist social relations and contributes to economic needs. It helps to guarantee capital accumulation, which is essential to the maintenance of the capitalist system. In this present study, education is seen not as part of the system of production but as part of the activities that are essential for the reproduction of the conditions of capitalism. The State is primarily viewed as central government in Britain, but from the perspective of investigating the ideological assumptions with which it operates in relation to education and the family.

The other school of thought which has influenced this study also has a Marxist framework. It is part of the current attempt to understand the position, and oppression, of women in capitalism. This interest stems partly from the recent wave of feminism and the growth of the modern Women's Movement, which have resulted not only in political activity but also in the exploration of women as a subject of study. One strand of theory suggests that the main emphasis should be the discovery of female achievements (Firestone, 1972); another, the understanding of the relationships between the sexes and the explanations for female inequality (Allen *et al.*, 1974). In this latter field, feminists have tried to locate the analysis of female disadvantages in capitalism to the sexual division of labour and particularly to the position of women within the family (McIntosh, 1978). It is this theoretical perspective which informs my study. Most of this feminist theory, though, is concerned to understand the contributions that women make to the maintenance of the capitalist system through their unpaid work within the home or their disadvantaged, but paid, work within the labour force (Gardiner, 1974 and 1975; Beechey, 1977). The interest in domestic labour, in particular, focuses on the ways in which women service their husbands and children. It concentrates on the nature of housework, and does not really involve a detailed consideration of the nature of child-rearing, or its corollary, mothering, although this is taken almost as given. As far as I know, there is only one feminist study, by Chodorow (1978), that begins to explore what it means to be a mother in a contemporary society (in her case the USA) and the implications that mothering has for child-rearing. Her study is informed by a psychoanalytic perspective and attempts to extend that theory to mothering within a Marxian framework. I am also interested in understanding how parenting, and especially mothering, has developed and been regulated by the State with respect to child-rearing and ultimately the formal education system. I, too, will explore the 'reproduction of mothering' (as Chodorow's book is entitled) but by investigating the State's interest in this question, rather than the social processes that bear upon mothering and child-rearing.*

Indeed, the major focus of this book is the role that the State plays in regulating family activities with respect to children and especially the relationships between men and women as parents, or rather as fathers and mothers. This regulation extends not only to parental activities with regard to their children's schooling but also to the ways in which children, within schools, learn about parenting. This learning does not necessarily occur through explicit curricular teaching but through the implicit processes of schooling and the ways in which education is organized. This has sometimes been referred to as the *form* rather than the content of schooling. The main materials which inform the book are the laws and official reports of successive governments and their explanatory documents. Commentaries on these legal and quasi-legal developments have also been combed to elucidate the assumptions that governments have worked with in regulating the 'family-education couple'. In fact, there are very few sources which adequately deal with the interconnections between the family and education. Perhaps this is because sexual divisions are implicit in both the family and schools and affect how they really work and what they stand for. This study will try to make explicit these fundamental assumptions, but it does not constitute a complete historical survey of educational developments within capitalism.

Research in the area of the family and education traditionally has not concentrated on the mediation of the State. There have been two

*Whilst this study was in the process of publication, another book was published, which looks specifically at the impact of theories of child-rearing on mothering. It, too, relies mainly on American material. It is *For Her Own Good: 150 Years of Expert Advice to Women* by B. Ehrenreich and D. English, London, Pluto Press, 1979. The book does not, however, deal specifically with the State's treatment of mothering or child-rearing.

main approaches. For sociologists of education the concern has been to understand the impact that the family has on the education system and, in particular, on the successes and achievements of children in school. In the last twenty years or so, a vast quantity of research evidence has been amassed, most of which points out that parents are far more influential than schools over their children's educational progress. Class differences have also been found to affect parental interest and its impact on pupil success. It is only the most recent study in Britain, by Rutter *et al.* (1979), that has tipped the balance of evidence in favour of schools' influence rather than pupils' home background. The results of this study have not had time to percolate down into the policy process and be used as a basis for policy prescription about how to improve the school system. Previous researches have been incorporated into the policy process and used as a basis for trying to improve pupil performance and standards of child-rearing. The best contemporary example of this is the way that a committee set up by the government's Central Advisory Council for Education and chaired by Lady Plowden (CACE, 1967) drew its recommendations from research evidence, both already available and specially commissioned. Its own research results suggested the importance of parental attitudes in the success of primary school pupils. The committee proposed that the government should find the means to encourage some parental participation within primary schools. By this it meant that working-class mothers especially should attend their children's schools to help with their work and also, as an indirect effect, learn how to be more effective with mothering.

Secondly, some sociologists of education have analysed rather than prescribed the differential impact that fathers and mothers have within the education system. The two most sophisticated analyses are those by Bourdieu (1973) and Bernstein (1975). Both begin by arguing that the importance of education and its link with the family lies in its contribution to social and cultural reproduction rather than to the possibilities of social change. Bourdieu, whose main fascination is with how the bourgeoisie is reproduced, does not emphasize sexual divisions but assumes their importance. In one, albeit obscure, statement he says (1971a, p. 170):

> The gradual rationalisation of . . . teaching could threaten cultural integration . . . if, so far as the (educated) class is concerned, education and more particularly what is known as general culture were not at least as much a matter for the family as for the school, for the family in the sense of parents and their progeny and also in that of the fields of knowledge (*many scientists are married to*

> *women with an arts background*) and if all types of training did not allot a place, always a fairly important one, to classical liberal education [my emphasis].

In other words, Bourdieu acknowledges the significant role that women, as mothers, play in the cultural reproduction of the educated classes.

Bernstein is much more explicit about the importance of mothers to social reproduction, through education, although his emphasis is on the mechanisms rather than the structure of reproduction. He states (1975, p. 3) that it is 'important to keep together in one analysis the interactions between the family and the school, and to show the variations in this relationship – both within and between social classes.' He then goes on to show that women's role in the family and in the economy has changed and affected the ways in which children are treated in nursery and infant schools. He argues that 'historically . . . the mother is neither important as a transmitter of symbolic or physical property'. She was 'a domestic administrator' and served only as a role model for her daughters. This traditional system generated two models for cultural transmission: the abstracted mother was a model for the nanny-babyminder and the governess for the teacher of elementary competences. Nowadays the mother is 'an agent . . . of cultural reproduction and unable to get away from her children'. This is now the basis of the 'invisible pedagogy' which underlies the form of 'cultural transmission in new infant and nursery schools'.

Feminists working on education have also explored the ways in which the family and sexual divisions have had an impact upon schooling. One theoretical framework has added to the role-model theory that Bernstein used and shown how girls are unequal to boys in schools because they have a lack of role models for certain secondary subjects such as science. (Most women teachers teach the humanities.) In addition, these feminists have explored notions of sex-role stereotyping of school subjects, and shown how girls, for instance, resist the sciences because they are masculine disciplines (Kelly, 1974 and 1976). Other feminists have operated within the traditional sociological framework, exploring components of girls' achievement as opposed to boys' (Blackstone, 1976b; Byrne, 1978; Deem, 1978). They have tried to account for female disadvantage in the economy given the relatively similar rates of success for girls and boys, within the same social class, in the GCE 'O' and 'A' level examinations. External factors, such as parental attitudes and socialization, have been used to explain the inequalities. On the other hand, evidence of lack of opportunities for girls within schooling has also been collected (Jones, 1977). It has been shown, for instance, that girls are subject to some different curricula from boys on the grounds that, as adults, they will have different roles and jobs (Wolpe, 1975). Few feminists, however, have explored in a systematic way the 'familial ambiance' of the school and its impact upon girls' work. Nor have they looked at the opportunities and restrictions placed on women as teachers which affect their possibilities of modifying stereotypes and role models. This study will attempt to fill in that lacuna.

There is now a growing tradition of research with regard to the relations between the State and education. Most of this is what the Americans have dubbed revisionist social history (Katz, 1973) or the political economy of schooling (Bowles and Gintis, 1976). It mainly shows that education has contributed in the past, or continues to contribute, in various ways, to the capitalist economy, but ignores its links with the family. Only Benton (1974) and Finn *et al.* (1977), who analyse, with different Marxian frameworks, the post-war educational developments of British Labour governments, allude to the impact that they may have had on the family and/or the sexual division of labour. Benton (1974, p. 27), applying an Althusserian framework, asserts that 'even more importantly, the education system plays a large role in the inculcation of the relevant skills and subjection to the relevant ideological dispositions of women in preparation for their role in the division of labour within the capitalist family.' The curricula of schools may contribute to girls' preparation for their roles as wives and mothers. Benton (oddly, since he was trying to apply Althusser's theory to British education) does not go further in examining the 'family-education couple' but instead shows how limited Labour governments were in trying to transform the education system for the working class. Finn *et al.* (1977) are also at pains to demonstrate the failure of Labour governments to provide a more egalitarian education system or a transformation through education of the social formation. Although they argue (ibid., p. 195) at the outset that, in order adequately to understand 'ideologies about schools', 'theory must grasp the relations between school and other sites of social relations. The most important of these can be specified: *family*, work and the formal political sphere' [my italics], they barely mention the family. They criticize the last Labour government's Great Debate only because it 'addressed issues which have been developed as *of* concern to parents, but which do not necessitate parental involvement to resolve them'. Here they assume that participatory democracy which includes parental participation in educational decisions would have been more progressive than Labour's emphasis on economic efficiency and a realignment of corporate capitalism. The main interest of Finn and his colleagues is in showing that education has been increasingly tied to the reproduction of a capitalist economy.

Bowles and Gintis's (1976) study of American education is perhaps the most comprehensive in its attempt to show the ways in which education reproduces both the capitalist economy and class relations. Their main argument is that socio-economic reproduction occurs through the 'correspondence principle', that is, the organization of learning mirrors the organization of economic life. They state (1976, p. 12): 'Specifically, the relationships of authority and control between administrators and teachers, teachers and students, and students and their work replicate the hierarchical division of labour which dominates the work-place.' They add (ibid., p. 9): 'The pattern of social relationships fostered in school is hardly irrational or accidental. Rather, the structure of educational experience is admirably suited to nurturing attitudes and behaviour consonant with participation in the labour force.' This analysis of how 'good workers' are reproduced ignores what Benton alluded to – how girls learn the habits of being good wives and mothers. Indeed Bowles and Gintis deny that girls learn this at school. They assert that 'the family's impact on the reproduction of the sexual division of labour, for example, is distinctly greater than that of the education system.' They use the 'correspondence principle' to demonstrate how such reproduction occurs: the family also mirrors the economic system. They then try to justify the growth of education and its necessity as a separate sphere of reproduction from the family. They argue (1976, p. 144) that

> the close personal and emotional relationships of family life are remote from the impersonal bureaucracy of the wage labour system . . . Indeed, it is precisely because family structure and the capitalist relations of production differ in essential respects that our analysis sees schooling as performing such a necessary role in the integration of young people into the wage labour system.

The family inculcates sexual divisions but is an inadequate mirror to the economic system for inculcating the work ethic. Hence a separate sphere has been developed. The main flaw in Bowles and Gintis's analysis is that they do not allow for contradictory developments within education and specifically conflicts between the need for female wage labour and the sexual division of labour in the family. To them the only conflicts that occur in schooling result from the contradictory needs in the productive system for capital accumulation. Nevertheless, their study does advance our understanding of the role of education within capitalist societies. This study will, to some extent, draw upon their thesis that education has been tied to developments in the capitalist economy.

By contrast there is little theoretical understanding of the relationship between the State and the family. There is a vast literature on the history of the family and much controversy about the origins of the family and its sexual division of labour. The major developments on the topic of the State and the family have been made recently by feminists, namely Cockburn (1977), McIntosh (1978) and Wilson (1977), who also work within a Marxist framework. In their different ways they all show how important the family and its particular sexual division of labour is for the maintenance of the existing socio-economic system. Moreover, they demonstrate just how the State uses the family, in a variety of spheres, to reproduce existing divisions and relations. Wilson, for instance, argues (1977, p. 9) that

> the Welfare State is not just a set of services, it is also a set of ideas about society, about the family, and not least important, about women, who have a centrally important role within the family, as its linchpin. To put it in a slightly different way, social policy is simply one aspect of the capitalist State, an acceptable face of capitalism, and social welfare policies amount to no less than the *State organisation of domestic life.*

She goes on to show just how social welfare policies and their ideologies have assumed a particular sexual division of labour in the home and in the economy, using both historical and contemporary examples.

McIntosh, too, in a very closely argued paper (1978) shows how critical the 'family-household' is in capitalism and how it has been used by the State to maintain the social conditions of reproduction and, at the same time, ensure the oppression of women. She recognizes, however, a fundamental problem in her formulation of the analysis, which is that it is functionalist in character. She tries to show how *this* might be overcome by reference either to contradictions in the mode of production or to class struggle as a way of mitigating ruling-class power. Both she claims to be unsatisfactory modifications of the essential functionalism. The former merely shows how 'the accumulation of capital intensifies the contradictions between the social character of production and the private character of appropriation. But this does not really help in making a more politically useful analysis since it still provides no space for welfare politics, or education politics or women's politics within capitalism' (ibid., p. 282). There is also a problem of counterposing 'working-class struggle to ruling-class efforts to satisfy the "needs of capital" . . . For if school dinners or a national health service help keep the working class healthy, they fulfil aspirations of the class as well as merely help to reproduce it' (ibid.). But she adds that 'the value of introducing the idea of class struggle can only be seen in concrete analyses of specific situations.' These problems are likely to be encountered in this book, too. The solution to the functionalist dilemma will be to try to provide evidence of class struggle only in relation to concrete situations.

McIntosh (ibid., p. 283) finally points to further contradictions in this sort of feminist analysis: 'those between the sphere of the family and the sphere of capitalist production.' Specifically, she argues that 'at any given conjuncture there may well be contradiction between the state policies needed for the reproduction of the [working] class and those needed for reproducing the relation of women as a reserve army.' She claims that the problem is created by 'the relative inflexibility of the family . . . as well as by state policy', but that the 'family-household' is not necessary for capitalism and that other systems of reproduction are imaginable.

I have mentioned McIntosh's caveats to her analysis in detail because they are relevant to the analysis in this book. My study, too, is unfortunately functionalist in character but I am not trying to argue, as a conservative might, that the 'family-education couple' is necessary for capitalism. Nor can I suggest, on the other hand, that there is any tendency to move towards alternative and possibly more progressive systems for the reproduction of class relations and labour power. But with McIntosh, I would like to argue that 'such contradictions mean that there are always a number of conflicting principles articulated in state policy, so that there is always room for change.'

This book draws upon these disparate approaches to the 'family-education couple' and to State policies which sustain social and economic relations. It is organized around two central themes: one is the relationship of the family *to* the education system and the other is family issues *within* the education system. In the first part of the book – chapters 2, 3 and 4 – the history of parental responsibilities for children, especially with respect to their schooling, is explored, together with an analysis of the justifications for the growth of mass education for both boys and girls. Having briefly reviewed familial and economic relationships in pre-industrial society, the chapters deal in depth with the developments of class differences in boys' and girls' schooling in the nineteenth century, including contrasts between day and boarding schools (chapter 2), extensions to compulsory education through the growth of special vocational curricula in the first forty years of this century (chapter 3) and the modifications of both parental duties and economic rationales for schooling from the Second World War to 1970 (chapter 4). These themes are returned to in part III of the book, where chapter 8 considers contemporary issues in ideologies about schooling, the economy and parenting.

Part II of the book takes up the second theme, family issues *within* the education system. Again the evidence is presented in chronological fashion, around two major aspects of the theme: first, the status of teaching and particularly the treatment of women in the teaching profession; second, the development of curricula, especially courses for girls to learn about their role in the division of labour in the family. Chapter 5 surveys nineteenth-century developments in these familial issues, such as the entry of women teachers into formal schooling and the courses they were required to teach, for instance, domestic economy; chapter 6 looks at the early twentieth century and the growth of teacher professionalism, which began to exclude married women but required more specialized teaching of motherhood; chapter 7, at the impact of the Second World War and the subsequent changes up to 1970 for married women teachers and for teaching about marriage, wifehood and mothering. This theme is taken up again in Part III, chapter 9, where contemporary debates about women's economic position (and as mothers) are studied both for teaching and for curricula. Finally, in chapter 10 the two themes are brought together, and an attempt is made to summarize how the family and education both together and separately reproduce the sexual, social and economic division of labour. Although the ways in which these processes operate is now more explicit and although there have been more struggles in the last decade or so centred around the position of women in the capitalist education system, the prospects for a more progressive resolution of how parenting and mothering should be learnt and performed look distinctly bleak.

Part I

The family, schooling and the economy

Introduction

This first part of the book explores the relationships between families and schools and presents the rationales for particular forms of schooling. It is argued that the education system, as we know it, is a relatively recent phenomenon which developed as the economy changed and became based on industrial production. But there is not a clear fit between education and the economy. Some developments in schooling occurred because of struggles between emerging social classes in the nineteenth century and especially the demands of the labour movement. Yet the education system was not designed merely to fulfil the economy's requirements for labour but is more generally linked with social and economic needs for particular types of adults. It has aided the reproduction of social and sexual divisions and the family itself. There is a wealth of literature on specific aspects of these educational developments, and mention will be made of the major studies in the following chapters. However, none of the literature highlights the way in which the State has affected the form of family relationships and responsibilities by providing schooling. Yet this has been a major issue in the growth of the education system.

Prior to the development of capitalism child-rearing generally, and schooling in particular, took a very different form, and the modern State, which is a result of the growth of capitalism, was not at first involved in the regulation of parent-child relationships. Indeed, childhood itself was not recognizable in the form in which it is today and the family was composed of more members. The history of the family is now an extensive field of study but the major works are those by Laslett (1971), Shorter (1976) and Lasch (1977). None of these studies is concerned, though, to explicate the relationships with schooling and the formal education system: in part, this is because education has been universally provided only in the last 100 years.

The issues addressed in the relationships between the family and schooling are not the same in each chapter. In chapter 2, I look at how the State was seen to intervene in the traditionally private family sphere by creating an education system. Thus the State, in Britain, was slow to provide educational facilities and wary of parental resistance. Moreover, the rationales for universal schooling were difficult to formulate and, in the early part of the nineteenth century, schooling outside the home was only provided on a limited basis either for the poor and destitute or for the very wealthy. It was mainly provided for sons; daughters tended, if schooled at all, to be educated at home. Parents themselves were slow to recognize the value of education. Accounts of schooling in the nineteenth century tend to focus on one of the social classes, or boys, or girls, or a particular period. To document the way in which the State gradually intervened in parent-child relationships, I have relied not only on official reports (which, in fact, are numerous) but also on a wealth of social histories.* The two most general and comprehensive are the two studies by Brian Simon (1960; 1965) and the three volumes of J.W. Adamson (1930). The former is a Marxist account of educational developments, stressing the part played by class struggles; the latter is a straightforward political history. There are many histories of boys' schooling, especially in public schools, but the most recent and novel is that of Gathorne-Hardy (1977); Honey's (1977) is perhaps now the classic academic account. For the history of women's education, the most readable account on which I have relied remains that of Alice Zimmern (1898). Kamm has published prolifically on the topic (1958, 1965, 1966, 1971). Recently feminists have begun to explore the issues in depth: Peterson (1972), Pedersen (1975), Sharpe (1976), Marks (1976) and Dyhouse (1976, 1977, 1978). There are also numerous studies of the growth of working-class and pauper education: I have relied on Silver (1965), Sutherland (1972) and Pinchbeck and Hewitt (1973).

In chapter 3 I look at the ways in which the State redefined and developed parental responsibilities as the education system was expanded to provide for older children, with specific vocational

*Since this book went to press a further important book dealing with the relationship between parents and elementary schooling has been published by Routledge & Kegan Paul. It looks at the impact of elementary schooling on working-class parents between 1860 and 1918. It is J.S. Hurt (1979), *Elementary Schooling and the Working Class 1860–1918*.

courses for the working classes and middle-class education increasingly aided by the State. Here the main secondary sources on which I have based my evidence have been Fleet (1976), Lowndes (1969), Banks (1955) and Barker (1972). Simon's (1965 and 1974) studies still remain the most detailed and comprehensive. There is a dearth of literature on women save for Kamm (1965 and 1971) and recently Dyhouse (1978). For bourgeois boys, Gathorne-Hardy (1977) remains the most lucid.

In chapter 4, I argue that parental responsibilities for schooling were further transformed partly as a result of the Second World War and partly because of new sorts of evidence used about child development. Certainly in the post-war period, parents were increasingly incorporated into the organization of the education system on an individual basis but, at the same time, the system was further diversified to cater for changing technological needs and industrial advances. The main secondary sources used have been Lowndes (1969), Barker (1972), Benton (1974), Finn *et al.* (1977), Marsden (1971) and Rubinstein and Simon (1969). Again there is little on either girls specifically or parental involvement, save for Appendix B of the Taylor Report (DES and Welsh Office, 1977) and limited comments in Saran (1973).

The history of the family and childhood

In order to demonstrate the modern characteristics of parent-child relationships, especially within schooling, it is useful briefly to survey the evidence on childhood, child-rearing and schooling in medieval times and early capitalism. Most of the evidence suggests that childhood was not a very distinctive phase in a person's life, that the average life-span was shorter than today and that, as a consequence, child-rearing was but a limited activity. Children were reared mainly within the 'family circle'.

Several writers, notably Aries (1974), have argued that earlier societies, especially the feudal, were probably more 'puerile' than contemporary society. It is interesting to note that Aries, in his book which is an analysis of games and pastimes, comments not that society was childish, but that it was *boyish*. The divisions that will concern us here, namely sexual divisions, predate capitalism, a fact to which Aries inadvertently draws our attention. Although they were a feature of feudalism, the form that they took and the ways in which they were reproduced differed from capitalism. Although Aries argues that society was boyish, it may be surmised from his analysis that the sexual division of labour was less rigid since the entire activity of society was more limited. But boys were brought up for posts in public life whereas girls were taught to be mothers. These sexual divisions, however, were mediated by class divisions. Although feudal society was more childish, there were distinctions in the position to be acquired. The training of the aristocracy and gentry differed from that of labourers and peasants. Peasants reared their children within the immediate family circle, where differentiation according to sex was apparent, though perhaps less blatant. Children of the yeomanry, gentry and aristocracy did not necessarily stay within their own family circle for their whole training. They may have been sent to board in another aristocratic household, to acquire certain skills and/or a vocation. This was especially true for boys but it also applied to girls. In all cases, the family circle may have been wider than that of the nuclear family today.

As capitalism began to take root, the home became more significant and forms of *household* training or apprenticeship were more formalized. Children's education was not the responsibility of their parents but of the church, town or professional guilds. The church was specially influential in this process, particularly for upper-class families. Schools began to flourish as one form of training. They were virtually always *boarding* schools. Aries, at this juncture in his analysis, presents his second concept of childhood – that children were to be treated as 'fragile creatures of God' who had to be disciplined and rationally brought up to play a part in society. In this case, the child became central to the family. Aries argues, however, that this concept *followed* the development of the notion, the family form, of domesticity and changes in the structure of social life, the privatization of family life. This was initially the prerogative of the slowly expanding middle, or merchant, classes and not of either the aristocracy or peasant class. For example, he argues (1974, p. 404) that the housing situation was a prerequisite: 'The concept of the home is another concept of the family.'

What he does not deal with explicitly is the changing place of women in relation to domesticity and child-rearing. This subject is dealt with by a number of authors, but most clearly with respect to the formalization of child-rearing and schooling by Joan Simon (1971) and, for the later period, Pinchbeck and Hewitt (1969), Clark (1968) and Hall (1974). It is still not a major theme in studies of the history of childhood or the family, and there is very little detailed evidence of these early capitalist forms of upbringing in terms of sexual divisions.

Simon (1971) tries to show that, until the thirteenth century, there was little clear sexual differentiation in the rearing of children. With the expansion of social and economic life and, in particular, the development of cities and a merchant class, a sexual division in teaching began to appear, mediated by class divisions. Only the upper class had access to 'learning' in the academic sense: vocational training was the lot of the majority of children (or rather boys). Moreover, there was a distinction in the duties of parents towards their children's learning. Mothers were responsible for young boys and girls, and for girls over the age of seven. Fathers were responsible for the forming of their sons. But the detailed teaching was not conducted by parents. Special places of learning, separate from those of the church, began to develop on a businesslike basis. Children, especially boys, were removed from their own family circle after the age of seven and treated as adults (with criminal liability, for instance) whilst in training for some profession. The training often took the form of an apprenticeship in another household.

Pinchbeck and Hewitt (1969) argue that the development of welfare for children was linked to the state of the economy. Thus the sixteenth and seventeenth centuries were times of relative prosperity, and concern for children was strong. Indeed, children came to be seen as valuable assets and training was therefore applied to ensure each child his proper place in society. This analysis seems to be in broad agreement with Aries.

Clark (1968) and Hall (1974) have both looked at women's position in early capitalism. They have shown that, although women were primarily responsible for child-rearing, since this was a limited activity women were also engaged in productive, and hence social, activities. They were not confined to being mothers but there was a clear sexual division in parental responsibilities.

As capitalism developed, especially in the eighteenth century, social and sexual divisions gradually became more obvious. In particular, childhood was slowly recognized as a distinctive phase in the life-cycle. This was as a justification for the changes in the social and economic order and was initially based on the tenets of religious teaching. Shipman (1972) has argued that 'there was a growing awareness of "moulding the man" and not precipitating him to be an adult but holding him from society until he had some elementary skills.' The family was slowly becoming no longer central as a unit of productive activities and women were as a result increasingly excluded from economic activities. These processes were uneven throughout the country and varied according to the type of industry and economic change. Pinchbeck (1969) has shown how prevalent women workers, including mothers, were in the early years of the Industrial Revolution and especially in agriculture.

By the beginning of the nineteenth century economic activities had become very diverse, and the unit of production was increasingly the factory rather than the home. Activities within the family were also becoming divided along both age and sex lines. Children were treated differently from adults and a sexual division in parental responsibilities was more apparent. Moreover, social divisions in the wider society were emerging. Williams (1961, p. 156) has argued that 'the change from a system of social orders to one of social classes was complete by the end of the eighteenth century.' Schooling, however, had not yet become universally available or justified.

2

Schooling: a revolutionary invasion of parental rights over children?

This chapter surveys the development of schooling in the nineteenth century and the ways in which the State eventually ordered parental responsibilities for children, to fit them for the socio-economic system. At the beginning of the nineteenth century, capitalism was well established as Britain's economic system and industrialization was developing apace. The change to a mechanized, factory system of production was also slowly taking place and the family, as a unit, was gradually being excluded from productive activities. But these changes were by no means uniform and the country was still dependent upon its agricultural system. Nevertheless, an economic division of labour was in the ascendant and social divisions were predicated upon these new forces and mode of production.

Schools were not very common and none was provided by the State. The Churches – both Church of England and non-conformist – were the major providers of the various different types of school. Charitable foundations and endowments were the other chief means of supporting schools. However, many children, and especially girls in the growing middle classes, did not leave home to attend school but were educated within the home. Education itself was not compulsory: there was no obligation laid on children to attend school or on their parents to compel them, but parents had to pay for any education they acquired for their children.

Sons of the aristocracy tended to be educated at home, at first, by women and later by male tutors whom their parents employed. Some did attend schools away from home, at which they boarded. These schools were generally financed through ancient endowments or charitable foundations but at the beginning of the nineteenth century they were in a run-down condition. The daughters of the aristocracy also were mainly educated within the home, as infants by their mothers and subsequently by governesses.

The sons of the aspiring middle classes on the whole received the most formal education. A variety of other schools, provided either by religious or charitable foundations or by private endowment, began to spring up to cater for their needs (Gathorne-Hardy, 1977, chs 3–4). Such boys were sent either to the local ancient grammar schools, which were mostly day schools, or to boarding schools, which usually were what the Secondary Schools Inquiry Commission (1868) later termed 'proprietary schools'. These latter were schools set up by individuals or companies to provide a 'modern' education and fit boys for the professions or elite positions in the newly forming social order. Many schools were provided by rationalists and gave a scientific bias to the education; others were provided by non-conformists or Roman Catholics, for parents who were reluctant to send or excluded from sending their sons to the ancient foundations, dominated as they were by Anglicans. A feature of these schools was that children from a wide geographical area began to attend them. As transport systems improved and the railways were introduced, proximity to home was no longer a criterion for choice of school (Honey, 1977). Parents therefore began to relinquish to the schools their direct control and influence over their sons. They did retain the right to choose a school which they believed suited their wishes for their sons. They also retained the duty to pay for their sons' attendance at school. Indeed, one of the main ways in which these newly established schools differed from the grammar schools was over the costs that they imposed on parents. They also differed from the academic foundations in the emphasis they put on their purposes: the traditional schools trained for social character; the new schools laid the foundations for a 'useful' professional training (Williams, 1961, part two).

The daughters of the middle classes either attended private, 'family' schools or, if their parents could afford it, were educated at home by governesses. The schools provided for such girls tended to be run by women who owned the school, taught in it and may have made a profit from so doing. As the century wore on, it became more fashionable, as Peterson (1972) has argued, for girls to be educated within the home. It was a proof of the fathers' respectability and station in life that they could afford staff both to run their homes and educate their daughters. Moreover, to have an idle and leisured wife confirmed this status.

Poor and working-class children were treated very differently. At the beginning of the nineteenth century there was virtually no schooling for them, especially not on a daily basis. In the seventeenth century, the Charity Schools Movement had been set up to provide some schools for the poor and peasants as a form of 'moral rescue'. By the end of the next century such schools had lost any popularity they once held. Many children could find work either in agriculture or in the expanding factory system. Indeed, children were often used as labourers in the early years of industrialization because they were both dextrous and nimble. Their parents frequently exploited their talents and abilities and relied on their wage-earning capacity for economic survival (Musgrove, 1966). However, very young children or infants could not be used in this way. Where their parents, and in particular their mothers, worked outside the home, they were sent to what were called schools, but were institutions barely meriting the title. These 'dame schools' were really early equivalents of child-minders or day nurseries: older married women, in their own homes, looked after large numbers of children while their mothers worked and charged fees for the service. Pinchbeck (1969, p. 107) has stated that 'a woman out in the fields all day was glad to use the school as a nursery and to send her children to school as soon as possible.'

Sunday Schools, established by religious philanthropists such as Hannah More, also gained in popularity and provided the rudiments of a moral education for poor and working-class children.

Pauper children were treated differently again. On the whole, they lived in workhouses either with their unemployed parents (usually mothers) or as destitutes. Schools of industry were set up alongside the poor-houses, where these children were taught to be useful citizens and to earn a living (Pinchbeck and Hewitt, 1973, p. 414). The aim in educating boys was to bring them up (Silver, 1965, p. 60) 'at the utmost distance, as from vice in general, so in particular from idleness and *effeminacy*' (my italics). Girls were taught domestic skills and had to work in the poor-house to learn such useful skills as cleaning, knitting and sewing. All pauper children in these schools were also given a moral education to prevent them from either pursuing a life of crime or becoming insurrectionists. Such schools as were provided were seen as 'an antidote to crime' (ibid.).

The pioneers of education for the new middle classes also sought to influence how the children of labourers, peasants and the poor were brought up. This was part and parcel of their attack upon the ruling classes and attempts to become dominant in a changing society. They tried to win over both their own children and those of their inferiors. Early attempts to establish a national school system were easily thwarted since they did not have sufficient political power to take control. But they continued to argue for extending education to the working classes in their (the middle classes') own interests. It would enable these children to earn their own livelihood and not be a drain on society and, more important, it would inhibit insurrection and probably create a supportive populace.

The two main protagonists of these views, whose ideas appear to have influenced the course of educational history, were James Mill and Jeremy Bentham. They both argued, in the early nineteenth century, that education was 'essential for the well-being of the nation' and that the nation should not leave anything to chance (Simon, 1960, pp. 74–9). According to Simon (ibid.) they both drew on Adam Smith's (1776) earlier ideas that education was essential to capitalism. Indeed, Bentham tried to go further and argue for the enfranchisement of men of the working class, although not their attendance at Parliament, in order to mould them to willing co-operation. But these ideas were opposed by both the representatives of the old aristocracy, the Tories, and the Whigs, who mainly represented the aspiring middle classes. The one Tory exception was Hannah More, who helped to develop the Sunday School movement. The majority of Whigs and Radicals were also opposed to the use of the political organs of the State in establishing education but they did support the efforts of the Church of England and non-conformists in founding charitable societies to promote education for the poor.

In the first two decades of the nineteenth century, a voluntary organization, with the financial support of wealthy dissenters and liberal Whigs, established schools for the poor. This was the Lancastrian Society, formed in 1808, which in 1811 became the British and Foreign Schools Society. The Church of England also helped establish schools through the National Society, set up in 1812, with the purpose of providing moral teaching and rescuing children from the vagaries of the harsh new economic system. These were day schools, at which parents had to pay fees for their children's education. There was apparently no distinction in admission between boys and girls, although they were usually taught separately (Gordon, 1974, chs 1 and 2). Pinchbeck (1969, p. 107) has argued that there was a difference in the rates at which boys and girls actually attended schools, depending on alternative sources of employment and mothers' opportunities for labour:

> As a general rule in rural areas boys were earlier employed in the fields than girls who remained longer at school. In towns and especially in factory districts the opposite was the case. It often happened, however, that far fewer girls than boys were sent to school in the first place, partly on account of their greater usefulness in domestic occupations and also from the general impression

> that education was not so necessary to girls as boys. Again, although girls remained longer at school, their attendance was much more broken, especially where the mother was engaged in agricultural work away from home. After the age of 11 or 12 girls were kept at home entirely, either to take charge of the house in the absence of the mother or to become nurse girls in other families.

In 1819 a Whig presented a Bill to Parliament for State support of universal education for the working classes. It failed to gain support, for both Whigs and Tories argued that the capitalists still required child labour to develop industry. Thus, in the early years of industrialization, children were seen as the sole property of their parents, to be exploited by them, and by capitalists and industrialists too. Parents could use their children for financial gain and as an insurance against their own misfortunes, especially in later life (Musgrove, 1966). Indeed, there is evidence to suggest that in the early period of industrialization parents were dependent on their children (rather than vice versa), especially in the towns, because children, who were more dextrous and nimble and could perform tasks more easily than their parents, were more likely to be employed. Since children were useful both to their parents and to capitalists, their labour was not regulated and, more important, education was not seen as socially necessary or useful. Thus compulsory education was spurned.

It was not until the last third of the century that the need for universal education was accepted and the political will was there to enforce it. The need was only recognized as a result of changes in the economy and their effects on labour force participation. The changes had an impact upon the demands for both child labour and that of women, especially married women. Women's position in the labour market changed not only as a result of the demands of capitalists for types of skill, such as dexterity, but also with the impact of organizational changes and male pressure on the availability of work for men. Gradually, men's wages came to be regarded as a family wage, which resulted in the increasing exclusion of married women from the labour market and a stress on domesticity as an alternative form of employment (albeit unpaid). However, this exclusion of mothers from labour force participation varied from industry to industry. As Hewitt (1958) has shown, women continued throughout the century to work in the cotton industries. (I will return to the specific impact that changes in employment had upon the supply of teachers, particularly women, in chapter 5.)

With the changes in employment patterns came changes in the nature of child-rearing and the part that both the family and State should play within it. Until mothers began to be excluded from the labour market there was very little emphasis on the role that parents played with regard to their children or upon their parental duties. Musgrove (1966), for example, argues that the changes in provision signalled a move from parental power to parental influence. The State did gradually intervene in what had hitherto been a private parent-child relationship and took over certain child-rearing activities; in the process, it *created* duties for parents *vis-á-vis* their children which may not have been exercised before. It began to create a concept of the family that was enshrined in law and administrative practice. This concept supported a clear sexual division in parental duties and rights and, moreover, required general parental responsibilities. The concept was a clear explication of the notion of the nuclear family which had not necessarily been the standard for the family of any class previously.

Indeed, the duties of parents, either father or mother, with respect to their children which became the norm for proletarian families were not based upon imitation of bourgeois, middle-class or aristocratic families. Both much less and much more were expected of the latter in respect of child-rearing. Upper- and middle-class families were not bound by standards set by the State. They were not compelled to provide a particular form of education for their children. The majority of parents chose to exercise their responsibilities by relinquishing power to schools and schoolteachers. They sent their sons away from home to schools on the grounds that they would benefit more (Honey, 1977).

Schooling for middle- and upper-class children was extended and improved before consideration was given to education for the masses. This schooling did not require extensive parental involvement but did rely on parental wealth. Schools for boys became very expensive. Girls, however, were still excluded.

It was not without considerable struggle by some women of the middle classes that education for daughters was recognized as at all important. Even so, girls' education was not to be the same as boys' because men and women had different functions to play in adult life. Education was increasingly recognized as being to provide for a particular economic and social organization of adult life and not only for character or moral training. Thus the moves to improve schooling were based on its links with both new forms of political leadership and the needs of business and industry. The initiatives came from the leaders of the middle classes, who by the 1850s had gained positions of political dominance within Parliament but had not necessarily received extensive schooling. Engels, for example, as quoted by Simon (1960), described the English middle classes at that time as 'quite uneducated upstarts'. They had gained ascendancy by the

1850s because of the changing relationship between agricultural land and industrial capital in the economy. This particular change was signalled by the Repeal of the Corn Laws, which revoked the unmitigated powers of lords over the land (Simon, 1960).

Class and changes in schooling in the 1860s

This changing balance of economic power had a significant impact upon educational development. There were three immediate effects which occurred in the 1860s. Indeed, this was the main decade of the nineteenth century for changes in the form of schooling for all social classes. One was the reform of the universities, especially Oxford and Cambridge, which had hitherto dominated the intellectual life of the country. Internal reforms were made to individual universities and a Royal Commission was set up, which eventually called for changes in the curriculum. Theology was no longer to predominate, and diplomacy and politics were introduced. This had the long-term result of more social exclusiveness in terms of those admitted to university. The middle classes continued to attend but the children of the poor were excluded by means of financial changes. New criteria of merit and efficiency were also applied, through the development of more rigid and bureaucratic examinations. The second policy change, attendant upon the ascendance of the middle classes and part of their attack upon the social hegemony of the aristocracy, was the reform of both the public and grammar schools. The third change was the introduction of education for middle-class girls. In 1861 a Royal Commission, chaired by Lord Clarendon, was set up by Parliament to look at the finances of nine schools, which were considered to be the great public schools. These had traditionally been schools for the sons of the aristocracy or gentry and operated on a fee-paying basis. However, they did provide some places, free of charge, for the poor but able children of the locality. The declared reason for the Royal Commission was that the schools were ineffective and had declined in status (Adamson, 1930, p. 236). The aims of the Clarendon Commission were to make the schools more financially viable and to modernize their curricula, for they were still regarded as 'the schools of the governing classes' (Adamson, 1930, p. 237).

In 1864 the Commissioners recommended the abolition of 'free' places and limitations on local entrants, known as Oppidans, to ensure the social exclusiveness of the schools. They also suggested reforming the governing constitutions of the schools. The recommendations were put into effect in 1868 through the Public Schools Act, which required seven of the nine schools to submit to a new statutory commission new constitutions for their governing bodies.

Parents were to play a limited part in the running of the seven transformed public schools. They were not to be included in the newly constituted governing bodies. Moreover, they were expected to send their boys to the schools and trust the teachers to act *in loco parentis*. Indeed, parents' objectives in sending their sons to such schools were commented upon by the Public Schools Commissioners (1864, p. 40). If the real object

> is merely or chiefly that he should make advantageous acquaintances and gain knowledge of the world, this is likely to be no secret to him, and the home influence which ought to be the Master's most efficacious auxiliary becomes in such cases the greatest obstacle of progress.

Although for a time there was an attempt to resist the changes, the schools slowly began to alter in character and by the end of the nineteenth century they had become the preserve of the upper- and upper-middle classes. This was mainly achieved through increasing fees charged to parents and reducing the numbers of scholarships available to local and poor boys.

In 1864 an attempt to reform the rest of the schools for the middle classes was set in train. Another Royal Commission, chaired by Taunton and later known as the Schools Inquiry Commission (SIC, 1868) was established to investigate the bulk of secondary schools for boys. It had to examine the endowed grammar schools, proprietary schools and private schools. The aim was to inspect all such schools, excluding only those endowments that had been covered by the Education Commission chaired by Newcastle, which had reported in 1861 on the state of popular education.

The main exclusion from the terms of reference for the Taunton Commission was the inspection of middle-class girls' schools. Some active campaigners for women's education, who were later said to constitute the Women's Educational Movement, exerted pressure on the Commissioners for girls' schools, albeit very few, to be included. They wanted the inadequacies of such schooling to be exposed, to gain support for their then unfashionable argument that many women, mainly single, needed to be prepared 'to earn their own bread'. These women campaigners had already begun the fight for the opening up of the universities and their courses to women and had managed to establish in London a training centre known as Queen's College, for women wishing to teach in girls' schools (see ch. 5). The result of this campaigning was that a few girls' schools were included in the scope of the report, but the inspectors covered only twelve girls' schools as opposed to 800 boys' schools.

The Taunton Commission's recommendations were that an organized system of education for middle-class boys be established. The two key features of the system suggested were the ages at which boys should leave and the fees to be charged to parents. It did suggest, however, that scholarships be provided to enable clever children of the lower-middle and working classes to attend the schools without paying fees. The schools were to continue to rely on their endowments for most of their finance. Some of the old endowments were now to be used towards the education of girls. It had been discovered, during the course of the Commission's inquiry, that most of the old endowments had been devised for the 'children' of the community and had subsequently been subverted to provide only for boys.

The new system proposed by the Commissioners would demarcate clearly between classes of children, even within the middle classes. They suggested three types of school, differentiated by length and breadth of school life. The *first grade* of school, as they termed it, were to be *boarding* schools for children of the wealthy – the upper and middle classes and those living on unearned income. These schools would provide an education to enable boys then to attend university. The usual school-leaving age would be eighteen or nineteen years of age. The *second grade* of school would be *day* schools, with a school-leaving age of sixteen. These should be provided in every town of over 5,000 population and would cater for the sons of merchants, businessmen, shopkeepers, larger tenant farmers and army officers. The Commissioners (SIC, 1868, p. 20) added that 'the first and second grade seem to meet the demands of all the wealthier parents of the community'. The *third grade* of school would be *day* schools providing for the sons of 'small tradesmen, superior artisans and small tenant farmers', with a leaving age of fourteen. '[This school] belongs to a class distinctly lower in the scale but so numerous as to be quite as important as any' (ibid., p. 20).

The type of school bore with it a conception of family commitment and responsibility. Parents who were not wealthy had not only to pay for their sons' education but ensure their daily attendance. Wealthier parents were divested of their regular responsibilities to their sons by the provision of boarding education (ibid., p. 42): 'The schoolmaster should be in the parents' place and to do his work properly ought to be clothed with *all the parent's authority*' [my emphasis]. Moreover, the Commissioners argued that boarding education was preferable to day schools for the 'formation of character'. Day schools had certain advantages, in particular the closer relationship between father and son. But, lest that impede the schooling process, the Commission tried to define parental and teachers' rights over education and used as its example religious education. It was stated (ibid., pp. 41–2) that the system of general education should be in accordance with *parental wishes* but that

> parents ought to be protected against any systematic or persistent inculcation, in his son's presence, of doctrines of which he disapproves. But, on the other hand, as the parent ought to be free to withdraw the scholar, so ought the master to be free and unfettered in his teaching.

In cases of dispute between parents and teachers, the Commissioners recommended recourse to legal tribunals. But the assumption on which the Commissioners operated was that, the wealthier the parents, the more likely they were to be in sympathy with the aims of education. It was stated that 'those who can afford to pay more for their children's education will also, as a general rule, continue that education for a longer time.' But the aims of this education were not at all vocational. 'Parents are ever asking for this or that kind of instruction with a view to this or that business in life. The answer should be "Your boy comes here for instruction, not for apprenticeship" ' (ibid., p. 15). The instruction was to be in accordance with future class positions and hence the three grades of school. The Commissioners stated that 'it is obvious that these distinctions correspond roughly, but by no means exactly, to gradations in society' (ibid.). They added that 'the wishes of the parents can best be defined in the first instance by the length of time during which they are willing to keep their children under instruction.'

However, the Commissioners did not stick to that principle for girls' education. They felt that they could 'not classify so accurately for girls as boys partly because there were not enough funds available' (ibid., p. 16). The funds available should mainly be used for boys. In any event, girls were much more often educated at home and the Commissioners did not argue ardently for this system to be altered.

The recommendations were mainly accepted by Parliament and passed into law through the Endowed Schools Act of 1868. Girls' education in the Act was not to be thwarted but encouraged. This Act formed the starting-point for a 'rational' system of secondary and higher education for middle- and upper-class children based on the notion of social merit. Children were now to be trained for particular purposes in life and to respect a rigid system of social ordering. They were to learn about their class position in the social hierarchy, as well as its attendant social and familial values. At the same time they were to learn, implicitly rather than explicitly, their places *within* the family as mothers and fathers. Indeed, their own parents acquired very real responsibilities through the consolidation of the division between day and boarding education.

The Act did signal the extension of formal schooling for middle-class girls. Not only were some of the old endowments opened up for girls' schools but new schools were established for both day-girls and boarders. Eighty endowments were achieved in the next decade. In addition, new proprietary schools were started, for instance, through the establishment of the Girls' Public Day School Company (GPDSC) in 1871. This helped to establish low-fee day schools in many large towns for middle-class girls, but not without much hard campaigning work on the part of its key founders. It was a joint-stock company with ordinary shareholders and not based on endowments. The women educational campaigners also established in November 1871 the National Union for the Education of Girls of all classes above the lower (National Union), to further press the case for women's education. They were often thwarted in their efforts by both men and unsympathetic women. For example, Roman Catholics were deeply suspicious of predominantly secular education and refused to join, and the Duchess of Northumberland argued that all that girls really needed to know was 'something practically of cooking, washing and ironing, nursing both of sick and infants and . . . needlework' (Kamm, 1971, p. 43). She did not agree that 'the object of women's education *ought* to be to enable a woman to fill her position in after life as wife, mother, mistress or servant' (Kamm, 1971, p. 43). Indeed, in order to gain support for the movement, Emily Shirreff (one of its leaders) had to put forward the 'shirt-button and slipper' argument that a man's house would not be made uncomfortable by the presence of an educated wife (Kamm, 1971, p. 48). Because of the opposition, the schools had to be cheap, 'to induce parents, too ignorant themselves to know what is good, to prefer sound teaching which is also cheap, to bad teaching which is expensive' (Kamm, 1971, p. 41).

It was slowly, over the next twenty years or so, that the arguments for women's education came to be acknowledged and parents stopped being indifferent to their daughters' rearing. The main expansion of GPDSC schools was in the Company's first six years, at the end of which time there were 1,000 pupils in nine schools. The schools were very harsh in their treatment of the parents: they were expected to buy shares in the company, as well as paying fees and buying curricular extras such as stationery. Kamm (1958, p. 52) claims that 'more than once parents had to be threatened with legal proceedings before they consented to pay for it [education] '. Also the hours of schooling were limited: in no way did they approximate a working day. They were 9.30 a.m. to 1.30 p.m., followed by a midday dinner for girls who could not go home. Mothers therefore had to ensure that their children were looked after in the long period after school.

The reforms to secondary schooling, for both boys and girls of the middle classes, laid down in the two Acts of Parliament in the 1860s heralded major changes in the school system and its relationship with parents. By the end of the nineteenth century a reformed system of middle-class schooling had been put into effect. New schools for boys and girls had been established on both a day and boarding basis. The majority of bourgeois girls attended schools, mainly proprietary day schools, by the turn of the century. Few of them were any longer educated at home. Boarding schools for girls had also been established in this last third of the nineteenth century, modelled on the boys' public schools and catering for both the aristocracy and the bourgeoisie (Zimmern, 1898). The boys' schools established followed the lines recommended by the Taunton Commission (Gathorne-Hardy, 1977).

Towards the end of the nineteenth century, when Britain was emerging from an economic depression that had lasted almost twenty years, the government again established a Royal Commission to inquire into secondary education. This, the Bryce Commission, was set up in 1894. The main reason was to establish the need for financial and curricular changes and to tie the schools more closely to the changed state of the economy. This Commission's terms of reference automatically included girls' schools and, furthermore, a number of women (three teachers) were included among the Commissioners.

The Commissioners did not find it necessary, in the short time that they investigated the schools, to make any radical changes to the system, save to recommend a central governing body to guide the whole education system. They did, however, endorse the arguments that girls should be educated, and pointed out (Royal Commission on Secondary Education, 1895), that in the twenty-five years since the Taunton Commission had reported, 'the idea that a girl, like a boy, may be fitted by education to earn a livelihood, or at any rate to be a more useful member of society, has become more widely diffused.' But they also pointed out (ibid.) that 'although the world has now existed for several thousand years the notion that women have minds as cultivable and worth cultivating as men's minds is still regarded by the ordinary British parent as an offensive, not to say revolutionary, paradox.' The recommendation of a central body was followed and in 1899 a Board of Education was established as a central government body to oversee the organization of the education system. In order to encourage the education of girls the Commissioners recommended that governing bodies of girls' schools should include women. Indeed, they added (ibid., 1895, para. 110): 'the proportion must vary according to circumstances but there should be no obstacle in the way of a body composed mainly or exclusively of women.' They did not, however, advocate the specific inclusion of parents.

Compulsory education and parental rights

Schooling for working-class boys and girls was also organized during the last third of the nineteenth century. By the 1890s it had become both universal and compulsory and mainly provided by the State. This process of achieving universal and compulsory education was both slow and politically difficult. The arguments for the State to provide education for the working classes only won acceptance as the economy became more diversified, the need for skilled and trained labour more critical and the demands of the working class too pressing to ignore. Indeed, the provision of such education in the first instance was to pacify the demands of the labour movement and to prevent potential conflict and crime. By the 1860s, youth unemployment was considered as much a problem as parental exploitation of child labour (Musgrove, 1966). But State intervention in parent-child relationships was not readily acceptable and needed to be justified on both moral and economic grounds.

The provision of a national system of elementary schools for the working classes had been debated in Parliament as early as 1818 but was rejected because child labour was still socially necessary to capitalists and it was argued that the State should not intervene in market relations, whether between employer and employee or between parent and child. However, there were stirrings of concern about child employment because of the high rate of injury and the lack of effective skills. The first attempts by the State in the nineteenth century to regulate child-rearing were over the conditions of child employment. Thus, measures were taken to exclude children from certain industries, either totally or for part of the day. The first legal measure was also a reaction to working-class pressure. Until 1830, the working and middle classes had apparently shared political interests. As a result of the enfranchisement of men of the middle classes and the punitive Poor Law Amendment Act of

1834, which hit the poor and paupers severely, the working and middle classes no longer were united in their political interests or activities.

Activists from the working classes began to campaign for changes in their working conditions. Their main aims were for, initially, a reduction of the working day to ten hours and the stopping of child labour. These issues were debated in Parliament but the liberal argument, that the State could not interfere with the 'free' contract between capitalists and labourers, was repeated. However, child labour could be limited. The Factory Act of 1833 specified that children should be protected, and educated, within factories. They should be taught for two hours a day, six days a week. But the Act did not set up any administrative machinery to this end and factory schools were rarely implemented. At the same time, the government did agree to provide grants to the voluntary societies for school buildings. The 1833 Education Act was to provide 'school houses for the children of the poorer classes in Great Britain'. These finances, however, were clearly tied to religious teaching and attempts to protect against working-class radicalism. The grants were given only to the two voluntary societies and not to private schools.

Throughout the 1830s the working classes continued to campaign for improved conditions, such as a shorter working day. The political organization of the Chartists united demands for a ten-hour day with enfranchisement and educational demands, because of the legal limitation of child labour in particular localities and industries which had just been implemented through the Mines and Workshops Acts. Sutherland (1971) regards these Acts as forms of 'indirect compulsion' for schooling. The Chartists also began to establish their own schools (mainly in the evening), called Owenite Halls of Science, to counter the Mechanics' Institutes, which Engels, for example, had argued were for 'the dissemination of the sciences useful to the bourgeoisie' (1969, p. 264). The Chartists tended to argue that those who exploited workers had a duty to educate the children of such workers.

Although the State was gradually taking an interest in providing education, its purpose was to stem such radicalism. In 1839 a committee of the Privy Council was set up for education and shortly afterwards it provided further financial help to the voluntary societies. Only four years later, the committee was given powers by Parliament to provide grants for furniture and apparatus, in return for the voluntary schools being inspected by HMIs and ensuring particular standards of schooling, which included religious education.

The State itself did begin to make educational provisions for paupers during this period. The arguments used to justify such provisions were utilitarian and yet even these had difficulty in gaining political acceptability. Most Whigs and Tories advocated the principle of less eligibility as an effective way to discourage pauperism. However, some philanthropists, such as Sir James Kay-Shuttleworth, argued that the Poor Law Commissioners stood *in loco parentis* to pauper children in workhouses (Pinchbeck and Hewitt, 1973, p. 504):

> The dependence of certain of these classes of children cannot be transient. The care of their natural guardians is at an end . . . [so] that the children have claims on the Boards of Guardians . . . to enable them . . . to attain independence . . . The duty of providing a suitable training for pauper children is simple and positive . . . Education is to be regarded as one of the most important means of eradicating the genus of pauperism from the rising generation, and of securing in the minds and morals of the people the best protection for the institutions of society.

In the 1840s these arguments finally found acceptance and in 1844 an Act was passed to set up residential district schools for pauper children, financed through the poor rate. But the Act was slow to be implemented

The notion that children should be withheld from the labour force until they had been provided with particular training, skills and indoctrination was gradually being translated into administrative practice (Pinchbeck and Hewitt, 1973, ch. 8). For example, in the 1850s a government department – the Department of Art and Science – was set up specifically to finance voluntary schools teaching these kinds of subject. In this same period, the Poor Law was amended to ensure that pauper children did attend workhouse schools, to enable them to earn their own living.

During the 1850s middle-class radicals began to support the Chartist demands, which were for proletarian franchise and a national system of education. Other non-conformist Whigs and the Tories still refused to provide political support on the ground that children were needed in the factories. The battle was over the religious rather than State influence in education. However, in 1858, one of the first of the Educational Royal Commissions, this one chaired by Newcastle, was set up to inquire into the possibility of providing 'sound and cheap elementary instruction for all classes of the people in England'. The pressure was still not sufficient for universal and State education to be justified.

The Newcastle Commissioners took four years to report, during which time they thoroughly surveyed the provision of schooling by the voluntary societies, which by 1860 had grown to six, by the Poor Law, by charitable endowments and that for vagrants and criminals. On the whole, they approved of this system of schooling and argued that (Education Commission, 1861, p. 74) 'the feelings which tend to make the offer of gratuitous instruction unpopular tend also to incline the parents to pay as large a share as they can reasonably afford of the expense of the education of their children'. The Commissioners claimed that there were, therefore, sufficient numbers of school places but that the length of school life, being less than six years, was too short. They pointed out that less than 20 per cent of children stayed at school after the age of eleven. This was because 'parents want schooling not for moral elevation but to be profitable to the child in life' (ibid., p. 34). In that case, the Commissioners were able to justify the types of schools already available. For instance, they stated that (ibid., p. 28)

> the infant schools discharge, in fact, the functions of public nurseries towards very young children . . . in the family of a mechanic or day labourer, to say nothing of the ignorance of the parents, the father is usually out at work from 6 in the morning to 6 at night. The mother has to perform personally all household operations. Stationery and books are too valuable to be made into toys . . .
>
> An infant school of some kind or other is thus the only means of keeping children of such families out of the streets in towns or out of the roads and fields in the country. These schools are therefore of great utility as places of security as well as of education . . . They impart knowledge, which though apparently small in amount, is of high value and habits of docility and submission to discipline, which are of still higher.

They also tried to estimate school attendance, its distribution by sex, and reported that of the 1,895 schools inspected 48.9 per cent were mixed, 22.2 per cent were for boys, 18.1 per cent for girls and 10.1 per cent were mixed infant schools.

The Commissioners recommended that further government grants be provided to the existing schools, especially to enable children to stay on after eleven years of age. They did not consider making schooling compulsory. The first President of the Council on Education appointed at this juncture, Robert Lowe, took up the recommendations and, for example, argued in Parliament against compulsion on the grounds that it was not for the members

> 'to struggle against early labour, not to interfere between a parent who is oppressed by poverty and the labour of his own children but to make the education of the child during the time he remains at school as perfect as possible'.

The 1860s also witnessed more pressure from the working class, especially through the expanding trade union movement, for education as a political necessity. For example, miners in Wales began to provide education for their young children through trade unions. In 1864 the first international working men's association was established, which pressed for political education and enfranchisement. In 1867 working men were finally conceded the vote. This set the stage for the possible extension of State education.

Technical and demographic changes also provided the context for universal educational provision. First, changes in technology meant that machinery was increasingly capable of performing the dextrous skills for which young children had originally been required. Musgrove has argued (1964, pp. 72–3) that 'advances in technology were . . . displacing the young worker.' These changes also affected particular types of industry, especially agriculture and lace, and thus displaced not only the young but also women. There was a gradual shift to domestic service. In a Manchester survey of 1865 (according to Musgrove, 1964, p. 76) it was found that, of the three- to twelve-year-olds, over half were neither in school nor in work. The percentage of the occupied population under fifteen gradually began to decline. Thus children were becoming marginal to the working population, outcast and neglected.

Demographic changes accentuated these developments. By the middle of the century, because of the economic value that had been placed on children, there was a superabundance of young people. But an imbalance in the sex ratio of the young occurred, since many young men emigrated through war or colonization, leaving an excess of spinsters. (I will return to this point in part II, ch. 5.) Because young people had been highly valued and by the 1850s could not find work to occupy themselves, they became highly visible and a political problem.

In the political arena, arguments such as those presented by James Mill earlier became more acceptable, i.e., that to educate the working classes would result in their being supportive to the social and political system. There was also by then a stronger fear of working-class political action. According to Sutherland (1973), Mill's son, John Stuart Mill, provided a new rationale for a State educational system in political terms: 'It is an allowable exercise of the powers of government to impose on parents a legal obligation of giving elementary instruction.' Mill added, as the reason for this political intervention, that the community would gain. Whig parliamentarians began to campaign for support for an Education Bill. In 1867, Forster, a Whig, obtained the support of the Bradford Chamber of Commerce to put forward such a Bill. Children were no longer a necessity to these capitalists and indeed ten- and eleven-year-olds were regarded by them as a nuisance.

In 1868 Forster introduced into Parliament a Bill for the State to provide universal, elementary education for the poorer and working classes. Such schooling, however, was to be limited in several ways. It was not to be free, compulsory or entirely provided by secular bodies. It was to be provided for all children aged five to ten, with a possible extension to thirteen years, but was not to be free – parents would have to pay fees of 9d. a week for each child, boy or girl, attending school. Also, this schooling was only to be made available by elected school boards in localities where the voluntary societies were deemed to be deficient. Thus the schooling provided would vary in content and type from area to area. The main similarity would be in the ages of children attending school – and the age of five was set as the beginning of schooling advisedly, although not debated for long in Parliament (Szreter, 1964). Forster argued that such a young age would prevent parental exploitation of children at home. In fact, many infants had been attending school much younger, escorted by older sisters, in lieu of child-minders, as the evidence of the Newcastle Commission had shown.

Parents were not given any rights over their children's education. Indeed, this Bill was condemned as 'a revolutionary invasion of parental rights over their children' (Musgrove, 1966, p. 3). Parents were not expected to contribute to the running of schools. The system of control that had developed out of Lowe's proposals in 1863 for the voluntary societies – managing bodies – was to be used by the school boards, and parents were not to be included among the managers. But neither were parents yet to be compelled to educate their children. Sutherland (1973, p. 123) argues that:

> direct compulsion could be seen not simply as an attack on the vested interests of the employer and parent in the child's labour. It could also be seen as an attack on the long-cherished notions not only of the duty and responsibility of parent to child but of his complete authority over him, the child being more of an adjunct or possession of the parent than an individual in his own right.

The Bill met much opposition on three grounds – interference in market relations, in parent-child labour relations and in authority relations – but especially the first, from Tories and farmers who still needed child labour. However, it was rushed through Parliament and became law in 1870.

Education, although now universally provided for the working classes through a mixed system of finance (fees, grants and the local rate), was not yet compulsory. Legal enforcement of school attendance did not reach the statute-books for another ten years, although other measures increasingly made it indirectly compulsory. For example, as another result of working-class campaigns, the age of ten was set as the minimum age of employment, further excluding children from the labour force. Parents still had to pay fees for their children's education, with the result that schooling was hard to enforce. Sutherland (1973, p. 122) points out that the case for direct compulsion had frequently been debated before 1870 : 'and each case [of non-attendance] that came before magistrates raised the question about the authority of the parent over the child.' This problem of not being able to compel parents to send their children to school continued because fees continued to be charged. In 1880 an Act did make education compulsory for five- to ten-year-olds but again, because of fees, it was still impossible to enforce. Eventually, in 1893, when more children were attending school board than voluntary schools, school boards were empowered not to charge fees on the grounds that fees inhibited the adequate provision of education. In 1872 one million children were in voluntary and only 8,700 in school board schools. By 1896 almost half of the 4.5 million attending school were in board schools. Voluntary schools had been able to exclude children by the level of fee. The expectation was that board schools would educate all children. They therefore had problems in establishing standards.

During this period of developing an administrative system that would ensure compulsory schooling, the government appointed yet another Royal Commission to inquire into the workings of the Elementary Education Acts of 1870 and 1880. Politicians were gradually adopting the view that education was important to the nation and the smooth running of the economy. This Commission, chaired by Cross, did consider the problems of making education viable and therefore looked into the question of school management. It found that the existing systems, in both school board districts and the voluntary schools, were inadequate. The managing bodies tended to be drawn from the leisured and moneyed classes (Gordon, 1974, pp. 161–3). The Cross Commission suggested various changes to this system, including the *representation of parents* on the committee of management, 'so long as they were not a preponderating element' (Elementary Education Acts, 1888, p. 67). But, although this view was widely debated in school districts and the voluntary societies, it was always roundly defeated. School managers wanted to be free of parental control and able to exercise their own discretion.

The question of women on school boards and bodies of managers was also controversial in this period. The 1870 Act had allowed for female representation on school bodies, and voluntary societies had themselves set up ladies' committees to oversee girls' schooling (Gordon, 1974, pp. 173 ff.). Nevertheless, although women were elected to school boards, attempts were made in the late 1880s to exclude them, especially married women. The courts argued, in 1889, that a married woman was not a personality; 'she was merged in the personality of her husband and therefore disqualified by sex and couverture' (DES and Welsh Office, 1977, p. 180, para. 123). This problem was not fully resolved until the second decade of the twentieth century, with the Sex Disqualification (Removal) Act (ibid.).

Thus, compulsory universal education was a long time in the making and forming. It only emerged as a result of economic change and social pressure, and when it was clearly useful to enforce certain parental behaviour and a commitment to position in the social hierarchy. The new system did enforce certain standards on parents. At the beginning of the nineteenth century parents were regarded as solely responsible for their children and with unequivocal rights over their earnings. But as the need for a more docile and differentiated labour force became apparent, with political, economic and technical changes, standards were forced upon working-class parents through the nature of schooling for their children. First, parents had to make financial sacrifices both directly through the payment of fees and through the opportunity costs of a loss of children's earnings. Second, as a result of compulsion in 1893, parents had to ensure their children's regular attendance at school. The hours of schooling, although more extensive than today, imposed burdens on working-class mothers, who had the dual responsibility of ensuring their children's regular attendance at school and of arranging their out-of-school activities. Not only was a particular standard required but it was expected that mothers would perform the necessary duties.

Changes in women's employment, especially married women's, facilitated the growth of universal and then compulsory education for the working classes. One argument, used especially in debates about the 1870 Act, was that a child of five was too young to attend school and should be with its mother. This was not based upon any evidence. On the contrary, until the second half of the century most infants had not been cared for by their mothers, evidence for which had been collected by the Newcastle Commission. In the working classes the mothers worked, as both Pinchbeck (1969) and Hewitt (1958) have shown. In the upper and middle classes, servants were the chief carers (Gathorne-Hardy, 1977). Nevertheless, this argument about maternal care was beginning to be accepted, because of the desire to exclude mothers from employment as well as their young children. But even by the turn of the century it was by no means universal that mothers, or their children, did not work. First, the earlier children attended school, the younger they could leave to find employment, and children's earnings were still valuable. Second, in certain industries and areas there was still some work for both married women and young children (Hewitt, 1958).

The notion of a family unit, with parents having particular responsibilities towards and standards for their children grew up in accordance with the changing but diverse demands of the economy. It was not a common standard at the beginning of industrialization and was not even universal by the end of the century. Mothers did not always care for infants, for example, between 1870 and 1900 the proportion of infants, that is, children under five years, in school was consistently higher than it has ever been since. It has been estimated that in 1870 one quarter of all three- to five-year-olds were in school and by 1900 almost half (Blackstone, 1971, p. 69). Nevertheless, this attendance at school made demands upon parents, and mothers in particular, that were novel and were not rights but duties.

By 1900 the relationships between parents and children, and between parents and the State, over schooling were entirely changed from the beginning of the century. Parents were no longer solely responsible for their children. But different classes of parent had different responsibilities: working-class parents had to submit their children to education and, in return, were required to behave in particular ways towards them before, during and after schooling. In particular, rearing was becoming more professionalized, and mothers were having demands made upon them. Children were also shown their position and future place in the social order. Increasingly, developments were made in vocational education, to ensure children a more precisely delineated place in the social hierarchy. Upper- and upper-middle-class parents were not required to reach the same standards as working-class parents. Even at the end of the century the employment of servants and tutors to care for young boys and girls remained the norm. These parents were only expected to obtain the adequate upbringing of their children, especially their sons. Again the actual teaching was to be left to professionals.

3

Parental responsibility for 'national efficiency'?

This chapter considers the developments in the relations between the family and schooling over a forty-year period, from the beginning of the twentieth century to the start of the Second World War. Although the first twenty years of this century witnessed major educational innovations, it has been argued that, for the inter-war years, 'there is little to write about' (Gilbert, 1970). However, as Brian Simon (1974, p. 9) has observed, 'failure on the part of government to implement policies which, at least, had widespread support is as much a matter of history as achievement of the most forward looking programme', and he has written a lengthy, scholarly book dealing with those twenty years.

In the first twenty years of the century (including the First World War) the education system was extended, both in terms of the time during which children were expected to attend school and in the types of welfare provisions made. Class differences in provision were somewhat eroded, as middle-class schooling came under greater State financial control, and schools for the working classes were modelled on such schools. Parental responsibilities were increased, not through legislation, but through the concern that the State began to show for the welfare and physical well-being of its citizens, and its use of these concepts to modify schooling. Sex, however, remained a crucial division in the form of schooling. In the inter-war years, there was considerable official and political discussion of how to transform schooling but, because of economic crises throughout the 1920s and 1930s, few of the proposed policies came to fruition. They are, however, vital for understanding educational reforms during the war and the post-war period. And parents were heavily implicated in the form of child-rearing which the State pursued.

Schooling in the early twentieth century

When the twentieth century opened, the State was involved in major debates about how to modify and reorganize schooling for both the middle and working classes. During the 1890s, there had been a number of important proposals through Royal Commissions, which were possible because of economic developments, such as Britain's recovery from the Great Depression of 1870–80 and its involvement in the Boer War. All children were now provided with at least a modicum of schooling, which was intended to help them become national assets. From 1893, all working-class children had to attend school for at least six years, from five to eleven, and over the age of eleven they were entitled to a total or partial exemption from school only if they obtained proof of employment. However, as Sutherland has pointed out (1971, p. 44), in 1895 the majority of schoolchildren had been provided with exemption from attendance by the age of twelve: only 14 per cent of the children on the registers of inspected schools were aged twelve and over. Moreover, only 2.4 per cent of those remaining at school were to be presented for examination in special subjects: the rest were 'either handicapped, or not very bright and had suffered from defective schooling earlier' (ibid.). The majority of schools provided for the working classes were merely elementary schools, although in the large industrial cities the school boards did also provide for the more able, industrious or technically-minded what were known as higher-grade schools. These schools were of some official concern in the 1890s because they were popular with the children of those in the labour movement and they provided a sound technical education. The school boards in the major cities also created, at the request of local labour movements, industrialists or employers, vocational and special technical evening courses or classes in special institutes, using money from their elementary education grants and with help from county councils through the Technical Instruction Act 1889. Extra resources provided from a new customs tax in 1890 helped county councils to establish separate technical instruction. However, by the end of the 1890s, the voluntary societies were still influential in the provision of elementary education: only slightly over half of the almost 6 million children in such education attended school board schools, the others were in voluntary schools (ibid.).

Schools for the middle classes had also become numerous by the turn of the century, although, as Lowndes (1969, p. 39) has pointed out, there is no evidence either of how many schools or how many children there were. Secondary schools (endowed, private or proprietary) were entitled to some grant income for teaching special or technical subjects but they did not have to be inspected in the same way as elementary schools were. Also parents were not in fact compelled by law to send their children to these schools, although there was an expectation that they would do so. The Bryce Royal Commission, which in 1895 reported on the state of secondary education, found that over one in ten (11 per cent) of the entrants to Oxford and Cambridge Universities had had private tutors instead of attending school. These two universities, however, catered for only a tiny proportion of even the secondary school-age population. It is generally claimed that the majority of middle-class boys and girls received an education in this period, and that it was usually in school.

The political situation at the start of the twentieth century was somewhat in flux. Although the Tories were in power, both the Liberals and the newly formed Labour party posed real threats to their control. The Labour movement had wrung several concessions from the Tories, especially over educational provisions, and they were at this point loath to concede any more. The Tory administration therefore tried to reform the elementary education system to ensure the maintenance of the old social order. The first object of its attack was the school boards. Halevy (1929) has argued that in the 1890s they were seen as 'citadels of radicalism'. In the big towns and cities, many of the elected members were trade unionists, radicals or Fabians, although in rural areas school boards still tended to consist of members of the gentry and aristocracy. But, on the whole, all the school boards posed a real threat to the established system. Lowndes (1969, p. 55) has argued that working-class parents were also wary of them because of their rigid enforcement of the school attendance laws. The voluntary schools were in financial difficulties, being dependent upon voluntary contributions, small grants and parental fees, and as a result, school boards were gradually increasing their share of educational provision and extending their facilities.

The first critical political event in this educational controversy was the establishment in 1899 of a reorganized Board of Education in central government. One of its first actions was to question the activities of school boards. This was achieved initially through one legal case. The government auditor refused to sanction the accounts of the London School Board over the Camden School of Art. In the now famous Cockerton Judgment of 1901, followed by those of the Queen's Bench and Court of Appeal, the School Board was pronounced to be acting illegally in providing specialized courses which were not defined as elementary education. The attack was, first, on the use of the rates and, second, on the legality of the courses. This legal decision provided the basis for the framing of the Education Bill which subsequently became law in the 1902 Education Act.

The Education Bill of 1901 proposed to streamline the administration of education by abolishing the school boards and bringing the voluntary schools under more direct State control. The numerous school boards were to be replaced by local education authorities (LEAs) based on the recently created (in the 1880s) system of local government, composed of county and county borough councils. The reduction in number and increase in size of authorities were used to claim that the LEAs would achieve greater administrative efficiency (David, 1976). In fact, the reduction in number of authorities was not to be huge, since what subsequently became known as 'Part III Authorities' – parishes and boroughs – were to be empowered to make basic educational provisions. The local authorities, which were bodies elected to provide a range of public facilities were to provide schooling out of their rates and capitation grants from the Exchequer. Voluntary schools providing elementary education were to come under the LEAs through similar financial measures: they were to be aided by the rates of the Exchequer. This provision would mainly consist of elementary schools for five- to thirteen-year olds. The LEAs would also be able to provide some 'higher education' through three new mechanisms. They could provide their own vocational or special classes for those staying on at school after the school-leaving age, or they could give financial aid to endowed or voluntary secondary schools, or they could pay fees to enable some working-class children to attend secondary schools. The second solution implied that some voluntary schools might come under LEA control and thus be 'municipalized'.

Parents were still to be charged fees for their children's secondary schooling, save for those children who were chosen for LEA places at fee-paying secondary schools. The Bill did not propose to alter the place of parents in the education system, although it did propose a system of managing bodies for all schools. Parents were not mentioned as potential managers. Women, however, were. Section 23(b) declared 'that a woman should not be disqualified by sex or marriage from being on a body of managers' (DES and Welsh Office (Taylor Report), 1977, p. 180). The system of managing secondary schools was also to be modified, but not through the Act. The new Board of Education started to issue Codes of Regulations for secondary schools, the second of which, in 1905, dealt with the question of school government.

This Education Bill was highly controversial and was fought out in Parliament for almost a year. The main contentious issues were the subsidization of religious schools through public funds such as the rates and the limitations on the expansion of elementary education *per se*. The TUC had since 1895 been demanding more comprehensive and extensive elementary schooling. It had, for example, called for 'a staircase, not a ladder' to secondary education and put forward the principles of equality of educational opportunity and secondary education for all.

The explicit issue addressed by the Tories was how to provide for greater 'national efficiency' through the revamping of the education system. the Boer War ended on the day that the debate on the Bill began. The Liberal Party was concerned to be reunited after its disastrous internal splits. It was pledged to oppose the religious clauses of the Bill. But the Bill was finally pushed through Parliament by the Tories, with the support of some of the Fabians – namely the Webbs – though the working classes opposed it. It became law in 1902.

The Education Act of 1902 has frequently been described as a major piece of social legislation. Sidney Webb, who supported it, wrote that 'the Bill of 1902 [is] epoch-making in the history of English education'. It certainly was important in shaping the contours of English education and yet rigidly set its limits. Secular instruction was not to be the main form of education. Nor were the working classes to be provided with the system that the labour movement demanded. The 328 new LEAs were expected only to 'supply or aid the supply of education other than elementary'. No new network of secondary schools for the working classes would be created. LEAs could, however, provide capitation grants to existing private, voluntary or endowed secondary schools and pay the fees of LEA children to attend such schools. This latter scheme of scholarships came into effect in 1904.

As a result of the Act, class differences in the education system were reinforced. Elementary and secondary education remained parallel rather than consecutive systems. On the other hand, the limitations of the elementary schooling of the nineteenth century were increasingly recognized. Children were gradually being regarded as autonomous from their parents and of *use* to the nation as a whole. The fact that the country was ill equipped to fight the Boer War – which had cost, in the terms of 1900, £27 million – gave added political incentive to the need to improve the lot of working-class children. Children were being seen as valuable national assets, not only to be controlled but to be moulded into useful citizens. This type of idea slowly germinated and became a major influence on the form of education. The change was expressed most succinctly in the 1904 Elementary Code of Regulations (Lowndes, 1969, p. 110), which laid down the new curricula for elementary schools.

The new notion of childhood also affected subsequent policy initiatives. From the late 1890s, part-time continued education had been vigorously debated. After the passage of the 1902 Act, there was in Parliament a constant spate of Private Members' Bills calling for its consolidation and compulsion. This policy was aimed at improving 'national efficiency' variously defined, in contrast to the policies espoused by the labour movement, such as secondary education for all. The Fabians vigorously opposed the latter and argued that a more feasible and more workable policy, given that most children had to leave school to earn a living, was that of 'a ladder not a staircase'. In other words, only clever working-class children should have extended educational opportunities such as scholarships to secondary schools. Limited numbers of scholarships had been introduced in the 1870s. These 'national efficiency' arguments thus led to proposals for a national minimum of education. Others, especially the Liberals, favoured the extension of part-time education.

The idea that education should be more explicitly used to fit the needs of industry, commerce, business and the war effort continued to dominate the political arena in the early 1900s. Education was the major political issue on which the general election of 1906, for example, was fought. Simon (1965, p. 53) has stated that 'once more on the issue of education . . . major political conflicts came to be fought out.' The Liberals were elected to office in 1906 and the Labour Party for the first time gained a small number of seats. The 377 Liberals were pledged to repeal the 1902 Act. It had been vehemently contested since its enactment and 'it gave rise to a substantial passive resistance movement involving 70,000 prosecutions for non-payment of rates, and took some years to gain acceptance in Wales' (Lowndes, 1969, p. 48). It was resisted both by the working classes (but not their political advocates, the Fabians) and by non-conformists, who resented the financial help given to the Church of England, which at this point held the majority of the voluntary schools. Nevertheless, the new Liberal government failed to repeal the Act, since the House of Lords rejected the amendment bill.

The Liberal administration and 'national efficiency'

The Liberals, although opposed to the 1902 Act, had not intended to provide secondary education for the working classes. Their aim was to prepare children for 'different walks of life' or social functions. They recognized that, given the changing economic system and the growth of white-collar, skilled and service occupations, education should be more fitted to employers' needs. More working-class children should be trained to be 'handymen' for the lower ranks of commerce and industry. To this end, the Liberals tried to improve the 'ladder' for working-class children to secondary education. Of course, this was also in the interests of the middle classes, whose secondary schools, run as private ventures on a fee-paying basis, were by now experiencing financial difficulties. In May 1907 a new 'free-place system' for secondary schools was created to give financial help to the schools. Secondary schools would be provided with an Exchequer grant if they made 25 per cent of their places available to children from elementary schools. The children would be selected for the schools by a test of attainment and provided with free, that is, non-fee-paying, places: there was no test of parental means, since it was not even considered that such a system would have widespread popular appeal to working-class parents. It was presumed that the majority of working-class children would still need to leave school at fourteen or earlier, if they were entitled to exemption for part-time work at eleven or a full-time exemption at thirteen.

The Liberal government also felt that parents needed more encouragement and help towards their children's education. Because education was now assumed to be not only in the national interest but of economic significance, the Liberals introduced a series of further measures to change parent-child relationships. Under the 1907 Education Act, children were to be entitled to scholarships in exceptional circumstances to prepare for teaching careers, if they could not afford to remain in school after the school-leaving age. These were to become known as maintenance allowances (Banks, 1955, p. 48; Fleet, 1976, p. 231). This provision was a sop to the demands that the labour movement had been making for an increase in wages to help the family or maintenance allowances to enable children to remain at school past the age of fourteen.

The most important measures taken by the Liberals, however, were not direct financial provisions. They concerned the health and welfare of children. A number of local authorities had established their own school medical officers in the 1890s. This system was to be extended and each LEA was required to create a school medical service. These were to check on, and also help to maintain, the health of children. To this end of ensuring the maintenance of *healthy* schoolchildren, the Liberals also introduced a school meals service, which allowed LEAs to provide free school meals at lunch-time. The argument used to justify this welfare measure as part of the school budget, was that teachers could not teach starving children. For the first time a measure to alleviate an aspect of poverty was deemed to be so vital to the nation that the fathers of such children would not be disfranchised (and thus discouraged from taking up the benefit). Hitherto, recipients of Poor Law provisions were automatically disfranchised. The measure was not intended to help mothers and enable them to take paid employment, but was, instead, an indictment of the care they had shown to their children. Indeed, this type of approach to parental responsibilities was not the only one introduced by the Liberals.

The Liberals also condemned mothers of younger children by the actions they took to regulate the schooling of infants. The Liberals' welfare measures were in part the result of an inter-departmental committee report published in 1904 on physical deterioration (Board of Education, 1904b). Evidence was produced for that committee (Whitbread, 1972, p. 64) that 'working mothers sent very young children to school to get them out of the way, and [it was] suggested that school attendance was responsible for physical deterioration when young children were forced to sit still and quiet on benches, doing work that was too fine and hence injured their eyesight.' Although the committee did not condemn the schools, the Board of Education immediately asked its women HMIs to check on the education of infants. Their report was published quickly, in 1905 (Board of Education, 1905a). It attacked the elementary schools and argued that children under the age of five should not be in 'schools of instruction', but in special nursery schools. The women HMIs were highly critical of the ways in which mothers discharged their duties to young children, judging from the appearance of the children in infant and nursery schools. Indeed, the HMIs' report had to be censored. As a result of this report, in the elementary code of 1905, article 53 (Board of Education, 1905b), LEAs could refuse to admit children under five to infant classes. The LEAs were not provided with any money to supply alternative nursery schools. The Consultative Committee to the Board of Education in 1908 also condemned mothers and argued that young children should be at home with their mothers (Board of Education, 1908). In urban areas, though, LEAs should supply special nursery schools to rescue poor, slum children from their adverse home circumstances. Nursery schools would fulfil certain social needs, where mothers were deemed to be inadequate. Again, no financial support was made available from the State and all the nursery schools that were created in the next decade resulted from voluntary effort. They were all concerned with the health and welfare of poor children and not their educational needs.

The Liberal government's major concern was with the physical efficiency of the nation. To ensure this, it instituted a series of health and welfare measures, which took over certain parental responsibilities and imposed particular standards and duties on parents, especially mothers. It did not extend educational provision *per se*. But a number of Liberal MPs submitted Private Members' Bills during this administration to improve national efficiency through other educational measures. The main thrust of these bills was to extend compulsory schooling, but not on a full-time basis. Since most working-class children needed to work after the age of thirteen, for their income was important to their families, it was proposed to provide part-time education for them in what were termed 'continuation schools' for fourteen- to eighteen-year-olds. Children were now being differentiated according to their capabilities and potential involvement in the labour market. The notion of adolescence was becoming accepted as a separate stage of children's development. Children of fourteen would not be treated automatically as adults on leaving school. They would become *'citizens in training'*. It was also important that they be prepared not only for citizenship but also for work life and particular aspects of it. Continuation schools would provide the means of such training.

Although sixteen Bills were presented, with four by the government and one in the House of Lords (Fleet, 1976, p. 42), they never gained the full support or attention of Parliament until economic circumstances forced a recognition of the issues. The Tories argued fervently against the aims, in particular of compulsion. Liberals were not convinced about the means until the outbreak of the First World War. In the meantime, LEAs were steadily limiting the age of exemption from school attendance to fourteen, using their own by-laws: they also restricted the use of labour certificates to those with the requisite qualifications (Lowndes, 1969, p. 112).

By the end of the first decade of the twentieth century, education had become an issue of great national concern. Children were no longer merely to be controlled but were to be prepared for the labour market and the family. Parents were increasingly obliged to care for their children in particular ways and to co-operate with the State in rearing the country's children. Because of rising unemployment, in 1909 the abolition of both partial and total exemptions from school attendance was proposed (Fleet, 1976, p. 40). As Barker (1972, p. 23) has argued, the justification was that 'little children were being used to keep men and women out of work.' The Liberal government tried to abolish cheap labour, but many workers who were also parents were opposed to such measures. They feared the loss of wages that would result from their children having to continue at school. In this case, parents managed to resist the State's incursions into their rights.

The concern about middle-class children was not so very different in this decade. Private secondary schools were brought into the State ambit, if they wished, through the capitation grants provided by LEAs from 1904 and by central government in the Free Place regulations of 1906. The only conditions attached to this financial aid were that they had to accept a majority of LEA governors and have 25 per cent of their places filled by elementary schoolchildren. Some of the endowed grammar schools, especially boys', willingly entered into these arrangements, because of their financial problems. The Girls' Public Day School Trust (formerly Company) schools were rather more equivocal because they sensed that the parents would fear working-class infiltration. Kamm (1971, p. 114), in her history of the Trust, has pointed out that, when a similar issue occurred over the schools providing places for girls to study for teacher training (a point to which I return in ch. 6), 'to ward off potential *parental opposition* they were reluctant to accept as pupil-teachers many elementary school girls' [my emphasis] .

Nevertheless, it is clear that the class differences which the State supported in schooling were being slightly eroded. Because schooling was seen as vital to the economy, the State was becoming involved in middle-class education. Moreover, these secondary schools were explicitly gearing their pupils to particular types of occupation. Banks (1955, p. 4) has argued that the expansion of secondary education during these years was clearly linked to new occupations and the chance for children to obtain higher economic rewards: 'the driving force in the demand for secondary education was *status* and not education as such.' Secondary education conferred exclusive privileges in the way of middle-class occupations.

The impact of the new ideas about 'national efficiency' was that LEAs created new schools for older elementary schoolchildren that were modelled on secondary schools for the middle classes. From the early 1900s, there began to develop a diversity of types of school – – higher elementary, central, junior technical and senior schools – which were financed in three ways by the LEAs. LEAs also began transforming the old higher-grade schools into LEA grammar schools (Banks, 1955, p. 48). They all served the children of the expanding occupational groups such as clerks, managers and technicians, known as the lower-middle classes. These schools provided both strictly academic and vocational curricula. They began to compete with the now traditional secondary schools: endowed grammar, private and proprietary schools, which were still financed variously through parental fees, shares and endowments. The impact of LEA secondary schools, as Banks has shown (1955), was much greater on boys than girls. The vast majority of girls were still expected to prepare for 'home duties' and their parents did not encourage them to attend such schools (Dyhouse, 1978; Davin, 1978).

Until the First World War, two different policies were pursued for post-elementary education: one was the campaign for secondary education for all on a part-time basis, and the other was selective provision for the 'aristocracy of intellect' from the working classes, alongside the middle classes. In 1914, at the outbreak of the war, the chances of a boy from an elementary school going on to a secondary school at eleven had increased somewhat to 40 to 1 (Lowndes, 1969). The proposals for compulsory part-time education still had not won approval. Children could be exempted from school on a part-time basis from twelve years old, or full-time from thirteen, and provided they had passed the Standard VI examinations and had obtained employment, a labour certificate was issued. So although more children from the working classes were provided with education, a large proportion had far less than ten years' education. Nor were these children any longer able to enter school young in order to leave early. The codes on elementary education had effectively sealed off that possibility by rigidly enforcing the age of five as the minimum age of entry. They had not substituted, in its place, extensive nursery schooling. Between 1900 and 1910, for instance, there was a considerable drop in the proportion of children aged between three and five in 'maintained' schools, from 43 to 23 per cent. Two-year-olds had been totally excluded from such schooling by the 1902 Act. In 1901 there were 2,500 children of this age reported in these schools. Ten years later, none was reported.

Education in the First World War

The First World War had a dramatic impact on family life and its relation to the economy and schooling. The major changes were, first, that married, as well as single, women took paid employment in unprecedented numbers and, second, that 'war wages' increased dramatically, enabling families in which the husband was a soldier to obtain better education for their children. Although little is known about secondary education during the war it is clear that demand for it increased. By 1920 there was what Lowndes (1969) called an 'outburst of demand', which led to the exclusion of 20,000 pupils from secondary schools, half of whom would have been fee-paying and half free-place scholars. Even with this exclusion, the odds of an elementary boy of eleven going to a free place at secondary school had been improved to 21 to 1. Secondary education had thus established its popularity because of its perceived value in the labour market. War wages had enabled even wage-earning parents to pay the fees required for attendance at secondary school.

More important, however, is how this change in standard of living affected the growth and expansion of education. Although a middle-class type of education was being extended to more of the working classes, the principle of secondary education for all had not been established. Indeed, it was during the war that the extension of part-time compulsory education reached the statute books. Reconstruction was a theme of government social policy from 1916. The 1918 Education Act, passed by Lloyd George's administration, was a major piece of legislation, mainly devoted to the 'education of the Adolescent', who should henceforth be regarded as 'the workman in training and the little wage earner' (Fleet, 1976, p. 30). The Bill of 1917 had provided for the raising of the school-leaving age to fourteen and the abolition of exemptions from school attendance below that age. The establishment of continued education (originally termed continuation schools) for all fourteen- to eighteen-year-olds on a part-time basis was also proposed. Fleet states (1976, p. 34) that 'there seems to have been general agreement that it should prepare adolescents for adult life, both for work through appropriate training and for the exercise of civic duties and *parental* responsibilities' [my emphasis]. Indeed, in the previous years there had been parallel recommendations to prohibit adolescent labours, and the Act was heavily influenced by the Consultative Committee on Juvenile Education in Relation to Employment. This documented the severe problem of adolescent exploitation, aggravated by war work. The Education Bill of 1917 proposed that there should be eight hours a week of continued education for all those over fourteen.

The Bill also proposed a major reconstruction of the rest of the education system. Not only was it to extend educational provision upwards, but also allow for it to be extended downwards to younger children. LEAs were not to be mandated, but allowed, to provide nursery education. The other major 'health' measure that the previous Liberal government had introduced – school meals – was also to be extended. Apart from these two health measures, parents were to be more directly aided. Fees in elementary schools were to be fully abolished, but not those in secondary schools. But LEAs were to be provided with new ways of 'aiding' secondary education, through percentage rather than capitation grants.

The original Bill proved so controversial that it had to be withdrawn, but because of the continuing demand for educational reform, in the new Parliamentary session it was slightly amended and reintroduced. What became law, in August 1918, was a hybrid scheme of previous proposals. Education was still to be extended both up and down the age range: nursery education permitted, the school-leaving age raised to fourteen and continued education provided for adolescents from fourteen to eighteen. Financial measures were also included: the abolition of parental fees for elementary education and aid to secondary schools. The Act also dealt with administrative ways of enforcing its proposals. Sanctions would be placed on potential participants in continued education if they did not co-operate. Penalties were to be imposed on parents, employers *and* the young people themselves (Fleet, 1976, p. 73): 'on the grounds that parents could not have the same control over a young person aged 14 to 18 as they could over a child and that a penalty on the young person was necessary for the enforcement of compulsory attendance.' LEAs had to provide the schools but were not empowered to charge fees. Maintenance allowances for continued or full-time education were included in a form slightly modified from the 1907 Act. The Liberals would not accept Labour's proposals for full maintenance allowances, but provided merely for the costs of attending school rather than of foregoing work. The Labour Party regarded maintenance grants (Barker, 1972, p. 31) as 'a form of compensation for working class parents for the nationalization of some of their property – the earning capacity of their children'.

The main significance of continued education was the change in emphasis over family responsibilities as well as the contribution of the adolescent to the nation and its economy. Adolescents were no longer to be treated as the sole responsibility or right of their parents, but were to be seen as relatively autonomous. On the other hand, leaving school did not signal adulthood: such children should still be in *training* and withdrawn from the labour market to that end. But the recognition that children were in part necessary to the family and a right of parents was also clear; hence the part-time employment. Parents were not completely divested of their rights over their children or their earning capacity; nor were they to be totally responsible for their misdemeanours. Nevertheless, continued education was not the only post-elementary policy proposed by the Liberals in the 1918 Act. Secondary schools were to be supported through a changed financial mechanism, but were to remain outside full State control. They were to continue to charge parents fees, although they were now entitled, if they chose, to a grant for their running costs from either central or local government.

The Education Act of 1918 created new concepts of parental responsibility towards adolescents, confirmed by increasing State involvement in educational provision. Parental responsibility was also redefined by other sections of the Act. The government sought to confirm the trends, partly as a result of the war, towards early child care outside the home. The war had created demands for women's paid work and therefore many mothers took up employment. Their young children had to be cared for. Creches or nurseries were demanded. Some mothers in the labour movement also argued for them not on the grounds of economic necessity but as part of a campaign to improve family health and welfare. This campaign had begun well before the war, in the early 1900s. The Act only partly satisfied the demands of the campaigners for preschool provisions. The Act included clauses to *empower* LEAs to provide nursery *education* for two- to five-year-olds, emphasizing nurturance and health rather than actual instruction. Indeed, one clause stated that the schools or classes should be provided 'as necessary or desirable for healthy physical and mental development'. It also added, 'or attending to the health and nourishment and physical welfare of children in nursery schools'. The Liberal framers of the law clearly envisaged a national network of such nursery schools eventually, for it was also written into the Act that the age of entry to elementary schools should be raised to six when there were sufficient nursery schools. Nevertheless, the Act gave only permissive powers to LEAs. It did not mandate LEAs or provide finance and it assumed that LEAs would rely on voluntary effort. It was clearly formulated in a wartime situation when mothers were forced to rely on State help, since their husbands were away. In this situation, the State pledged itself to help and share with parents, or mothers rather, some of their child-care responsibilities.

The 1918 Act, in sum, defined a clear new framework whereby the State and parents together cared for and reared both young children and adolescents. Children were increasingly regarded as useful to the State and therefore to be moulded towards the nation's needs. Parents had to be shown how to treat their children and were seen as, on the whole, inadequate to discharge all their responsibilities for rearing children. Neither provision – nursery or continued education – was intended to divest parents of their responsibilities but to point up their ineffectiveness and limitations.

Although the war had a dramatic impact upon parental responsibilities and family life and led to a changed course of social policy, it did not have lasting effects through these educational provisions. Neither nursery nor continued education was ever fully implemented. This was mainly because of the economic crises which almost immediately succeeded the resumption of peace. The measures taken to restore the economy were concentrated in education, which was used as one of the most important of the government's domestic policies. In 1921 and 1922 the Lloyd George Coalition government felt it had to reduce its proposed expenditure: the so-called 'Geddes axe', a form of public expenditure cut, fell heavily on nursery education. Two circulars prevented LEAs from providing such schools. Even before that drastic attack, though, there had been little initiative: in 1918–19, for instance, only thirteen nursery schools had received grants. The cuts in the early 1920s effectively prevented the expansion of any nursery education. Continued education also never became a reality. This was because no administrative framework had been devised by the Liberals. There was still pressure from the Labour government for secondary, rather than continued, education.

The other policy proposal which had been viewed, ever since its introduction in 1907, as a 'dangerous' change which would lead to 'the break-up of family life' was also not effectively implemented – school meals. Indeed, well before 1918 there had been a decline in LEA provision although in 1914 the limit on the rate to be used for school meals had been lifted. 'War wages' and servicemen's allowances which took into account family size probably enabled mothers to buy their own adequate food. The LEAs' limited efforts – only one-third of the LEAs were providing meals in 1918 – were briefly increased in 1921 during the coal stoppage, only to be severely curtailed by the public expenditure cuts. Moreover, a new constraint on provision was introduced, that the Guardians of the Poor Law should pay the LEAs for the meals provided for children whose parents were on out-relief. Children's home and parental circumstances became the criterion for a free school meal (Land, 1978, p. 4).

The inter-war years

The early 1920s witnessed a setback in the developing partnership between the State and parents over child-rearing. Parents were once more forced to rely on their own resources for the care of their children. Mothers, in particular, were forced to bear the brunt of this responsibility by both looking after very young children and providing meals for their school-age children. At the same time, they were decisively excluded from a rapidly shrinking labour market. There was, however, a brief attempt in 1924 by the first Labour government to reintroduce nursery education by withdrawing the two circulars curtailing expenditure. It was not generally an educational priority, and with the fall of the Labour government it lost all political support. Members of the labour movement still campaigned vociferously for nursery education. The Nursery Schools Association was founded in 1923 as a propaganda movement of women, mainly teachers, but it had little impact on policy development. In 1929 another Labour government again announced its support of nursery education, but did not provide the funds.

The main priority of the labour movement and Labour party was the development of secondary education for all. Improvements in LEA provision continued apace. The LEAs extended schools for post-elementary education and by the early 1920s there was a myriad of types of school. In 1924, parental fees for grammar school attendance were abolished in some LEAs. Both central and local government continued to provide grants to secondary schools outside the LEAs, in exchange for free places, scholarships and LEA governors.

In 1926 two kinds of secondary school emerged, one of which received a direct grant from central government and the other a grant from the LEA.

This confused system was the subject of much concern in the mid-1920s. Extended education was considered to be both a direct remedy for unemployment and a general solution to Britain's economic problems. Raising the school-leaving age to fifteen was suggested as one policy (Barker, 1972, p. 53). The Consultative Committee to the Board of Education, chaired by Hadow, was asked to consider the broad issues and it produced a number of reports. The most significant in this respect was the one produced in 1926, entitled *The Education of the Adolescent* (Board of Education, 1926), which recommended critical reforms of State schooling. First, it suggested the rationalization of elementary and secondary education into one system. For the first time in official circles, although it had frequently been suggested by trade unionists, socialists and others of the labour movement, secondary education was declared to be consecutive to elementary education. The Committee also proposed that the latter be officially renamed primary education and that it end at eleven. All post-primary schooling should be called secondary education.

This was, of course, to be more than a titular change. The whole orientation of education and its relationship to the socio-economic system was to be altered. The class basis of schooling was no longer to be that of separately governed institutions. The Committee proposed that all children – not a few children selected by parental background or their means to pay – would be able to follow a type of secondary education best suited to their capacities and 'bent of mind'. It planned different types of school, all providing at least four years of post-primary education. Another recommendation to achieve this was that the school-leaving age be raised to fifteen. The Committee did not set out a clear pattern of secondary education but, on the other hand, did not intend it to be the extension of traditional, academic grammar schools. There would be junior technical schools for those hoping to enter skilled careers and 'modern' schools which would provide the continued education of the commercial, literary and evening institutes. The Hadow Report, although recommending *secondary* education for all, retained a notion of different types of children. This was based on a new form of reasoning, psychology, which was subsequently consolidated in later reports of the Consultative Committee.

The Report was not immediately translated into practice, but some secondary schools (endowed and private) were given more State support. In 1926 the grant and free-place regulations were revised. Schools were compelled to choose between having a direct grant from central government in exchange for providing free places to LEA children, or coming under more direct LEA control, or remaining entirely independent. These regulations applied equally to boys' and girls' schools. In the event, there were 235 schools which opted for direct grants from central government. These new regulations led to a clearer distinction between LEA and other secondary schools. The majority of secondary schools receiving State financial support chose LEA help. Those that opted for direct grants did so either because of religious affiliation – mainly the Roman Catholics – or from a desire for autonomy and predicted parental opposition to working-class infiltration.

By the end of the 1920s, there had been a tremendous growth in educational provision, but this was almost totally concentrated in the secondary schools. The schools established were mostly maintained by the LEAs and were day schools. The schools supported with direct grants were also mainly day schools. Lowndes (1969) has pointed out that there was at the same time a gradual decline in both private and boarding schools, which reached their lowest numbers in 1935. The boarding school had become popular in the previous century with the introduction of a vast network of railways, among other things. With the improvement in the early 1920s of more individual or personal methods of transport, especially the bicycle, the day school gained in popularity. It was, of course, also more accessible in terms of cost to a wider range of parents. Lowndes adds the point that the odds against an elementary school boy of eleven obtaining a free secondary education had been reduced to 13 to 1. (He does not give the chances for girls.) In total, there were 169,254 pupils paying no fees at 1,341 direct-grant and LEA schools.

Although proposals to transform secondary education had been made, a more immediate political solution to continuing economic problems was to raise the school-leaving age. The Labour Party fought for it in the 1929 general election as a solution to unemployment. In the election there was much political rhetoric in favour of more social unity and an end to class divisiveness. The Tory Stanley Baldwin, in an appeal to the teachers during the election, even argued (Lowndes, 1969, p. 94):

> One of the strongest bonds of union between *men* is a common education, and England has been the poorer that in her national system of schooling she has not in the past fostered this fellowship of the mind. The classification of our schools has been on the lines of social rather than educational distinction; a youth's school badge has been his social label. The interests of social unity demand the removal of this source of class prejudice and the drastic remodelling of the national structure to form a coherent whole.

It was indeed the case that during the 1930s the extension of secondary education continued. However, class barriers were certainly not removed: they were modified as the class system changed. Many LEAs did reorganize their higher elementary education into senior departments or schools; junior technical schools developed alongside the county or maintained grammar schools. But parental background became a renewed factor in access to a secondary or private school. With yet further expenditure cuts in 1931, the National Government made a proposal for the imposition of a means test on the parents of scholarship winners to secondary schools. The free places were to become known as special places. This created a huge furore and the National Government asserted, in response, its ideal of moving towards a less restricted system of secondary education in which *all* parents would be tested for their means, not merely the parents of scholarship holders. This means test would be attendant upon a general competitive academic examination. In other words, the access to secondary education in future would be based upon academic merit *and* parental means and not only the latter.

This remained but an ideal until the end of the Second World War. So, too, did the other issue which dominated the educational horizon of the period – the raising of the school-leaving age. The age of fourteen for leaving school had been effectively set by the 1918 Act. In the early 1930s, as a response to chronic unemployment, the vexed question of continued education was transformed into one of raising the compulsory full-time leaving age. In 1930, 1931 and again in 1932, it was proposed that children should not leave school until fifteen. The third Bill, of 1932, reached the House of Lords before it was rejected. Three years later yet another attempt was made by the Conservative government to give effect to the recommendation of the 1926 Consultative Committee. In 1936 the Bill was passed, raising the age to fifteen, to take effect in 1939, but because of the outbreak of the Second World War, it never came into effect. Yet the figures for youth unemployment up to 1935 were very alarming. Even more distressing was the apparent chronic decline in the birth rate which led to fears that by the 1970s there would be widespread economic stagnation.

The 1930s were years of educational frustration and stagnation. No new policies were effected and the school system remained an administrative muddle. Consideration was given frequently to extending and reorganizing education for adolescents. The Hadow recommendations had had sufficient impact for children now to be differentiated not only by class but according to their ages. Sex differences in schooling were to continue because another of the Consultative Committee's reports (Board of Education, 1923) on the secondary school curriculum relegated co-education to an appendix. Adolescence was accepted as a distinct stage, separate from childhood *per se*, and school pupils here were to be treated differently. Parents' responsibilities towards adolescents were not the same as to young children. It was at this stage of life that children could be prepared for their adult life and the world of work. How that preparation should occur was still not formulated and, indeed, the problems of the economy loomed larger than the preparation for work. Nevertheless, the State's responsibility for the regulation of the labour market was being more accepted and adolescents' removal from it was of prime political importance, even if never actually fully achieved.

The nature of the preparation for the labour market remained a problem, because of the question of the types of skill required and how to allocate children of different social classes to them. At this time, different members of the labour movement advocated a diversity of versions of the common secondary school. The first proposal, from the National Union of Teachers (NUT) in 1928, was for the 'large multiple bias school'. The National Association of Labour Teachers, a year later, favoured multilateral schools, that is, schools on one site catering for a variety of needs – academic, technical, commercial.

In response to pressure from the labour movement and because education was regarded in political rhetoric as vital to solving economic crises and coping with economic development, the Conservative Government in 1934 asked the Consultative Committee to the Board of Education to report on secondary education. In evidence to this Committee, chaired by Spens, both the TUC and the NUT advocated the multilateral school with 'grammar and modern' sides. The NUT stated that 'differentiated studies in the same school' would be 'the ideal arrangement'. As a result of these suggestions, in 1935 the Labour Party formally adopted the policy of selective development of multilateral schools.

The report of the Consultative Committee in 1938 (Board of Education, 1938), however, was not so unequivocal in its support of this form of secondary school. It based its recommendations on the psychological needs, abilities and capabilities of different types of children and argued that the multilateral school, incorporating so many needs, would be too large to be viable (David, 1976). The Spens Committee recommended instead three different types of school. These would be for children of different academic abilities or aptitudes and would prepare them for different 'worlds of work'. In fact, the implicit recommendation was about work preparation for boys. Oddly, the Committee did not take account of girls at all. The presumption must be that girls were to be prepared to take their part alongside men as their dependents. Wolpe (1975) discusses this in more detail.

The two important points about the Spens Report were, first, that the class basis of the system was clearly rationalized in terms of psychological abilities being predispositions in the preparation for work and second, education was linked not merely to exclusion from the labour market but entry to it. As Banks (1967) has argued, it laid the basis for the selection of 'the aristocracy of intellect'. More sophisticated forms of selection by intelligence testing were developed.

Two earlier Consultative Committee Reports, with Hadow as chairman, also laid emphasis upon the contribution of children to the world of work and the family. They were concerned with nursery and primary schools (Board of Education, 1931 and 1933). Indeed, the Reports re-emphasized the trend towards more *home* care for very young children. Although the Labour Party from 1926 had been in favour of mandatory nurseries, especially on health grounds, because of the Slump this had never found general acceptance. In 1929 the Labour Party had included nursery schools in its election platform. After Labour came to power in the election, a circular on nursery provision from the Board of Education and the Department of Health called for 'a fair start' and outlined alternative methods to achieve preschool provision. The Slump of 1931 prevented full implementation, but some LEAs, as Blackstone (1971) has shown, continued to support nursery education.

The Hadow Report of 1933 called for nurseries for three- to five-year-olds, but set the age of five as the compulsory school starting age. The grounds for advocating nursery schools were health and not education, since the Report was heavily influenced by the Chief Medical Officer to the Board of Education. The Committee did not accept the principle of a universal system of nursery education on educational grounds. The *home* was deemed best for children under five, except where this was proved to be unsatisfactory. In this latter case schools would contribute to young children's physical, mental and moral development. Parental (or rather maternal) responsibility for children was now, almost by default, being more strictly defined and a clear evaluation was made of types of preschool care. By refusing to share early childhood education with mothers the State was locking women into particular positions in the family and the economy. Following this Hadow Committee Report, in 1936 the Board of Education published a pamphlet on nursery schools and classes which called for the 'physical and medical nurture of the debilitated child'. However, the declining birth rate, a characteristic feature of the 1930s, was just becoming apparent. As a result, spare capacity in infant and elementary schools was slowly used for nursery classes. One way of trying to stem the decline in the birth rate was to show public dissatisfaction with home-based socialization. Yet, even by the start of the Second World War, there were places for only 1 in 10 preschoolers in nursery schools. During the inter-war years, middle-class mothers did not send their young children to nurseries or kindergartens. They therefore provided little support for this demand to extend State provision *down* the age range.

Similar developments took place in allied education services. They were argued for on health, not educational, grounds. The school meals service was expanded during the 1930s, along with the provision of milk. The rationale for school meals was again the health and nutritional needs of children. Indeed, children were selected for free *meals* on medical grounds and not only parental means. For those rather less malnourished, the Chief Medical Officer to the Board of Education suggested *milk*. This was not a purely humanitarian measure but one clearly linked with the vagaries of the farming industry in a situation of economic crisis. Schools provided a steady market for milk and helped the unhealthy farming industry. By the end of the 1930s three-quarters of LEAs were providing free milk to nearly half a million children and milk at 1½d. a pint to a further two million. The school meals industry had not expanded nearly so rapidly and in 1939 only half the LEAs provided any free meals.

When war broke out in 1939, schooling had changed dramatically since the 1914 war. In some respects, there was a clearer partnership between the State and parents over children, but this partnership was specified in such a way as to define rigorous standards of behaviour towards children from their parents, especially from mothers. The standards of home life were more clearly circumscribed. The net effect of the extension of schooling, especially at the 'upper age margin' (to borrow Fleet's phrase), was to exclude more children from a tightly defined labour market. Mothers, especially those with preschool children, were also excluded from the labour market because of the *lack* of extension of education at the 'lower age margin'. There were still, however, class distinctions in educational provision, although the trend in the 1930s was towards an acceptance of the ideology of secondary schooling for both middle and working-class children. Private schooling had certainly not disappeared. It increasingly became the preserve of the upper-middle and ruling classes, for whom boarding education remained an essential characteristic (Gathorne-Hardy, 1977). Mothers, in this case, were expected to play a more distant role in their children's rearing.

Education and economic life: A matter of parental right or duty?

The origins of the contemporary education system lie in the Second World War. It was during this time of social and economic upheaval that major reviews of the nature of education were initiated. The reviews considered not only the social organization of education but the relevance of specific features of the system to the economy and, in particular, to industrial and technological development. They also covered the partnership between the State and parents in child-rearing. This issue was made the more stark by the way in which the State dealt with educational provision in war. Schemes of evacuation, which involved separating children from their parents, were a hallmark of the wartime education system.

This chapter examines first, educational issues during the war, which culminated in the Education Act of 1944; second, the consequences of this legislation and its ideological bases for peace-time educational provision; and third, the modifications in the relationships between education, the economy and the family in the 1950s and 1960s. By 1970, two major changes had occurred in educational organization. One was that the education system no longer merely reinforced the social division of labour but for the older age range it was used to impart knowledge of, and skills for, the economic division of labour. Education was being used to enhance economic growth, through its contribution to technology and industry. The second change was that parents were increasingly involved in achieving the State's objectives through education: in particular, duties were imposed upon mothers of young children. On the other hand, parents of adolescents were divested of some of their financial responsibilities for schooling to enable the State to exploit their children's talents and abilities.

Educational organization in the Second World War

When war broke out in 1939, the government was not so unprepared as it had been in 1914, in part because the war had been predicted for several years. Indeed, in 1938, a year before the war began, the government had devised an ingenious and probably unique scheme of evacuation, which centred on schoolchildren and pregnant women or nursing mothers. The aim was to transfer these women and children to places of safety and to continue the education of the schoolchildren as undisturbed as possible. The scheme had revolutionary implications for the relationships between the family and the State : the State took over major responsibility for supporting women and children. What is fascinating today is that the scheme was accepted with very little political discussion or dissension. Yet it was evacuation on an enormous scale. During the course of the war, *all* schools in 100 areas, mainly London and large cities, were dispersed to small towns and villages over 100 miles from London (Lowndes, 1969, p. 194). Children were taken, not with their mothers, but with their school-teachers, to new schools. They were removed from their parental homes and fostered out in families in small towns and villages. Lowndes claims that this was seen as the only way of ensuring their safety (1969, p. 197): 'The best, if not only, way to do this would be to send them out as schools under the control of their teachers and board them out with foster parents in the country.'

Although this was an unprecedented break with past policies – and ideologies about the care of children – it was achieved with the minimum of controversy. In London, according to Lowndes (ibid.), in 1938 'at parents' meetings 80% of parents agreed to allow their children to leave with the school and practically every member of London's 20,000 teachers volunteered to take them.' Moreover, in one month (January 1939) 4 million homes were visited in the countryside and offers were received to care for 2¼ million unaccompanied children In the first evacuation over half a million children from the LCC area were removed. During the whole war, about 4 million mothers and children were evacuated.

The initial intention of the scheme was to link a city school with one in the place of evacuation but in such a way that the local and visiting school would retain their own identities. This did not happen because the scheme was administered, not by the Board of Education, but by the Ministry of Health, which was more concerned with residential than educational questions. With this concern, it created a vast network of nurseries and nursery schools for evacuated children, especially those without parental care. It set up 230 residential nurseries and 430 residential nursery schools for 60,000 children under five. Day nurseries – 450 providing 14,000 places – were also set up in reception areas (Ferguson and Fitzgerald, 1954, ch. 4).

Evacuation schemes revolutionized the relationship between the State and families over the care and education of children. The State took full responsibility for many preschool children and all schoolchildren, radically altering parental duties. Moreover, it recognized the financial burden of parental care. Foster-parents, that is, women who took in evacuees as boarders, were paid a weekly allowance for their services.

The scheme also threw up questions about children's welfare. A whole series of new measures were developed whereby children received welfare services as of right. For example, milk was distributed to all schoolchildren. Clothing schemes were developed to ensure that all children were adequately clothed for school. Youth welfare centres for children of school-leaving age were developed. Most important, school health services became more extensive and efficient: children were immunized and vaccinated, and they were screened for medical and emotional problems.

Health was a major criterion for State intervention, together with the need for women to participate in the labour force. Indeed, it was the grounds for the extension of the school meals service. The original concern over the declining birth rate in the 1930s increased anxiety about the health of the existing population, especially as competition between nations became a real problem towards the end of the decade. The 'state of the nation', and its preparedness for war, forced consideration of the health of children. Means were considered to prevent, rather than merely cure, malnutrition. School meals were argued for on the grounds of prevention of ill health and this changed the basis of the implementation of this policy. Free school meals were no longer to be provided only on medical grounds, but were to be more widely available. R.M. Titmuss later wrote (1956, ch. 4) that 'it needed a second World War, employment demands for mothers in factories and another food shortage to achieve what 24 years of peace and thousands of nutrition investigations had failed to do.' School meals gradually became a normal feature of school life to all children whose parents wanted them to have a midday meal on payment, or free if necessary. In 1940 only 1 child in 30 had a school meal; by 1945 it was 1 in 3 children. However, many parents needed reassurances from the LEAs that the scheme was not just for 'necessitous children', who had in the past been fed in special 'feeding centres'. Indeed provision expanded most rapidly in areas where *no* children had been fed previously. Parents were wary of the stigma of State aid and the abrogation of responsibilities previously demanded of them.

The government also had to find ways of bringing women into the labour force. To facilitate women's employment, the war government provided a number of incentives. Chief amongst them was the provision of nursery centres for children under school age, as well as school meals becoming more abundantly available for those at school. The State was prepared to take over what had hitherto been mainly regarded as maternal duties – the looking after young children, providing meals and care – to enable mothers to participate in the labour force. Preschool children were cared for in a number of ways. First, LEAs extended nursery schooling, in either voluntary or LEA schools, to educate young children. In 1938 there were only 8,000 places in about 114 schools; by 1946 there were over twice that number – 19,000 places. Second, the Board of Education tried to co-operate with welfare authorities to extend nursery, rather than school, provision. In 1940 it urged joint action by LEAs, welfare and reception authorities in the setting up of nursery centres in reception areas for the evacuated. This proved to be unworkable, and the following year the creation of special war nurseries was urged instead. These were to be financed by the Maternity and Child Welfare Department of the Ministry of Health. They were to provide not education but *care* for preschool children, to enable young married women to join the labour force. They were full-time nurseries and were open for up to fifteen hours a day.

These provisions helped to popularize the idea that young mothers could and should take paid employment, and that their children could be looked after by the State. Although mothers had worked in previous generations, the Depression of the 1930s had created a climate for the ideology of the non-employed housewife. The war situation enabled an alternative ideology to gain credence. It set the context for the new legislation and for defining a new partnership in child care. However, the form of most wartime provision for young children was that of care not education. Indeed, in the nursery centres there was much disagreement over how to treat children between those who advocated educational schemes and those who favoured health measures. There were, in fact, three different schemes used during the war. Nevertheless, by 1944 there were 1,000 day nurseries providing for 71,806 children of war workers.

The major policy concern of the war years was the *future* of education and its link to social reconstruction after the war. This was associated with other social policy issues such as health, welfare and housing, as well as family responsibilities and rights. Indeed, no sooner had war begun than civil servants at the Ministry of Education, evacuated to Bournemouth, began to plan for the future peace. Their plans and those of the politicians were slow to mature. In 1941 they produced *Education after the War*, popularly known as the 'Green Book'. In the meantime, the government's plans for a whole range of new social welfare provisions began to take concrete form. The report *Social Insurance and Allied Services* written by Sir William Beveridge, which formed the basis for many of the changes, was published in 1942 and overnight became a best seller. It included education as one of the five key issues for social reform. This provided confirmation of the need for restructuring education.

Children were recognized as a national resource and the connection between their future work and education was acknowledged. The existing educational system did not seem to fit contemporary or future needs. In particular, the education of the vast majority did not fit them for their part in the labour force. Nor was the State getting the best out of all children, since many were denied access to educational opportunities. This situation could not be allowed to continue. The 1936 Education Act had been the first attempt to reform secondary education, by a partial raising of the school-leaving age. Its planned date of implementation was the day war broke out, so it never came into effect. It also had a dual objective which became the basis for the wartime debates. The first was to link the school-leaving age with employment opportunities. Any adolescent who could produce evidence of an offer of 'beneficial employment' could leave before the school-leaving age, but there were problems of defining the term. The second objective was to revise the relationship between voluntary authorities, LEAs and central government by providing a new financial system of grants for extending school buildings. This also would have become a thorny administrative and political problem. The question of the status of religious schools was one of the most controversial issues in framing new legislation.

Throughout the war there was much political review and debate about how to reconstruct the educational system. Both the content of curricula, and the attendant examination system (see ch. 7), and the organization of schools were hotly debated. Agreement on reform in principle did not extend to agreement on method. It was agreed, in principle, that education should be extended for *all* children and should be *free* of charge to parents. The distinction between primary and secondary education should hold for all children. Universal secondary education with a raised school-leaving age would be finally a reality. It was regarded as of national value, and the abolition of a charge, or fees, was not highly contentious for State-maintained schools, although it was for the endowed and public schools. The public benefits of an educated population weighed more heavily than the private or individual benefits. Nevertheless, the public value of education was not the sole argument for universal secondary education. Class and religious (which paralleled class) differences were not to be entirely obliterated. The main debate, therefore, centred upon what privileges to maintain within the system. In particular, the question revolved about the incorporation of private or endowed schools into the State-maintained system and the role of the religious, voluntary authorities. Parental rights over their children's education remained a vexed problem. The new balance to be struck was contentious, since it affected what privileges parents would be able to pass on to their children and whether their income should weigh heavily. This was the subject of an official report, on which legislation was based. In 1943 a Commission chaired by Fleming was set up to investigate the public schools for the first time since the nineteenth century. Two other reports bore on the general issue, those of the Spens and Norwood Committees.

At the other end of the social scale, there was more unanimity about a minimum standard of provision and opportunity. Children of poor parents would not be denied access to secondary schools on the grounds of income. Moreover, such children would be entitled to educational opportunities after the statutory age for leaving school. The opportunity costs of such education were openly considered and questions were raised about providing parents with financial aid (educational maintenance allowances) to enable their adolescents to continue to attend school. Although this question had been discussed by previous framers of legislation, namely by Fisher in designing his Act in 1918, the full extent of indirect exclusion from educational benefits or rights had not been acknowledged. It could only be an issue when children's abilities to participate more effectively in the labour force were under critical review.

Not only secondary education was scrutinized politically. So, too, were primary, nursery and further education. The political ideal of equality of educational opportunity was not contended, and was to be implemented throughout the educational spectrum. The operational definition was contentious, then and throughout the 1950s and 1960s. Serious consideration was given to extending educational provision to younger age groups, on both health and educational grounds. Moreover, children's participation in education was also in need of revision. Concern was expressed, as a result of war experiences, over access to welfare services such as milk, meals, clothing and medical inspections as a right and not as a concession.

The Act that was eventually passed in 1944 has occasionally been nicknamed 'the Children's Charter'. In fact, the word 'child' hardly appeared in the statutes and there was certainly very little about children's rights. These rights were the main issue but were dealt with indirectly, in terms of the relative rights and duties of parents and the State acting *in loco parentis* through teachers, the LEAs, governors or managers and central government itself. Children were the object of concern in that child-centred education was the ideal but they were not regarded as having any needs or wishes which could not be catered for by others. The question of balance between public and private benefit from education was crucial and similarly the question of what the parents and the State had to do to further these interests. The issue was about children and their future *uses*. In this legislation, children were clearly of paramount importance to the well-being of the nation and its economic productivity. They had therefore to be excluded from the labour market until they were capable of participating in it efficiently and effectively. The concern was no longer with ensuring a social order but with the supply of individuals to actual positions within the economy. Nevertheless, social ordering still played a part. Education was not only for supplying the economy but also for reproducing the social order and hence sustaining parental rights to pass on their positions and privileges. The arguments about the importance of education became extremely complicated.

The legislation did not follow the exact guidelines laid down by any of the reports on education commissioned within the previous decade. The Spens Committee (Board of Education, 1938) had explicitly argued for matching secondary education to the world of work. The organization of such education was not to be uniform but predicated upon children's differing psychological abilities, a rationale provided by academics such as Cyril Burt who advised the Committee. This type of reasoning was also taken up in the Norwood Report published in 1943, which had been commissioned from the Secondary Schools Examinations Council (1943, ch. 1) to consider examinations in the two existing types of secondary school, grammar and technical. It too advocated separate types of school, stressing the importance of child-centred education. The ultimate aim was to fit children to the adult world (ibid., ch. 2) as 'citizens and workers with hand and brain in a society of fellow citizens and fellow workers'. It argued that children could 'roughly' be divided into three groups on the basis of their aptitudes, not measured ability. Groups of children could be identified (ibid., ch. 3) as those who 'could take a long view and hold in their minds several ideas at one time', those for whom 'the subtleties of language were too difficult' and those who could only cope with concrete ideas ('he often fails to relate his knowledge or skills to other branches of activity . . . he may be incapable of a long series of connected steps'). On the basis of this judgment about *types* of children (in fact, only *boys*), the Committee recommended (ibid.) three types of school: 'The needs . . . should be met within three broad types of secondary education . . . each school offering alternative courses which would yet keep the school true to type.' Dent (1961) has argued that it 'translated tripartism from a proposal into a doctrine.' In fact, this division was based upon the Norwood Committee's knowledge of existing facilities and the division between grammar, technical and secondary modern schools. Yet only 40 per cent of LEAs had technical schools. In the remaining areas no children presumably could be grouped into that type! The division seemed appropriate for the reproduction of labour requirements. Grammar schools (ibid., p. 21) were for the 'learned professions or [those] who have taken up higher administrative or business posts'. The second group were to be the technicians needed by industry and the third prepared for semi-skilled or unskilled jobs. In fact, as Wolpe (1975) has pointed out, the division was one for boys only. Girls' interests were to be divided in terms of their preparation for the family and home, what the report termed the world of citizenship, rather than work.

This report was not fully translated into statute, although its ideas were of importance in the framing of legislation and, more important, in its subsequent implementation. It affected the White Paper entitled *Educational Reconstruction*, which was published in 1943 and from which the Act derived (Ministry of Education, 1943a). Both the Labour Party and the TUC had disagreed with the proposals, arguing in favour of multilateral schools, that is, common secondary schools, but subdivided on the lines of the Norwood proposals. They also argued for a common school to the age of thirteen. In fact, some of the Labour Party admired the traditional grammar school and really wanted that to be the model for secondary education, free for all children (Parkinson, 1970). The White Paper, produced by a coalition government of Tory and Labour, was able to argue for tripartism in secondary education with the proviso that each type of school be of 'equal standing' and enjoy 'parity of esteem'. Both political parties were concerned about the economic objectives of education and how grammar schools could help in achieving them, so that multilateralism was not hotly defended (Banks, 1955).

The other important issue in the framing of legislation was the role of parental means in educational distribution and public schools. In 1942, at the public schools' request, a Commission chaired by Fleming had been set up. The schools 'were conscious of the social changes which were taking place and anxious not to be isolated' (McClure, 1968, p. 210). The Fleming Report (Board of Education, 1943b) argued for the social importance of education and the view that access to types of school, such as day or boarding, should not be always influenced by the financial circumstances of parents. It was argued that day schools had three features which were not mirrored in boarding schools: a larger share of interest in pupils' education was left to the home; day schools developed a measure of co-operation with parents and local institutions which could not be a feature of boarding schools; and children learnt more about their fathers' trade or profession and their mothers' household tasks and care of children. Boarding schools, on the other hand, developed a perspective wider than the home background. The Committee recommended that all secondary day and boarding education should be 'freely available and without financial bar' (ibid., p. 100). It proposed the replacement of direct grants to certain endowed and proprietary schools by a scheme whereby LEAs would reserve places at independent day or boarding schools and pay the fees for their pupils to attend. This would enable children from poor home circumstances to attend. In addition, the Committee suggested the provision of bursaries for children from primary schools to attend boarding schools. The LEA would pay the fees and recover a part from parents on a sliding scale, according to income. Third, it was proposed that boarding education should not be the preserve only of the wealthy and of the independent sector, but that maintained schools should provide some boarding places. The thrust of the Fleming Report was to alter the nature of the partnership between parents and schools. Parents should neither act as a barrier to nor fully control their children's education. Thus fees should not be the main channel of access to certain types of school. Boarding schools, in which parents inevitably would have less continual control, should be more easily available.

Although both of the measures proposed by the Fleming Committee had been used in a modified version earlier in the war, when the evacuation solution had not been opposed, they were not incorporated into the 1944 legislation. The argument was that to terminate direct grants would be to frighten off these schools from the State system, make them independent and might lead to more social exclusivity in terms of school composition. Instead, the direct-grant system was extended, parental fees continued to be charged in those schools and no large-scale measures were taken to extend boarding facilities.

The 1944 Act was very much a compromise measure, spearheaded by a Tory minister (R.A. Butler, now Lord) and a Labour secretary. There was unanimous agreement over the importance of education for the nation as a whole. Churchill's sentiment, expressed in 1943, that the future of the world is in the highly educated races', was accepted. The division of the education system on the prewar recommendation into three stages – primary, secondary and further – was pursued without question. The extension of secondary education by raising the school-leaving age to fifteen initially and sixteen as soon as possible thereafter was also acceptable, as was the abolition of fees for secondary schools maintained by LEAs.

The organization of secondary schools was most controversial, with several issues to be settled: how to finance the schools and the role of parental means; the relationship between religious authorities, LEAs and independent schools; and the influence of central government in schooling. Tawney's plea in 1931 (1964, ch. 3) that 'the hereditary curse on English education – the association of educational opportunity with the vulgar irrelevancies of class and income' be abolished was only partially heeded. A right to secondary education was established but it was not to be an equal right. Education had to fit the world of work, and although tripartism was not written into the Act, the policy prescribed was education suitable for children's 'ages, abilities and aptitudes'. However, poor children were no longer to be denied access, through lack of finance, to educational opportunities. Under Section 81, educational maintenance allowances, to enable children to remain at school over the age of sixteen, were to be extended on a new parental income scale. This solution for poor parents did not mean that all parental circumstances were equalized.

After much bitter wrangling, the voluntary religious authorities, which were slowly becoming poor, were given financial support for buildings and/or maintenance from the LEAs in exchange for some loss of control of governors to the LEAs. Four financial types of LEA school were in effect created – those with sole financial maintenance from the LEA, called county or maintained schools, and three with varying degrees of LEA aid, called voluntary aided, voluntary controlled or special agreement. The political row had been over State aid to religious bodies. In fact, some parents of particular religious persuasion were enabled to pass this on to their children. Voluntary authorities were given the choice of entering the LEA system. So, too, were endowed schools in receipt of a direct grant. Their system of LEA places was slightly modified but not on the lines recommended in the Fleming Report, which had argued that it was illogical for central government to pay fees in circumstances where parents could afford them. On the other hand, it was a technical duplication to have both central and local government involvement. Yet this duplication was retained, on the grounds that to abolish it would lead to more social exclusiveness, since most schools would choose independence. Direct-grant schools were given three choices: to enter the LEA system, to become independent or to remain with changes in the proportion and type of LEA places and the parental means tests for remission of fees in non-reserved places. These changes were to meet the ideal of being 'fully accessible to parents without regard to income'. The central government would no longer only subsidize the schools through capitation grants, that is, by numbers of pupil, but also by the remission of fees for 'residuary' places (those not reserved for LEA pupils).

Parents were to be given financial support if they chose to opt out of the system organized by LEAs. They were also entitled to send their children to schools which received no direct financial aid, except by virtue of their charitable status. The system of public and private or independent schools was regularized in that it was to be subject to inspections and an assessment of standards, under Section 3 of the Act.

Thus universal secondary education by no means implied equal or similar education. It merely meant allowing working-class children access to such education as had been previously denied them. Parents, and their financial circumstances, still influenced children's opportunities. Indeed, *parental choice* became a central axiom in the provision of LEA schools. Neither the LEAs nor the voluntary bodies were to be allowed a monopoly of provision in an area. LEAs were charged with the responsibility to provide schools so that 'pupils are . . . educated in accordance with the *wishes of their parents*' [emphasis added] but they were to have 'regard to the general principle that, so far as is compatible with the provision of efficient instruction and training and the avoidance of unreasonable public expenditure' (Section 76). Parents were still able to treat their children as their possessions, and different types of school provided for different classes of parent. The crucial social class distinction between day and boarding education for secondary pupils also remained. The Act did not take up the Fleming Committee's proposal for extending access to boarding schools to children of modest home circumstances. Parental rights were an important underlying assumption in educational provision.

On the other hand, the Act modified the State-parent partnership by legislating for more parental obligations with regard to children's overall welfare and in setting standards of provision. The school medical and dental service was extended; milk, meals, clothing and transport were provided to all schoolchildren, but they were *not* to be free except through tests of parental financial means.

The spectrum of educational provision was greatly increased. LEAs were given powers to provide not only for the compulsory school years but also for preschoolers and post-school further education, either technical and vocational or non-vocational. LEAs could also provide financial awards to enable students to enter university, thus extending the State scholarship system that had been introduced in 1920. These latter were parental means-tested maintenance allowances together with the payment of fees, for pupils from State-aided secondary schools. In 1926 the age limits for the awards had been raised from nineteen to twenty, for one year, to take account of the recession. A year later, this age limit was retained for women students. In 1930 more grants were awarded, but the boy to girl ratio remained as unequal and was based on the number of candidates. This arrangement was subsequently retained.

The expressed aim of all these additions to educational provision was to increase access to educational opportunity. The expansion of further education and financial support for university education was clearly linked to the growing, diverse needs of the economy, industry and commerce in particular. But there was little enthusiasm for central control of further and higher education and few guidelines were specified. The LEAs were given *carte blanche* to proceed as they and local employers and industrialists wished.

The partnership between State and parents was altered not only through the specification of parental rights and duties but also through the redefinition of the government agencies involved in educational provision. Teachers' duties were not well defined (a point returned to in ch. 7), but the whole political organization of education was redefined. Central government took more power for itself through the Minister, and Ministry, for Education. Although the State took no powers over the curriculum or appointment of teachers, it did give the newly titled Minister of Education power to 'direct and control'. Resources for education were also to be determined centrally. New LEAs were defined, the Part 3 authorities being abolished, and the educational authorities were to be only counties and county boroughs. Although the political bodies of these latter became the LEAs, they could co-opt educational experts to the education committees. The LEAs were chiefly responsible for the supply of education. Their actions and those of their key agents, the teachers, were to be monitored by a third political tier – governors or managers of individual schools.

This latter tier of government was not redefined in the Act itself, but through legal Instruments and Articles a year later in 1945 (see DES and Welsh Office (Taylor Report), 1977, pp. 158–72), although during the discussions on the Act much consideration was given to the problems of management. Parents, however, were not a topic for attention since the problems were mainly with the role of religious authorities and the public schools. So parents were not vouchsafed a say in this tier of government. Teachers were also more or less excluded.

The system became extremely complex and bureaucratic, in order to ensure an education system suited to the needs of the nation and its economy. Parents shared the rearing of their children with a vast army of bureaucrats, professionals and welfare officers who were responsible for their care. Parental standards were to be more closely monitored, in that standards for children's school participation were specified in detail. The 1944 Act, heralded as establishing educational rights, in fact determined parental duties in painstaking detail; children were clearly defined not only as their parents' property but as that of the nation. The nation had to find ways to reproduce itself advantageously.

Education in the early post-war era

The new legislation did not have full or instant effect. The ravages of the war and the changes in government in 1945 meant that, in the immediate aftermath of war, priorities had to be selected from the range of new statutory duties. Initially, attention focused on getting the education system back in working order. The major problem was that many school buildings had been destroyed through bombing attacks. All LEAs were galvanized into building construction programmes. The raising of the school-leaving age to fifteen was deferred until buildings were suitable and available, and was set for 1947; raising it to sixteen inevitably became a political dream. LEAs were fully occupied with what became known as the hutted operation for raising the school-leaving age to fifteen (HORSA) (Griffith, 1966, ch. 3). Building problems also affected the *type* of secondary schools developed. What is more, the new Labour government's vacillation over multilaterals or tripartism was clearly shown in its early post-war circulars about secondary education (Rubinstein and Simon, 1969). It recommended tripartism *and* academic selection for secondary education. It argued, on social grounds, that secondary modern schools were suitable for the working classes. Multilateralism was not pursued in the late 1940s, since tripartism was justified as more suited to the needs for a diversified labour force. In 1950 when a Conservative government came to power, few LEAs had been brave enough to abandon academic selection. The new government clamped down on future attempts, advocating academic selection.

Although the post-war Labour government equivocated over the *type* of secondary education, its main interests lay in this level of education. It did not actively pursue policies for primary or nursery education. On the contrary, immediately after the war many nurseries and nursery schools were closed. Women were no longer required for work: they could and should be replaced by returning soldiers, sailors and airmen. In 1945 the Labour government stressed that a comprehensive system of nurseries had to be worked out with the welfare authorities, to determine their character, needs and custom. The assumption was that such facilities would be needed only in certain circumstances, where mothers needed to work or children needed care and attention because of inadequate mothering. Indeed, LEAs had only been granted permissive powers in the 1944 Act: nursery schooling was not to be universally available. The problem of the supply of infant and junior teachers became acute in the late 1940s, especially with the growing demand for places caused by the rapidly rising birth rate. The first post-war circular on nursery education, therefore, accepted the need for nursery places for children of teachers as working married women, but on a temporary basis (see ch. 7). But only a year or so later, the apparent need for economy cuts meant that nursery education was affected. In an enabling Act to the 1944 Act, passed in 1948, the ages of entry to types of schooling were more clearly defined. Five years old was set as the age of entry to infant schooling and eleven for secondary education, further limiting nursery school expansion. The Conservative government of the early 1950s was even more parsimonious over nursery education. The State was barely involved in sharing with mothers their early child-care responsibilities.

The other major policy change of the 1944 Act was over county colleges for further education. This was also a permissive power for LEAs and it was not pursued vigorously at first. Much attention needed to be paid to another aspect of further education: technical and technological education.

The Percy Committee, which reported in 1945 on higher technological education (Ministry of Education, 1945), recommended a series of special LEA colleges for higher technological education and a local structuring of further education requirements within the framework of regional advisory councils (RACs) to advise on the distribution of facilities. Initially, such developments were to be left to local initiative and the demands of local labour markets. A Special Committee, chaired by Barlow, was set up in 1945 to examine the question of Britain's *scientific* manpower (*sic*) requirements and it advocated in 1946 an increase in skilled technologists, as the major way of improving the economy (Lord President of the Council, 1946). It focused its recommendations on the expansion of the universities. It argued that there was nothing sacrosanct about the existing number. It suggested the setting up of a new university 'which would give the present generation the opportunity of leaving to posterity a monument of its culture'. It also proposed doubling the output of scientists from universities. Its other proposals were to attempt to increase the productivity of the labour force. The very specific needs of the economy for a more diversified and technically and technologically skilled labour force affected developments in the education system. The government did not rigorously pursue a central policy, but it accepted the Barlow Report's suggestion on universities and left other colleges to the vagaries of local industrial and commercial demand. Although the 1944 Act had been an attempt to reconstruct the whole education system, the economic effects of the war focused concern on secondary, further and higher education and their expansion, with respect to the new demands of the post-war economy.

The Conservative legacy

Throughout the 1950s, Conservative governments were in power, determined on the consolidation of a system which matched education to the changed class structure and to specific needs of the economy (Lowndes, 1969). Nursery education was gradually squeezed and the ideology that a mother's place was in the home when she had pre-school children was ostensibly confirmed by research evidence available to the Tories. The expansion of further and higher technological education continued to take place only at the request of industrialists, employers and those in commerce. Until the mid-1950s, when the impact of international economic competition became irresistible, the government did not intervene. In secondary schooling, tripartism continued to be pursued vigorously on social as well as on educational grounds.

Nevertheless, a tide of evidence was growing against the effectiveness of this system and its utility for the economy. Report after report in the 1950s demonstrated that the secondary school system was not fulfilling its promise to provide educational opportunities according to ability and not social class background and parental financial means. It was demonstrated in particular that there was a class bias in the academic selection tests at eleven and that furthermore these tests were a poor predictor of subsequent educational performance in secondary education. It appeared that the goal of 'parity of esteem' between types of secondary school was not being achieved. Vaizey (1958), for example, demonstrated that children in maintained grammar schools obtained a disproportionate share of resources. It was also argued that secondary modern schools neither served the needs for semi-skilled manpower adequately nor were morally just on social grounds. The Conservatives' one concession to this problem was a 1958 White Paper entitled *Secondary Education for All: A New Drive*. This questioned whether education was meeting its aims of 'producing citizens who are fitted by character, knowledge and skill to play their full part in an increasingly educated and skilled society.' It proposed a new system of examinations in schools to try to stem the 'wastage of talent' and allowed for some limited experiments with different forms of secondary organization, albeit retaining the idea of transfer at eleven.

The government also requested a series of reports from the standing commission set up under the 1944 Act, the Central Advisory Council for Education (CACE). The initial report (CACE, 1954) was the first to document the influence of social class and, in particular, 'home background' on educational performance, especially *within* grammar schools. It argued (ibid., p. 20) that 'a child's home background influences his performance at school' and that 'a boy whose father is of professional or managerial standing is more likely to find his home circumstances favourable to the demands of grammar school work than one whose father is an unskilled or semi-skilled worker.' It argued that such boys were *not* innately inferior but were limited by their class backgrounds and also showed both the low rate of working-class entry to grammar schools and the poor performance of those who did enter. It therefore recommended as remedies, first, the expansion of grammar school places and, second, better maintenance allowances to enable needy children to stay at school over the age of fifteen. It also called for legislation for the payment of family allowances in respect of *all* children still at school.

The government acted upon these proposals by setting up another, this time a departmental, working party. It commissioned a second report a short time later, in 1956, to look at the question of education for children in the post-school-leaving years: *15 to 18* (CACE, 1959). The Crowther Report was published in 1959, in a situation which had changed rapidly and drastically from that of 1956. There had been a sudden and rapid increase in population due to an earlier marriage rate and higher birth rate, which was leading to more children and fewer teachers. The report did, however, consider, and recommended raising the school-leaving age to sixteen but with implementation delayed until 1966–8. The reasons for raising the leaving age were a child's right to education and 'education as a vital part of the nation's capital investment' (ibid., p. 117). It also recommended implementation of another policy proposal in the 1944 Act – that of county colleges providing compulsory, continued part-time education for sixteen- to eighteen-year-olds. It set a timetable for this and for the provision of full-time education to eighteen, for *half* the school population, to be achieved by 1980. The main concern, however, was with 'wastage of talent' due to early school-leaving of children from the whole ability range, and the inadequacies of full- and part-time technical education.

The main thrust of the Report was the emphasis on the inadequacies of the educational system in meeting the needs of a transformed economy, although its arguments were rather convoluted (ibid., ch. 11, paras 190–201):

> What the best and wisest parent wants for his own child the community must want for all its children. A boy or girl of 15 is not sufficiently mature to be exposed to the pressures of industry or commerce . . . The onset of puberty is earlier than it used to be . . . but this is not true of the social and emotional consequences of puberty . . . This is surely the period in which the welfare of the individual ought to come before any marginal contribution he or she could make to the national income . . .

It mixed moral arguments with the declining needs of the labour market for juvenile labour and the small national cost to advocate raising of the school-leaving age. This was linked with a general upgrading of demand in the economy for types of skills which implied further training. Exclusion from the labour market was justified in terms of a moral or civic right to education and the need for more educated manpower (*sic*). Moreover, the actual rate of unemployment and lack of available jobs provided further and yet contradictory justification (ibid., p. 124, para. 191) :

> It is not only at the top but almost to the bottom of the pyramid that the scientific revolution of our times needs to be reflected in a longer educational process. The case for raising the minimum leaving age is further strengthened by the lack of opportunities for part-time day education for girls.

(This aspect of the report is discussed in detail in ch. 7.) It also added that school, in later years, should more reflect the conditions of industry (ibid., p. 126, para. 194):

> Now that the leaving age is 15, a good many people have doubts whether school conditions should not be brought for everybody (as they already are for a good many) a little nearer to subsequent working conditions . . . They apply, however, only where the

> actual hours spent in school are the sum total of work done by the pupils. Wherever homework is set, and conscientiously done, the balance is substantially redressed . . . Some at least of us feel that the raising of the minimum leaving age to 16 may increase the frustration of prolonged dependence on parents for every penny of spending money . . .

It justified a change in the relationship between parents and adolescent children, in terms of meeting the further needs of the economy for particular technical skills. Indeed, the Report also pointed to the historical evidence of the link between aspects of education and the economy (ibid., p. 332):

> Further education has grown up as a handmaiden of employment. For the overwhelming majority of boys and girls in further education, the choice of job (or at least type of employment) comes first and entry into further education follows as a consequence . . . English further education cannot be understood without realising that virtually everything that exists in it has come into existence as a conscious answer to a demand arising from industry or from individual workers.

The Report, therefore, tried to increase and improve on the connections between education and industry and thereby modify parental responsibilities. In being excluded from the labour market in order to fit them better for it, children would continue for longer to be dependent upon their parents. The Crowther Committee's specific recommendations were not, however, enacted, but merely left as suggestions for government policy.

Meanwhile, more consideration was given to higher technological education. In a White Paper in 1956 the government created new Colleges of Advanced Technology and reorganized on hierarchical lines the system of colleges of further education. It also continued to supply resources to the universities.

Nursery education, by contrast, either received very little attention or suffered specific reductions. In 1958, in a bid to effect national economies in public spending, LEAs were advised to reduce nursery schooling (Blackstone, 1971). Two years later, a more strongly worded circular, 8/60, was published, which *forbade* LEAs to expand nursery schools and classes. Those available should be for part-time not full-time education, in the children's interests. It was argued that 'only some mothers "by force of circumstance" have to work.'

In the 1950s, the changes in the British economy resulted in changes in family relationships enforced by educational policy. The education system was directed to suit the needs of the labour market for more highly skilled labour, and therefore children were to remain in school and be dependent upon their parents for a longer time than hitherto. On the other hand, mothers were not helped with some of their child-care responsibilities. For instance, nursery provision was drastically reduced.

Some consideration was given to the welfare of children at school and whether it should be provided by the State or parents. From 1946, milk had been provided free to all schoolchildren. Meals were to have become free on April Fool's Day, 1947, but they never were! Nevertheless, the school meals service continued to expand so that more and more children were receiving school meals at a cost subsidized by the State. Consideration was also given to providing financial support to parents to help their children to continue at school. In 1957 the Ministry's working party chaired by Sir Toby Weaver and set up as a result of the CACE's 1954 report reported on educational maintenance allowances (EMAs). It argued for three maximum rates of grant for fifteen-, sixteen- and seventeen-year-olds, but as Reddin has argued (1968, p. 10): 'its recommendations were subsequently emasculated by the then Ministry of Education, but were offered to the LEAs as suggestions for rates for the future.' The LEAs were able to use the new rates at their discretion and the result was considerable area variation in the rate of grant. Reddin has pointed out (ibid., p. 11) that, although there was considerable evidence of financial pressures on children to leave school 'to bring home a pay packet to add to the weekly income', there was little agreement on the 'extent the community should share the financial burden with the parent – if at all. And if this is to be a shared responsibility, then what proportion of the "burden" should be borne by the community and what proportion by the parents?' The Weaver Committee's proposal (Ministry of Education, 1958) was not that EMAs should compete with what a child might earn in the labour market, but that they should help parents to meet the costs of keeping a child in school, after allowing for subsistence costs of supporting the child. The residual sum would express the costs to the parent which exceeded the basic subsistence requirements of the child. EMAs, however, should be provided on a basis related to parental income.

The concern of the 1950s was to enable children to remain in school so that they would be better suited to labour force requirements subsequently. But the Crowther Committee's educational proposals were not sufficient to revamp the system. Worry continued over the purposes of secondary and higher education. The 1960s opened with two new reports commissioned. One was to investigate education for thirteen- to sixteen-year-olds of average or less-than-average ability. The other was a Prime Minister-sponsored study of full-time higher education. Both were still concerned with the defined problems of the wastage of talent throughout the education system and the need to link education more clearly to manpower requirements. Both committees reported in 1963, at a time when the Tories were also considering how to restructure primary education. (They asked the Central Advisory Council for Education (CACE), chaired by Lady Plowden to report on this last question.) The Newsom report, commissioned in 1959, followed the recommendations of the earlier Crowther Report (CACE, 1959), which had concentrated on the above-average ability range. The Newsom Report (CACE, 1963, pp. 6–7) argued that: 'Despite some splendid achievements in the schools, there is much unrealised talent especially among boys and girls whose potential is masked by inadequate powers of speech and the limitations of home background . . .' It therefore proposed (ibid., ch. 1) again the raising of the school-leaving age. 'The schools will need to present that education in terms more acceptable to the pupils and their parents, by relating school more directly to adult life and especially by taking a proper account of vocational interests . . .' Again, though the initial arguments were couched in terms of parental and civic rights, the nub of the argument (ibid., ch. 1) rested upon employment needs:

> Briefly it is that the future employment in this country will require a much larger pool of talent than is at present available . . . The need is not only for more skilled workers to fill existing jobs but also for a generally better educated and intelligently adaptable labour force to meet new demands . . .

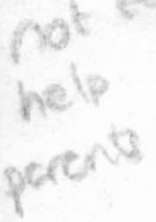

As had the Crowther Report, the Newsom Report recommended a closer matching of the school day for adolescents to that of the working day, as a preparation for their involvement in the labour force. It stated (ibid., p. 41):

> We advocate a rather longer school day for boys and girls in their last 2 years at school . . . All our evidence suggests that many pupils are capable of more sustained effort and show themselves able to respond to opportunities of a wider range of activities. The schools, on the other hand, find themselves short of time in which to undertake all the things they know to be profitable. Finally, young people still have to face a much longer working day when they enter employment, and some bridging of this gap seems desirable . . .

Schooling was not only to serve the needs of industry but to reflect the nature of employment in its *form* of organization. This was an explicit statement of what Bowles and Gintis (1976), in their analysis of the American education system, argue is the 'hidden curriculum' of schooling. Furthermore, the Report acknowledged (as did Lord Boyle in his introduction to it) that intelligence was not a fixed quantity, as had been believed by previous educationalists, but could be acquired through schooling. So the report was eclectic in its approach to theories of education. The Newsom Report specifically stated (ibid., ch. 1): 'intellectual talent is not a fixed quantity with which we have to work but a variable that can be modified by social policy and educational approaches.' Nevertheless, the Committee did not recommend changes in overall school organization. It merely proposed new solutions for teaching children in city and slum areas. The Report marked a new stage in educational debate and theory. Children were more directly malleable than previously it had been assumed, and there was much untapped ability amongst the working classes. The concept of *educability* became fashionable in academic research after the Committee had proposed it.

The Robbins Report of 1963 (Committee on Higher Education, 1963) also stressed the range of untapped ability in the population and the fact that intelligence was not a static quality. It, too, recommended extension of educational opportunities. Its major concern was the grounds for such extension. Three approaches were investigated – manpower planning and private and social 'rates of return' on investments in education. The first was dismissed as inadequate because the needs of the economy were no longer static. New professionals and technologists would create an environment in which social and economic needs were unpredictable. The social demand for, or rate of return on, education was likewise unpredictable and inexorable. The private demand, or rate of return, could suffice as a proxy for social needs. Thus the extent of higher education provision should depend upon the numbers of qualified, able students seeking such education. They would be defined in terms of the proportion of the eighteen-year-olds obtaining two 'A' level GCEs who wished to enter higher education. Parental circumstances were not to enter this equation, although they inevitably affected access to studying for GCE examinations, in terms of the schools to which pupils might go (as evidenced by the Crowther Report). They would also affect a student's ability to 'consume' higher education.

The Commissioners, therefore, discussed how to finance a student's attendance at university – through fees and maintenance awards as grants or loans – and the relationship between the community and the parent. They argued the case against student loans instead of maintenance grants, on the grounds that this would debar certain classes of student from participating in higher education, for instance, in the case of girls, they said (ibid., p. 210):

> In particular where women are concerned, the effect might well be either that British parents would be strengthened in their age-long disinclination to consider their daughters to be as deserving of higher education as their sons, or that eligibility for marriage of the more educated would be diminished by the addition to their charms of what would in effect be a negative dowry.

Apart from this facetious comment, they argued for special help for married women (ibid., p. 168, para. 515):

> In most cases a married woman returning to her profession is involved in extra domestic expenditure and must therefore earn from the state. We therefore recommend that adequate financial arrangements should be made to enable married women to take refresher courses: financial support should also be available for older women who wish to take initial courses of higher education.

They did not argue that students should, on the other hand, be autonomous and free from dependence on parents or their financial circumstances. Grants on a parental means-tested basis were suggested. These had, in fact, been introduced in a modified form, instead of the county awards and State Scholarship system, in the Education Act of 1962, the year before the Robbins Committee reported.

The Robbins Committee's reasons for an expansion of higher education – through the growth of the universities, the transformation of CATs into universities, the establishment of SISTERS (new higher technological institutes) and the conversion of teacher training colleges to colleges of education – were not limited to coping with economic growth. Indeed, it argued that the costs of such an expansion could be absorbed by the greater productivity realized (ibid., p. 201):

> A substantial fraction of the rise in expenditure could be carried without increased relative burden by the increase in productivity we have assumed; and although there would remain a proportion not so carried such expenditure would be well justified. On any broad appraisal of the return both in productivity and increased capacity for enjoyment, many items at present covered by public expenditure have less claim on resources than this . . .

Its argument was for 'the good life', as stated baldly later: 'the good society desires equality of opportunity for its citizens to become not merely good producers but also good men and women.'

The era of Conservative government ended with optimism about economic and educational advance, especially in the fields of further and higher education. Government measures were directed towards exploiting 'untapped pools of ability'. Nevertheless there was a slowly rising tide of criticism of secondary education associated, as Lowndes (1969) has argued, with changing parental aspirations. He called it 'the mums' revolution' (ibid., p. 265). Through the post-war expansion of educational facilities, women had been led to expect more from education for themselves and their children.

Social democracy and efficient education

The economy appeared to be reasonably buoyant when a Labour government was voted into office in 1964. One of its main electoral slogans was complete educational reform but this was only slowly achieved. Early policy measures consisted in relaxing the ban on nursery school expansion, if only to encourage back more married women teachers, for whom nursery schools would be their crèches. The government did not until the late 1960s consider a broader expansion of nursery schools. Its priorities were secondary and higher education until the CACE Committee chaired by Lady Plowden, which had been set up under the Tories in 1963, reported on primary education in 1967.

Changes in both secondary and higher education policies were announced in 1965. First, the Robbins Committee's proposals were modified so that expansion of higher education would take place in two types of institutions – universities and polytechnics, created out of LEA colleges of technology. The latter were to have a heavy emphasis on technology and vocationalism and were to be parallel, rather than subordinate, to the universities. The policy became known in 1965, after a speech by Anthony Crosland, as the binary policy (Burgess and Pratt, 1970). The rationale for polytechnics mirrored that for the change in secondary schools policy: it was that equality of educational opportunity should be provided on grounds of social-class mixing as well as academic access. The argument ran that the outputs from any educational institution should be equalized (see Halsey's definition below).

Second, in 1965 the Labour government set about officially dismantling the tripartite system of secondary schools and creating schools which would contain children of all abilities and without regard to parental or social class background. Experiments with what had become known in the 1950s as comprehensive schools had occurred in a few, mainly Labour-controlled, LEAs (Pedley, 1960). Indeed, the thrust to experiment had resulted in the Conservatives being forced to relax, in August 1964, the rules about the specific age of transfer between primary and secondary education, but this Education Act 1964 was only for experiments, as the explanatory circular stressed (David, 1977).

The Labour government's proposals for the reorganization of secondary education have been variously summarized, but Halsey's definition (DES, 1972b, ch. 1) brings out the emphasis that parental background was not to influence educational attainment:

> In this new interpretation a society affords equality of educational opportunity if the proportion of people from different social, economic or ethnic categories at all levels and in all types of education are more or less the same as the proportion of these people in the population at large. In other words, the goal should be not the liberal one of equality of access but equality of outcome for the median member of each identifiable non-educationally defined group i.e. the average woman or negro or proletarian or rural dweller should have the same level of educational attainment as the average male, white, white-collar suburbanite. If not, there has been an injustice.

The Labour government, although publicly committed to improving equality of educational opportunity by pursuing a policy of reorganizing secondary schools on comprehensive lines, did not move swiftly or forcefully. Indeed, it equivocated over the form both of the new schools and the administrative procedure. Believing that the 1944 Education Act was a sufficient legal framework, since it required LEAs both to satisfy 'parental wishes' and provide schools in accordance with pupils' 'ages, aptitudes and abilities', the government merely issued a circular (10/65) *requesting* LEAs to reorganize their secondary schools. It even set out *six* different, possible patterns, and did not favour any one pattern. And the circular did not have the force of law. Yet the government naively supposed that most LEAs would be willing to dismantle their grammar schools and abolish academic selection in order to improve educational opportunities. They appeared to reckon without the power of middle-class parents wishing to preserve their traditional privileges, which for the last 20 years had included obtaining 'free' selective education, financed by the State, for their children. They also assumed that schools which would contain pupils representing all ranges of either intellectual ability or social class would reduce class and hence parental privileges in education (Marsden, 1971). They no longer argued only for neighbourhood schools which would contain *all* children from a locality. On the other hand, it has been argued (Finn *et al.*, 1977) that Labour's strategy was weak because it was not really committed to the goal of eliminating class differences and parental privileges in education, but rather to pursuing a goal of economic and hence educational efficiency.

In fact, apart from publishing the now famous circular 10/65, the government did little else to achieve comprehensive schooling, save to limit expenditure on tripartite schemes through restrictions on building programmes, expounded in circular 10/66 (David, 1977, ch. 5). Instead, it took the view that the issue of reducing class privilege and parental rights in education could only be achieved fully by an attack on the independent sector of schooling – the direct-grant and public schools – which although numerically few were the schools that trained for élite social and economic positions. To avoid initial political conflict, the government set up a Royal Commission to report on these schools. Without changing the entire range of secondary schools, the government could appear merely to be finding more adequate ways to exploit 'the untapped pool of ability' to ensure a more suitable labour force. Indeed, there was much discussion in the mid-1960s of the need to produce more skilled workers, as the Prime Minister Harold Wilson put it, for 'the white-hot technological revolution'. The new comprehensive schools were to be modelled on the old grammar schools, since they provided for highly skilled man-power requirements.

The Labour government also revived the idea of raising the school-leaving age to sixteen, as recommended by both the Crowther and Newsom Reports. Problems with youth employment in the mid-1960s seemed to make the idea of removing children from the labour market doubly attractive. The effect would be to make children dependent for a long period on their parents, and on mothers in particular, although youth participation in the labour market would not necessarily imply lack of dependency on parents. Indeed, recent evidence has suggested that employed adolescents generally do not adequately recompense their mothers for the housework performed on their behalf. The raising of the school-leaving age was planned first for 1967 and then for 1968 but was eventually postponed until the 1972–3 school year, when it was finally implemented. Although it was seen as a solution to one aspect of Britain's economic problems, it was expected to exacerbate such problems since it involved additional, deliberate public expenditure – most of which was capital (on buildings) and with long-term implications. The plan was post-poned on these cost grounds, but the costs of juvenile unemployment to the Exchequer through social security benefits in the meantime were never calculated.

The other Labour initiative in secondary schooling was the investigation of the public and direct-grant schools. When the Newsom Commission reported (Public Schools Commission, 1968), its recommendations were so far-reaching that they would have required an Act of Parliament for implementation, and this never happened. The Commission suggested ending the charitable status of the schools, whereby both parents and the schools were indirectly relieved of paying taxes on school fees and costs. In addition, it argued that Parliament should provide fiscal policies whereby such school fees could be paid from sources other than parental income. Thus, on the one hand, it suggested a break from the dependence on parental income for access to these schools and, on the other, reducing the community's support to them. But, in addition, it did want closer co-operation between maintained and public schools and, to that end, suggested a process whereby half the places in public schools would be reserved for children in the maintained sector, over a period of seven years. It felt that the LEAs should identify children with specific 'boarding' needs, the criteria being social or academic deprivation of children at home. To co-ordinate the new schools, a Boarding Schools Corporation was to be created. The view that home circumstances were often inadequate for the rearing of working-class children was increasingly being articulated, and new solutions to these problems devised. The notion of extending boarding facilities to such children to rescue them was but one solution. It is a curious contradiction that boarding schools for children of the upper and upper-middle classes were seen as an extension of home. Such parents, and mothers especially, were not castigated for their inadequacies in child-rearing; rather it was recognized that parenting could not be achieved alone but should be shared with professionals and experts.

These recommendations were left pending until the Commission had reported on its second subject – the direct-grant schools. In 1969 the second report, which had been chaired by David Donnison, was produced (Public Schools Commission, 1969). It suggested that the direct-grant boarding schools be treated like the public schools, with LEAs taking up boarding places. The direct-grant *day* schools should no longer charge fees to parents and should lose their direct grants. A School Grants Committee should be set up alongside the Boarding Schools Corporation to meet the schools' capital debts. The schools themselves would fit into the comprehensive secondary school system either as ordinary schools or to fill special needs, such as boarding needs. If the schools were not willing to be incorporated, they would have to become independent. The Commissioners refused to sanction the State subsidizing parents' special needs, such as sending their children to selective schooling, since it was out of the financial reach of the majority of parents. They did not countenance the arguments that the loss of direct-grant schools would lead to more, rather than less, social exclusiveness. Their implicit aim was to exploit a wide range of children's talents to fit them more efficiently for an unequal labour market. Parents would be no longer able to pass on their privileges automatically through the school system. None of these proposals, however, was implemented in the 1960s.

The government also tried to improve equality of educational opportunity through the system of primary education. In 1967 the CACE Committee chaired by Lady Plowden reported, and its main attack was also on the inadequacies of certain home circumstances and parents in their child-rearing. The Committee was interested in this problem in so far as it had a bearing on the productivity of the nation. It was concerned with children's 'educability' and how this depended not only on the school but also on the home and parents. It suggested a new method for educating children – a closer relationship between home and school (CACE, 1967, ch. 4):

> Our argument is that educational policy should explicitly recognise the power of the environment. Teachers are linked to parents by children for whom they are both responsible. The triangle should be completed and a more direct relationship established between teachers and parents. They should be partners in more than name; their responsibility become joint instead of several.

It proposed imposing new duties on both teachers and parents to liaise over their children's primary education. It further identified areas of special need, arguing that schools in the older, inner-city areas were in need of particular attention, because social policy had up to that time been focused upon supplying new areas and newer towns. In the older areas there was a high turnover of both pupils and teachers and no necessary coincidence of values between parents and teachers. It, therefore, felt that such children were educationally deprived and handicapped and needed a 'new distribution of educational resources'. It argued (ibid., ch. 5):

> we ask for 'positive discrimination' in favour of such schools and the children in them, going well beyond an attempt to equalise resources. Schools in deprived areas should be given priority in many respects. The first step must be to raise the schools with

> low standards to the national average; the second, quite deliberately to make them better. The justification is that the homes and neighbourhoods from which many of their children come provide little support and stimulus for learning. The schools must supply a compensating environment . . .

The Committee proposed 'Educational Priority Areas' and suggested criteria by which they might be identified. The underlying assumption was the inadequacy of the family in coping with the problems of child-rearing; the report mentioned Sir Cyril Burt's notion, developed in the 1930s, of the lack of 'efficiency of the mother'. Having identified problems in society, instead of attacking the way the social and economic system worked as the root cause, the Committee blamed those who suffered society's ills. Mothers were explicitly accused. So the solution to the problem went further than merely to improve education for working-class and poor children at primary school. The Plowden Committee also recommended improving nursery education provision so that by 1980 75 per cent of three- and four-year-olds would have at least part-time nursery schooling. New nursery provision should initially be made in the EPAs. The argument was again couched in terms of maternal inefficiencies with early child-rearing. Children would benefit from being removed from these poor parental influences.

The Plowden Committee's ideas were translated into government policies in several ways. First, parental participation in schools was encouraged under the initial guise of providing community schools through buildings and the use of extra resources. Teacher-social workers were also promoted. Second, a programme of EPAs was inaugurated. In addition, special areas were designated as the basis for an evaluation, through action-research, to monitor the innovation. Six areas were studied and developed by mixed teams of academics and community workers (DES, 1972b). Third, nursery provision was initially promoted in 1969 through a government programme, sponsored by the Home Office, of Urban Aid and community development projects for inner-city areas. In all three types of programme, a major policy focus was the improvement of maternal behaviour through the development of a new partnership between the State and mothers over child-rearing. Mothers were to be shown, through attending school on a daily or regular basis, how to care for their young children. They were not enabled to take on activities such as paid employment while their children were in nurseries but were expected to be regularly involved in such education. The State's need to reinforce familial, and traditional maternal, values was now more explicit. It was necessary in a situation where the deprivation of inner-city areas contrasted starkly with the affluence of other residential areas.

The second era of post-war Labour government ended abruptly in mid-1970, when Britain's economic problems were stark and politically prominent. At that time much educational policy was in the melting-pot. For example, a bill had just been introduced to Parliament to reform secondary education, by banning academic selection for entry to secondary schools. It did not reach the statute books.

By this time, Labour had been forced to realize how politically controversial comprehensive schools were, and how hard middle-class parents would fight to retain grammar schools. Indeed, they had already been forced, through such pressure, to amend sections of the 1944 Education Act to clarify their procedures for allowing changes in secondary schooling (Saran, 1973, pp. 68–72). The amendments were contained in the Education Act, 1968. Labour was now hoping to be more forceful, but, not being overly committed to the issue, was voted out of office before it could succeed! But Labour's bequest to the new Tory government was important – it was a new partnership between parents and schools. Parents were to be more limited in their influence over their children, and schools were to play a larger role in inculcating both skills and economic values into children. Halsey, summarizing the priority area programmes in 1972, expressed the aims (DES, 1972a, ch. 1):

> What assumptions could or should be made about the world into which . . . children would enter after school? Were we concerned simply to introduce a greater measure of justice into an educational system which traditionally selected the minority for higher education and upward social mobility out of the EPA district . . . a modern, humane and even relatively enjoyed form of gentling the masses? Or could we assume a wide programme of social reform which would democratize local power structures and diversify local occupational opportunities so that society would look to its schools for a supply of young people to their communities not by failure of competition but by rich opportunities for work and life?

In other words, the Labour strategy had been to bring out children's abilities to criticize our unequal society but not necessarily to create an equal job market.

From the Second World War, and the 1944 Education Act which has not yet been superseded, education was seen by successive governments to be clearly tied not merely to the reproduction of the class system but to the supply of agents for positions in the occupational structure. Linked with that was an attempt to create appropriate family responsibilities over children in schools which would reproduce appropriate familial behaviour in adult life. Such adults would, then, rear their children for work in a capitalist system. Increasingly, therefore, the notion that parents could be taught, not merely through schooling itself, but through the responsibilities heaped upon them when they had their own schoolchildren, was a part of the educational system. 'The efficiency of the mother' was not an empty slogan. It was used as the basis for various reorganizations of the educational system. At the same time, separate education for girls from boys was more muted. Co-educational institutions were the hallmark of the comprehensive school system, even if their curricula have to some extent remained sex-specific (discussed in chapter 7). This question never surfaced as a policy concern in the twenty-five-year period under review. The major issues were the twofold relationships – education and the economy and education and parents. Parents were given few new rights but their duties to their children were considerably extended.

Part II

The familial ambiance of schooling

Introduction

This second part of the book examines family issues within the education system. Two key issues are considered: one is how the teaching profession grew and, in particular, involved the employment of women; the other issue is what and how the teachers taught – the development of the curriculum and the authority relations between teachers and pupils. These illustrate the ways in which schools act *in loco parentis* and take over certain parental responsibilities. In the first instance, the choice of teachers involved notions of how teachers and schools were to take on parental responsibilities. Specific structures were then developed for teachers to look after children. Curricula, too, were predicated on notions of how teachers would parent and, perhaps more important, how children would learn to be adults and parents themselves. Children would learn about their positions not just in the labour force but in the wider socio-economic system and in the family particularly. The economy had an impact on the development of schooling. Not only did it set the conditions for the products of schooling – the sorts of skills required and the numbers in the labour force – it also set the limits to the availability of personnel for the educational labour market. Indeed, this was one of the first areas where women, albeit single or widowed only, were able to find employment. This was because caring for children was seen to be a feminine activity.

In chapter 5, the developments in nineteenth-century teaching and curricula are examined. As shown in chapter 2, both class and sex were critical factors in the organization of early schooling. Teaching middle- and upper-class boys was seen as a profession, whereas the teaching of working-class boys and girls only required a limited apprenticeship, first as a monitor, later as a pupil-teacher and finally at a training college. Teaching middle-class girls as a governess was originally about the *only* respectable occupation for a middle-class woman, partly because it took place within the home and was second-best to being a wife. Later it became an occupation for many middle-class women. As teaching varied, so did curricula – boys were to train for their social and economic positions as adults, girls for their positions within the family and, only briefly and later in the century, to enable them to earn their own living. Middle-class girls would learn first to obtain husbands and later to be wives and mistresses of households; working-class girls would learn to be mothers and housewives doing domestic chores.

The evidence for the account in chapter 5 is drawn from official reports and various secondary sources. Gosden (1972) provides the most comprehensive account of teaching developments; Adamson (1930) is the most entertaining and lucid. Tropp (1957) and the Parrys (1975) provide evidence of working-class teachers, but Horn (1978) concentrates on schoolmistresses. For middle-class women I have drawn on Zimmern (1898), Burstall and Douglas (1911), Kamm (1958, 1965, 1966, 1971), Marks (1976), Peterson (1972), Neff (1966), Stenton (1957), Pederson (1975) and Holcombe (1973).

Chapter 6 looks at the ways in which teaching became professionalized, training was developed and divorced from elementary and secondary schools and women's employment limited. Curricular changes and developments in vocational and specialized training are also examined up to the Second World War. Class differences in teaching were gradually being eroded but sex remained a crucial division: equal pay and treatment were not afforded women teachers.

Interpretation of the State's policies is based on both official reports and the following sources. Gosden (1972) is again used for teaching developments, as are the Webb (1915) survey of the period to 1914 and Lowndes (1969). Holcombe (1973) is useful for early developments in women's teaching; Kamm (1965) provides a brief overview. Partington (1976) is a slight but informative study. As regards curricular changes, Banks (1955) is helpful, as are Simon (1965), Graves (1943) and Barker (1972). Dyhouse (1977 and 1978) and Davin (1978) provide information in girls' schooling and curricula.

In chapter 7, teaching and curricula developments during and after the Second World War, up to 1970, are appraised. Here the emphasis is placed upon how teaching was fully professionalized and attempts were made to turn it into a fully graduate occupation. The arguments for the exclusion of women, especially married ones were totally vitiated in this period as schooling became tied more particularly to the sexual division of labour in both the family and the economy. Curricular developments were now increasingly tied to technological and technocratic requirements.

There are few secondary sources on which to rely for this account. Lowndes (1969) and Partington (1976) are useful on developments during and immediately after the Second World War; Gosden's (1972) account remains vital. Burgess and Pratt (1970, 1974) are informative on the tying of education to the economy. There is a dearth of literature on modern education for girls, although Sharpe (1976), Wolpe (1975) and Blackstone (1976b) allude to some of the issues. Byrne (1978) is also of limited relevance.

The history of teachers, teaching and caring for children

The schools that existed in medieval society and early capitalism mirrored the organization of the household. A school was small in size and could be constituted with only a handful of pupils. The distinction between day and boarding schools was not held very rigorously. Children tended to attend schools at a short distance from home but, because of methods of transport, might spend nights at a time there. They did not live *in* the schools but were boarded out in local households. The schools were for special functions: they did not provide for all children, for infants or give a general education. They educated boys for a trade or a profession such as a chorister, clergyman or doctor. Young children were taught at home; older boys may have gone to university but more commonly went into a trade or profession or became a member of the gentry. The early medieval grammar schools were, on the whole, for training boys for a profession. Universities initially were established as guilds of scholars for the training of teachers, with a specific religious content. Indeed, from medieval times the church had had a monopoly control over education, since no man was allowed to teach without the licence of the diocese. After the Reformation, the Church of England assumed the control previously held by the Church of Rome.

The ways in which children were taught also differed from modern methods. Since schools were small, there was relatively little differentiation by age, but children were distinguished by their knowledge and learning. Teachers tended to help pupils individually rather than in large groups. Teachers in such schools were always men, usually clerics, trained at university.

Women in medieval times, either as wives or duennas, taught

only young children (boys and girls) and older girls within the household setting. They provided the model for the governesses of early capitalism who taught the daughters of the ruling classes. Slowly, in the sixteenth century, girls' boarding schools developed which were, as Gardiner argues (1929, p. 194), parallel but not identical to grammar schools for boys. This was at a time when grammar schools were becoming lay institutions, although the curriculum remained classical. During Tudor times, guilds of merchants provided the finance for the establishment of secular grammar schools, which trained boys for their particular trade. The girls' schools were established through Christian teaching. In the early days of these girls' schools, children were gathered together and taught by men, usually clerics. In 1710 an edict was passed (ibid., p. 201) forbidding such co-education. From then on, separate schools for the daughters of the newly expanding class of merchants, traders and professionals were established.

Howe (1954) argues that in the eighteenth century it became fashionable for the merchant classes to send girls to boarding schools, which required women teachers. Until then there were few female teachers: 'for the standard type of education in the home, women experienced in domestic and social life, the mother, the duenna were the obvious instructresses; book learning was the man's province . . . especially clerics to impart to girls and boys alike' (Gardiner, 1929, p. 202).

During the seventeenth century the schools for girls were what Gardiner calls 'family schools'. They were run by a husband and wife, but with separate responsibilities. The wives mainly supervised the care and government of the scholars and the household, and taught only elementary competences. Gardiner (1929, p. 206) adds, 'all that was now required of the headmistress was a matronly supervision of health, dress and good manners: scholarship was afforded by the visiting master and especially by the foreign professor.' Some women did teach during the seventeenth century, but not because 'they were qualified to teach but in order to earn their bread honestly.' In the 1620s and 1630s such private schools proliferated. They were solely for the girls of the gentry, aristocracy and of traders or merchants. Artisans and labouring people did not usually send their children to school. When they did, it was to what were known as dame schools: schools where married women with home responsibilities looked after, but generally did not teach, children.

The curriculum of the girls' boarding schools was consequently oriented to this wealthy class. 'Training in practical domestic duties is still of the first importance; efforts are made to improve such useful accomplishments as keeping accounts; needlework is regarded as having a direct influence on feminine psychology' (Gardiner, 1929, p. 229).

During the seventeenth century, with the increase in capitalistic industry and the growth of guilds, women were slowly excluded from influence outside the sphere of the family and home. Men, on the other hand, were more and more involved in the establishment of trades, guilds and associated schools. Alice Clark (1968, p. 286) argues:

> Coincident with a gradual curtailment of domestic activities may be observed a marked tendency towards the exclusion of women from all interests external to the family. The political theories of the seventeenth century regarded the State as an organization of individual men only or groups of men, not as a commonwealth of families: in harmony with this idea we find that none of the associations which were formed during this period for public purposes, either educational, economic, scientific or political, include women in their membership. The orientation of ideas in the seventeenth century was drawing a rigid line between the State, in which the individual man has his being and family matters. The [third] tendency was towards the deterioration of women's intellectual and moral capacity, owing to the narrowing of family life and the consequent impoverishment of women's education. The [fourth] tendency was towards an increasing belief in the essential inferiority of women to men.

Clark also argues that women had little access to knowledge and, where they did teach, as in dame schools or as governesses, only taught elementary subjects. She adds (ibid., p. 287):

> women were not incapable of teaching but as knowledge became more specialized and technical, the opportunities which home life provided for acquiring such knowledge proved inadequate, and consequently women were soon excluded from the higher ranks of the teaching profession.

Men continued to teach in schools and the universities. As capitalistic industry developed and trading and merchandising proliferated, more secular schools developed. Boys were prepared for their adult lives in the professions and trades or as part of the gentry or aristocracy. The emphasis in the grammar and public schools was initially on academic work and scholarship. Yet Clark (ibid., pp. 295 ff.) points out:

> It is difficult to estimate the respective shares taken by men and women in the art of teaching, for while the young were dependent on home training, they received attention from both mother and father and when the age for apprenticeship arrived the task was transferred to the joint care of master and mistress. With regard to learning of a scholastic character, reading was usually taught by women to both boys and girls, who learnt it at home from their mothers, or at a dame's school: but the teaching of more advanced subjects was almost exclusively in the hands of men, although a few highly educated women were engaged as governesses in certain noble families where the Tudor tradition still lingered. Generally speaking, however, when a girl's curriculum included such subjects as Latin and Arithmetic her instruction, like her brothers, was received from masters, and this was equally true in the case of accomplishments which were considered more appropriate to the understanding of young ladies. Women rarely, if ever, undertook the teaching of music, painting or dancing. From these branches of the teaching profession they were debarred by lack of specialized training.

The early effects of capitalism were therefore to increase the division of labour between productive work and the family *and* between men and women. Women were more and more excluded from life external to the family and had no need therefore to be fitted to it. Men, on the other hand, had increasingly to be trained for economic life away 'from home-life, to work upon the premises of the masters.' This further excluded wives from occupations. The other effect was the increase of wealth 'which *permitted* the women of the upper classes to withdraw from all connection with business' [my italics] (Clark, 1968, p. 298).

This process of capitalism and industrialization was accelerated in the eighteenth century. Schools for both boys and girls were not of great importance. The schools that were developed for boys, training them in particular professions, were mainly established not by the Church of England but either by rationalists for boys to learn sciences or by the Roman Catholics to provide a religious upbringing. Private ventures also gained in popularity, and the male teaching profession grew. 'Teaching became a good business when well managed' (Pinchbeck and Hewitt, 1969, p. 284). Girls' boarding schools became fashionable for daughters of the gentry, traders, merchants and professionals. Their aim increasingly was for girls 'to learn all things fitting to render them good and industrious wives'. Girls rarely learnt scholarly subjects but more usually feminine accomplishments 'such as needlework, dancing, singing, music, drawing, painting and other accomplishments such as French' (Zimmern, 1898, p. 9).

Children of the labouring classes still were not schooled except in dame schools, the major exceptions being pauper children – orphans or disabled, destitutes or children of 'idle and dissolute vagrants'. They were either provided with compulsory apprenticeships through the courts or sent to Poor Law, that is, workhouse, schools of industry, to prevent 'lawlessness and mischief'.

5

Rearing schoolchildren: paternalism or maternalism?

Developments in teaching and curricula, accompanying the establishment of schooling in the nineteenth century, are surveyed in this chapter. Schools were not provided on a universal basis: class and sex were critical divisions in the form that schooling took. They also affected teachers and what was taught. Teachers did not see themselves as a cohesive occupational group (the term itself was not applied to middle-class educators) and the fare that they provided varied according to what was expected of their pupils in adulthood.

Schooling was slow to develop in the nineteenth century (as shown in ch. 2). One reason was that it could not be justified in economic or moral terms. However, the churches and religious orders did provide some education for the poor and the very wealthy. Schools for the poor were established in the first two decades by two rival voluntary, religious societies. The Lancastrian (later the British Foreign and Schools) Society first addressed the problems of teaching method and teaching shortage. It did not have problems about curricula since it was concerned only to provide 'moral rescue' for poor children. Large classes of children were taught together in one huge hall. The teacher had as helpers some of the older children, who would act as monitors and instruct groups of children. This system was subsequently rationalized as a sound educational method. Silver (1965, p. 53) commented that 'many felt that the process of child teaching child was not merely economical and adequate but educationally the most desirable form of instruction.' These early teachers were drawn equally from men and women, and both boys and girls were taught, either together or separately. The National Society employed the same principles of the monitorial system. Early radicals, who supported the extension of education for the poor, justified their support through endorsing the monitorial system for its efficiency and economy. It was also seen 'not to confound the distinctions between the classes' (Silver, 1965, p. 45). Dame schools were also supported, although they were (Sutherland, 1977, p. 13)

> in the most deplorable condition. The greater part of them are kept by females but some old men whose only qualification for this employment seems to be their unfitness for every other. Many of these teachers are engaged at the same time in other employments such as shop-keeping, sewing, washing, etc., which renders any regular instruction among the scholars almost impossible.

Although there was no national movement in favour of schooling, the two societies quickly developed a network of schools. Lancaster, therefore, considered how to deal with the problems of both teacher shortage and teacher competence. He established, with his first school in Borough Road in London, a centre to train teachers. The entrants were mainly young adults, since a minimum age of entry, well above that of the age for leaving school, was set. They were usually Sunday School teachers, who were often financed by their religious employers.

Three other minor devices, according to Tropp (1957), were used to train teachers in addition to this school. 'Organizing masters' visited schools and inspected them; meetings of teachers were organized, usually for the harvest holidays; and teachers visited other schools, usually in the evenings. The system was thus very rudimentary. Furthermore, teachers' pay was not good and was subject to the vagaries of children's attendance, since the societies were not wealthy and were run on the basis of voluntary subscriptions. They also charged fees to parents. Hence the majority of recruits to such teaching 'were men who had tried other professions and failed' (Tropp, 1957, p. 10). Occasionally women were employed, too, teaching to support themselves.

Given fluctuating and limited attendance, what teachers were able to do with the children in school was severely limited. Rote learning of numbers, verse and catechisms was often the sum total of schooling.

The teaching profession, in the first decades of the nineteenth century, could hardly deserve that name. Indeed, there was little similarity between the teachers in these charity schools and the 'masters' in the proprietary, grammar and public schools. The schools were provided for different social classes, taught entirely different curricula, and their teachers were drawn exclusively from the relevant social classes. The teachers in the schools for middle- and upper-class boys were men, usually clergymen, educated at university. Their position, too, was difficult; for example, the masters in the ancient public schools were dependent upon the headmaster for their income. Very often they were badly paid for their main teaching, which remained the classics; they supplemented their pay by giving further private tuition to individual boys in return for additional fees. Moreover, the public schools were slowly transformed from local to national schools as a result of the problems of teachers' pay towards the end of the eighteenth century. Most of the ancient public schools were regulated by old statutes, dating back to the time of Henry VIII, which included teachers' salaries. Adamson (1930, p. 62) argues that:

> to secure a more equitable income, masters, where circumstances were favourable, availed themselves liberally of their statutory power to admit boarders, whose fees were not subject to statute. In the course of time these 'foreigners' from a distance outnumbered the foundationers, the sons of local residents, and the character of the school and particularly its studies tended to be governed by the requirements of the outsider rather than local needs.

By the 1830s, education was beginning to become more of a national issue. The middle classes were demanding more schooling for both the working classes and themselves in an attempt to transform the social system. Yet in 1836 Hill, for example (ibid., p. 30), stated:

> the education of the lower classes in this country is left, with few exceptions of the public charity schools, in the hands of ignorant and uneducated men, who are often destitute of every qualification for their office, and have undertaken it only because they found this the easiest means of gaining a subsistence and frequently in consequence of accident or bodily infirmity.

Early teaching systems

In the 1830s, then, the regularization of education centred on the problem of finding and improving teachers for schools for the working classes. As regards schools for middle-class children, the teacher problem did not become a public issue until the last third of the nineteenth century. In 1836 the Home and Colonial Infants Schools Society was founded with the object of training teachers for the working classes, mainly schoolmistresses (Adamson, 1930, p. 117). In 1837 a Select Committee of the House of Commons looked into the question of education of the poorer classes. It approved the voluntary society system but pointed out (ibid.) that 'amongst the chief defects yet subsisting may be reckoned the insufficient number of qualified schoolmasters, [and] the imperfect method of teaching which prevails, in perhaps the greatest number of schools.'

As a result much consideration was given to the question of training teachers and teaching methods. A system had already been developing in both Scotland and France, which formed the basis of official thinking. Sir James Kay-Shuttleworth, initially an advocate of welfare reforms, took Parliamentary responsibility for educational change. He became the first man in Britain to have deliberate educational responsibility when, in 1839, a committee of the Privy Council on education was established and he was made permanent secretary. His first scheme of teacher training was based on the French model – the normal school, defined (ibid.) as follows:

> A school in which candidates for the office of teacher in schools for the poorer classes may acquire the knowledge necessary to the exercise of their future profession and may be practised in the most approved methods of religious and moral training and instruction.

Teachers were to be known as 'candidate teachers' and were to board at 'normal schools'. Two schools would be attached: a day school for boys and girls of 150 to 200 pupils, in which candidate teachers could practise, and a residential model school, with 120 infants and 200 boys and girls. The curriculum would be for boys and girls to learn to be 'workmen or servants' and instruction in industry would be used as moral training. The scheme was to be financed by the government and be for the nation as a whole. However, the religious societies quarrelled over it and over the fact that there would be a form of secular control. The scheme was therefore utterly defeated by the Tories, backed by the Church of England.

Kay-Shuttleworth determined to find other ways to improve teaching and the prospects for teachers. He argued that at that time teachers could only look forward to 'hopeless indigence' and there were few material or social attractions to teaching. The first attempt to improve teaching was that the Privy Council stopped providing grants for buildings to the voluntary societies, which by the 1840s had grown in number from two to six. For example, the Roman Catholics and Wesleyans had also established societies for the provision of elementary schools. The Privy Council began to provide the grants to the managers of schools themselves in order to be able to check on the work of 'the unqualified masters and mistresses who directed the doings of the monitors'. This involved the setting up of a system of inspectors (HMIs) who would check on the schools. 'They were intended to be missionaries of education' (Sutherland, 1971, p. 19). In practice, clergymen became inspectors for the Church of England schools and laymen inspectors for the non-conformist schools. Religious teaching in dissenting schools was not, therefore, inspected. Women were not appointed as inspectors. The voluntary societies had, however, appointed ladies' committees to manage the affairs of girls' departments from their inception (DES and Welsh Office, 1977, p. 175). The non-conformists encouraged women; the National Society preferred men. In 1815 the British and Foreign Schools Society entrusted these affairs to ladies with the object (Gordon, 1974, p. 182)

> to excite a general interest in the minds of the sex on behalf of the lower class of females. The benefits which may be expected to arise are invaluable. It is well known that of female servants, the majority cannot read and it is very rare to meet one who is capable of writing a legible hand.

These committees acted more as managers than inspectors. The inspectors mainly investigated methods of teaching.

The second attempt at improving teaching was again made by Sir James Kay-Shuttleworth. At first he used a scheme privately, which then became the basis of a national system to train pupils to be teachers. In 1840 he established a normal school in Battersea, South London. The pupils who were taught there were all drawn from workhouse schools: boys from the Norwood Poor Law school were apprenticed to the workhouse schoolmaster and trained in the Battersea school for three years. They were also to practise in village schools. By 1842–3, this scheme had gained some Parliamentary approval from a new Tory government and grants were given to Battersea to train Poor Law teachers. At the same time the educational provisions of the Factory Bills were resoundingly defeated. Almost immediately, the scheme was widened to include other elementary teachers and the Church of England was provided with grants to run 'training schools'. It created separate colleges for men and women: by 1846 there were nine for women (Kamm, 1965, ch. 19). Very quickly, a network of colleges was established, providing training of a period between eighteen months and three years. This scheme was then extended to cover both apprentice teachers and their higher training.

In 1846 the Privy Council inaugurated the new scheme which became known as the pupil-teacher system. It was a two-stage system. Both boys and girls 'of at least 13 years of age and good moral character' were to be indentured for five years as apprentices to their headteachers in voluntary schools. The only provisos were that these boys and girls showed a capacity, according to the heads, to be teachers and that they passed a very elementary examination.

This was the first time that the government set out what the curriculum of a school should contain. Both boys and girls had to pass in reading, writing and ciphering, religious knowledge, geography and history. Boys had to pass, in addition, maths and mechanics. Girls, on the other hand, had to take examinations in sewing and cutting out, knitting, cooking and laundry-work. During their apprenticeship pupil-teachers were paid, and the headteachers were also paid £3 annually for their instruction. At the end of five years the pupil-teachers had to take a competitive examination and those who were successful became Queen's Scholars. They were awarded exhibitions of £20 to £30 per annum for up to three years to enable them to study at a residential normal school. Teachers who taught intending teachers were also paid to work there. Such trained teachers would then receive certification. Untrained teachers were also expected to take an examination.

This system of training was the first attempt to professionalize teachers. In addition, teachers, but not the managers, of voluntary schools were given an incentive to train. Certified masters would be paid, direct from the Privy Council, an augmentation of their salary of between £15 and £30 per annum, depending on the length of their training. The payment was to depend on the school managers providing the masters with a house rent-free and paying a salary of at least twice as much as the augmentation from the Privy Council. Although women were now entitled to become teachers and train to do so, they were not regarded as equal to male teachers. The school-mistresses who were certified were to receive only two-thirds the emoluments paid to men. Both men and women were to receive pensions (at different rates) at the end of their years of service, if disabled by age or infirmity.

This system was rapidly extended throughout the country and the more rigid monitorial system was abandoned. Indeed, even in the 1830s the latter was criticized. It was already being argued that the teacher should be a moral regenerator rather than hireling drill-master (Tropp, 1957, p. 8). Training colleges were established by private bodies and were nearly always denominational, residential and single-sex. By 1850, there were 16 colleges with 991 students (Gosden, 1972, p. 198). Between 1849 and 1859 the number of pupil-teachers rose from 3,580 to 15,224 and by 1859 12,604 certificates had been awarded. But, as Sutherland (1971, p. 2) has argued, this led to elementary education as a mode of social control: it formed a limited career ladder for working-class children to move to lower-middle-class respectability. However, it did not stem the religious or social-class controversies over the provision of education. These meant that the finance of such schooling could not be provided locally or out of the rates. Funds for education came from voluntary subscriptions and the tax grant. This system was not changed until the economic climate encouraged working-class agitation for the extension of schooling. Indeed, the pupil-teacher system exacerbated the conflicts between the middle and working classes. It was increasingly felt that working-class education was better than that for the middle classes and it should not be.

At about the same time, therefore, teachers in middle-class schools and the public schools tried to improve their status and standing. In 1846 the College of Preceptors was founded by a group of teachers from private and proprietary schools in an attempt to get similar social standing for teachers as for the medical profession (Parry and Parry, 1975). The initial response from such teachers was remarkable and by 1849 the College was able to apply for a Royal Charter. Subsequent developments were slow: frequent attempts were made to establish a register of teachers but because of the diversity in types of school, even for the middle and upper classes, such aims were not achieved. Instead, a whole variety of associations of teachers began to spring up.

Another middle-class response to the extension of working-class education was to try to improve the education of middle-class girls. Zimmern (1898, p. 20) argues this improvement also resulted from 1848 being significant as a year of revolution. Until the 1840s, the majority of middle-class girls were educated either at home, first by their mothers and then by governesses, or in cheap but inadequate, small, private boarding schools, mainly run by women but staffed with men for certain subjects. The term 'governess', however, applied to a variety of positions: women who taught in private schools, women who lived at home and travelled to their employers' home to teach (a 'daily' governess) or women who lived in their employers' home, who taught the children and served as their companion (Peterson, 1972, p. 4).

By the 1840s the position of middle-class women in particular had become problematic. There was a surplus of such women and there was no longer any guarantee of them marrying. The main reason for their overabundance was the fact that, with the international expansion of Britain's economic and military interests, more and more middle-class men were employed in the army and navy, the colonies and overseas. Men also tended to marry later than women and there was a differential mortality rate (Peterson, 1972, p. 6). The fortunes of these newly established middle-class families were not assured. Many middle-class women had to seek employment; teaching, especially as governesses, was a major source of employment. Howe (1954, p. 115) states that in the 1840s over 100 women advertised daily in *The Times*. Hewitt (1958, p. 70) shows that in 1841 there were almost 30,000 governesses and schoolmistresses, of whom only 1,500 were under the age of twenty. The only other fields of employment where more women worked were as servants (500,000), in the cotton industry (100,000), as dressmakers or milliners (89,000) and as launderers (45,000). None of these occupations was the rival of teaching for middle-class women.

By the 1840s, partly as a result of their overabundance, governesses were treated very badly by the families with whom they lived. They were paid a pittance, unemployment was always a possibility and they were scorned by the children whom they taught. Indeed, their position was, as Peterson (1972, p. 5) has cogently argued, contradictory: 'the governess was a testimony to the economic power of the Victorian middle class father, as were servants, carriages and the other "paraphernalia of gentility".' In addition, 'the governess was also an indicator of the extent to which a man's wife was truly a lady of leisure.' Therein lay the problem. Those women who had to seek employment as governesses, although from middle-class backgrounds, were seen as failures of that system. 'Society has thought fit to assert that the woman who works for herself loses her social position' (ibid.). However, as Peterson goes on to argue, 'the position of the governess seems to have been appropriate because, while it was paid employment, it was within the home. The governess was doing something she might have done as a wife under better circumstances. She avoided the immodest and unladylike position of public occupation.'

It was this position that became of some concern in the 1840s and slowly, through the next few decades, middle-class girls' education and employment was driven out of the home. The first attempt to deal with the problem was not to alter the family-based system but to give such women more financial security. In 1843 a Professor F.D. Maurice of theology at King's College, London University,with the charitable help of the Church of England, established the Governesses' Benevolent Institution (GBI): 'Its purpose was to provide placement service, temporary housing for unemployed governesses, insurance and annuities to aging governesses' (Peterson, 1972, p. 17). It was to ensure that such women, when destitute, would not have to rely on the Poor Law. It therefore maintained distinction between the classes. The second development, following from the GBI, was the establishment of some form of *training* for governesses. In 1847 Professor Maurice started to give lectures and in 1848 he and other professors from King's College opened Queen's College. Its purpose was to make governesses into better teachers, but the school was also open to ladies who were not governesses. The intention was not to expand the occupation but to improve its content and ensure that 'incompetent' women did not prosper. This did become the first step to providing new opportunities for women's employment outside the home. The college flourished; yet with a male principal as its head.

Two women who became key figures in the improvement of girls' education attended Queen's College shortly after it had opened: Zimmern argues (1898, p. 31) that it was 'a parent institution'. One was Miss Frances Mary Buss; the other, Miss Dorothea Beale. Together, and with other enterprising young women such as Miss Emily Davies, they began to campaign for changes in women's education. Miss Buss later stated that Queen's College began the Women's Educational Movement.

To improve middle-class girls' education, better-trained women were required as teachers. The recently established University College of London University, which was the child of radicals and dissenters, provided an impetus for women to start their own classes. At about the same time as Queen's College was established, Bedford Ladies' College was opened in London by a woman with a considerable fortune and non-denominational leanings. With six men and forty women on the board of trustees, it was to provide higher education for young women and be staffed entirely by women. Nevertheless, there were few women who were capable of attending, because of their deficient education and because they had been brought up to see their position in the social system as entirely different from that of men, mainly as leisured wives and mothers. The college's beginnings were tentative. It required the efforts of the women's educational movement to change that. Yet, in 1879 the college was incorporated into London University.

With the help of her parents, Miss Buss established a day school for young ladies in Camden, London, in 1850. It was specifically a school for the daughters of professional men, clerks, merchants and tradesmen and was established in an area where they were plentiful. When the North London Collegiate School opened, 35 children attended: less than a year later, there were 115. Miss Buss's aims were to provide a more rigorous (but home-centred) education for girls. She was an advocate of day rather than boarding schools: 'She advised mothers to send their girls away from home "only when it was unavoidable" ' (Kamm, 1958, p. 194). The curriculum of her school was broad but covered basic reading and writing, though not by the rote method since she wanted to cultivate 'habits of thought'. Music, painting and dancing were extras and were separately charged for; the main course cost 2 guineas a quarter. 'Callisthenics', or physical training, was part of the core curriculum. Kamm (1958, p. 35) has argued that Miss

Buss's 'chief instincts were maternal, and like many another good schoolmistress she sublimated them in a career which attracted her irresistibly.'

The first proprietary school for girls, Cheltenham Ladies' College, was opened in 1854, with shares of £10 each to the value of £2,000, for the 'daughters and young children of noblemen and gentlemen' (ibid.). It was established near to a boys' school for the same class of parents in Cheltenham; the town was chosen purposefully since it was the home of retired public servants from India and the East. The school was originally planned as a local one, to be governed by local people but it refused to admit daughters of tradespeople: 'The credentials of the prospective parents of pupils were rigorously inspected and a number of precautionary measures taken before pupils were admitted' (ibid.).

The school was more expensive than Miss Buss's – 6 to 20 guineas a year, including music and drawing. The subjects taught were the holy scriptures and liturgy, history, geography, grammar, arithmetic, French, music, drawing and needlework. German, Italian and dancing were extras. It was a Church of England school, which was now concerned with the education of girls. 'In founding this Institution . . . [it was] felt that due cultivation of girls' minds is not only desirable in itself but that the general welfare of society at large depends upon it' (Kamm, 1958, p. 52). This school had more difficulty than Miss Buss's in becoming accepted because day schools for such girls were still uncommon and 'parents feared their girls would become like boys'. Moreover, the question 'What is the good of education for girls? They have not to earn their living' was frequently asked. Examinations were disapproved of. In 1858 Miss Beale was appointed as the second headmistress. The college rapidly developed under her headship, although she had difficulty obtaining teachers since she insisted on women only to provide the right moral training. But the school gained a more than local reputation, so she began to accept boarders. In 1864 the first boarding house was opened. The curriculum was clearly linked to rigorous religious teaching and the aim of such education was 'service to God'.

Moves to rationalize teaching and courses in the 1860s

These two schools were becoming popular partly because parents were finding it increasingly difficult to afford private governesses. Indeed, during the 1850s private and public economy moves were more in vogue, although domestic concerns rarely sparked the political imagination. Yet another response to the extension of working-class education was therefore the demand from the middle classes that it be reduced! Middle-class parents were concerned about 'the inversion of social orders' and that teachers of the working classes were over-educated, conceited and ambitious. Non-conformists, alarmed by the spread of Church of England education, also wanted all education stopped. With the introduction of the pupil-teacher system for elementary education, the growth in public expenditure on education had been rapid. In 1853 spending was £150,000; four years later, in 1857, it had more than trebled to £541,233 and a year later it had increased by 25 per cent to £663,435; in 1859 it stood at £836,920. Between 1839 and 1860 the total Parliamentary grant to schools was £55 million, with most of the absolute increase going on pupil-teachers. There were greater percentage increases for certified teachers and administration, especially between 1851 and 1857. For certified teachers, public expenditure quadrupled, but by 1857 it was still only one third of that for pupil-teachers. In 1849 there were 3,580 pupil-teachers; ten years later this had increased to 15,224. Because of the overabundance of governesses many women became pupil-teachers and then schoolmistresses. In 1849, women constituted 32 per cent of teachers; in 1859, 46 per cent.

During this period the certified teachers also became more organized. In 1855 there were 2,770 such teachers and 51 local and district associations (Tropp, 1957, ch. 4). Fears of their influence were rife. The growth caused parliamentary concern, first, because of the massive cost of the Crimean War from 1854 to 1856 and, second, at the lack of control of education spending. In 1856 an Education Department was established, headed by a vice-president with a place in the government.

In June 1858 the government appointed a Royal Commission to investigate the state of popular education. One of its emphases was the efficiency of certified teachers; it tried to devise new methods of ensuring their competence and reducing their turnover. In 1853 grants to voluntary schools had been made dependent upon HMIs examining pupils in three age groups, seven- to nine-year-olds, nine- to eleven-year-olds and eleven- to thirteen-year-olds, but this was not satisfactory. The Commissioners developed a system which tied teachers' salaries to the successes of their pupils, who would be examined *before* their teachers were paid. Sutherland (1971, p. 24) argued that they wanted 'to make prospects and position of teachers dependent, to a considerable extent, on the results of this examination'. She went on to quote the Commissioners' claim (ibid.) that 'The object is to find some constant and stringent motive to induce them [teachers] to do that part of their duty which is at once most unpleasant and most important. The examination of only the 3 Rs (reading, writing and arithmetic) represented the "permitted maximum achievement".' The

Commissioners argued that this was the only way to stop teachers avoiding the drudgery of teaching younger and less able children, and it would stem the teaching of advanced work such as modern languages or elementary science. It would also improve education of pauper children.

While the Newcastle Education Commission was still sitting, the HMIs reported for the first time and more firmly advocated tying grants to examination performance. The government's new policy in 1861 was 'free trade in education', put forward by Lowe, the first President of the Privy Council on Education, who was a Whig but a firm advocate of reducing State expenditure. He changed the system for regulating elementary education from minutes to Codes of Regulations. In 1861, apparently as a result of the Newcastle Commission's findings, he produced, not an Act of Parliament, but the Revised Code, which seized on one aspect of the recommendations, that teachers were not to be considered civil servants: 'They would no longer receive any pay or augmentation direct and individually from the education department but from their several managing committees with whom all future arrangements respecting stipends must be made.' This would affect both certified and pupil-teachers. Children would be examined by an HMI or assistant in the three Rs, according to a fixed syllabus. Children would be grouped into four age groups – three to seven; seven to nine; nine to eleven; and over eleven. Failure in one element would result in managers' forfeiture of a third of their grant. Payment by the government to each school's managers would be 1d per child on the basis of minimum attendance of 140 days per year; morning and afternoon attendance would count as two attendances. Distinctions were not made between boys and girls.

There was dramatic reaction to this new Code from the teachers, with the effect that it was suspended. But in February 1862 Lowe introduced the ReRevised Code, which was still opposed by teachers and clergy (Tropp, 1957, p. 90). Children of three to six and those of twelve or older would obtain a grant on the basis of attendance only; other children would be tested. The proposed reductions for training now applied only to the training colleges and not to Queen's Scholars in schools. The scheme was postponed for introduction until March 1863 but then six standards for examination were defined: the standard I test was for six- to seven-year-olds and the standard VI test for eleven- to twelve-year-olds; and an attendance grant would be given for children under six. Subjects were specified for both boys and girls, with girls being required to pass needlework in addition. The final scheme did satisfy the demands for retrenchment in public expenditure and reduction in the overteaching of pupils and teachers.

But controversies in education remained – both teachers and clergy were dissatisfied with a scheme which left education to the forces of supply and demand.

This system of 'payment by results' had severe effects upon educational provision. By 1864 the education grant had been reduced to £706,000 and a year later to £600,752. There were drastic reductions in teacher training; most schemes lasted only one year and several colleges were forced to close. The pupil-teacher to pupil ratio declined: in 1861 it was 1 to 36 and by 1866 it had been reduced to 1 to 54. Many teachers left the occupation for a trade, for the new system meant they lost status and pay. They were now to be at the mercy of their school's managers and the HMIs, who became their inquisitors. Most important, the rump of the teaching profession gradually became predominantly *female*, for women had few alternative prospects to teaching as an occupation. Indeed, in the two years following the implementation of the new regulations (1863–5), male recruits to training college dropped from 1,167 to 860 and female recruits remained stable (Hurt, 1971).

Teachers learnt to exploit loopholes in the Code; for example, they feigned ignorance of the correct age of children in order to get the attendance grant for children under six, rather than submit them to inspection. The move to make teachers more of a profession gained popularity as they 'competed' with the Education Department (Sturt, 1967). The College of Preceptors had for twenty years been trying, unsuccessfully, to recruit teachers. In 1866 it formed the Scholastic Registration Association with four aims – to raise the social position of teachers, to drive out the unqualified, to promote the science of education and to defend children against untrustworthy teachers. It now won the support of certified teachers and, in the Association, there was a convergence of Church of England and non-conformist interests on educational and professional matters. Nevertheless, Parliament in 1867 still refused to sanction higher examinations for teachers.

Economies in working-class education were not the only issue of the 1860s. This was a decade which opened with retrenchment but developed into one of major parliamentary educational concern. The nine great public schools were investigated by a Royal Commission set up in 1861; all secondary schools – endowed, private or proprietary – were covered by the Schools Inquiry Commission, set up in 1864; and the working classes were provided with universal elementary education in 1870 (see ch. 2 for details). All these affected both the nature and content of teaching. In particular, women's involvement both in teaching and in the provision of education was greatly extended by these developments. Women were increasingly being removed from the home. Nevertheless, they were not treated on an equal basis with men. Class distinctions between men were also preserved and reinforced by the changes brought about in the 1860s.

First, the Public Schools Commission looked at only nine boys' schools and attempted to create an exclusive system of schools for the upper classes. It suggested a new system of competitive examinations and a new curriculum. 'The classical languages and literature should continue to hold the principal place in the course of study' but it advocated (McClure, 1968, p. 83) that every boy should be taught maths, one modern language, some natural science, and either drawing or music, with 'geography, ancient and a little modern history'. The Commissioners also recommended later specialization.

Although the intention was to train a new kind of ruling class, no moves were made to train the teachers for these schools. The fact of education at the recently reformed universities of Oxford and Cambridge was sufficient qualification. Training would have reduced the status of these men to that of the certified elementary teacher (Gosden, 1972, p. 216).

So it was, too, for the second set of schools inspected by the Taunton Commission between 1864 and 1868. The Commission recommended classification into three types of secondary school for different classes of the population and providing each with a different curriculum. Only the first grade of schools, mainly boarding schools, would educate boys to enable them to attend university and subsequently to become professionals or members of the gentry. The curriculum here would 'keep classics, but cultivate maths more carefully than at present and add modern languages and natural science'. The second grade of schools would be day schools, where the boys would be trained, through Latin (but not Greek) and modern subjects such as chemistry and physical science, for employment in the army, medical and legal professions, the civil service, civil engineering, business and commercial life. The third grade of secondary schools would educate the sons of small tenant farmers, tradesmen and artisans thoroughly in good reading, writing and arithmetic. The Commissioners also suggested new financial arrangements and teaching qualifications, which were codified in the Endowed Schools Act of 1869.

Neither the Public Schools nor the Endowed Schools Act spelled out the curriculum of the new secondary schools, although they did allow a 'conscience clause' for parents over religious teaching. The curriculum was presumed to be a mix of modern and classical. Nor did the Acts mention the training of teachers, although a member of the Taunton Commission, Fitch, had been concerned with this, arguing that 'almost all educational enterprise of the last few years has originated with private teachers.' The Taunton Commissioners also mentioned that 'the greatest hindrance to technical instruction was the lack of competent teachers of science and the government should train men to make good this want.' But the government did not aim to do this for another decade.

The heads of the more socially aspiring of the schools investigated by the Taunton Commission formed the Headmasters' Conference to discuss both teacher training and their curricula, since they were insulted at their exclusion from the Clarendon Commission's terms of reference. But they did not formulate official policy.

The 1870 Elementary Education Act, which provided universal working-class education, similarly did not specify either the curriculum for the school board schools or the training of teachers. Both these issues, it was felt, were dealt with by the previous Codes of Regulations. The standards for the scheme of payment by results were, however, revised in 1871, 1875 and 1882, when a seventh standard was added. The setting up of school boards under the Act did affect the pupil-teacher system. Gradually, as the boards extended their influence, it became usual in the larger cities to provide pupil-teacher centres for instruction of teachers in groups. The new practice of employing assistant teachers (not certified) also led to the development of separate classrooms, rather than a single one under the headteacher. This gradually led to more autonomy for teachers (Gosden, 1972, p. 196).

The questions of curriculum and teacher training were addressed when it came to women's education. This was perhaps the major educational issue of the 1860s. The numbers of women who were not dependent upon husbands had continued to grow, and women's education, to enable them to find employment, became their major concern. Marriage could no longer be a career for all women. In 1851, of a population of 18 million, 3½ million were women working for a subsistence, of whom five-sevenths were unmarried (Adamson, 1930, p. 323). Within the next ten years, the number of self-supporting women exceeded 20 per cent of the total population, which had reached 20 million. Indeed, in 1861 there were 6 million adult women of whom only slightly over half (3½ million) were wives, three-quarters of a million were widows and, more important, 1.5 million were spinsters (Best, 1973, pp. 119 ff.). In 1857, 120 governesses applied to the Governesses' Benevolent Institution for financial aid and asylum. All were over fifty; 99 were unmarried and 83 were destitute. The impact of these demographic changes were pressure for women's education, employment and the *vote*. The women who began to demand educational changes were not, however, all pursuing the same aims. Marks (1976) identified three strands of thought: women who wanted equal but parallel education to that of men, those in favour of education to make women into good wives and mothers, rather than 'husband-seekers', and those who saw education as necessary morally, for 'dutiful womanhood'.

All the women were concerned to extend educational provision for middle-class women and their first aim was to ensure a plentiful supply of competent teachers, who would then be able to teach other women. To this end, in 1862 'a committee for obtaining the admission of women to University examinations' was established by two major pioneers, Emily Davies and Annie Clough. They campaigned for women to be able to sit for the 'competitive examinations' to Oxford and Cambridge at the ages of sixteen and eighteen. These entrance examinations had been set up in 1857 and 1858 for young men not members of the University, the effect of which was to help raise the status of small schools. The women campaigners were initially successful at Cambridge, in 1865 informally and by 1869 officially (Zimmern, 1898, ch. 3). The curriculum which was set for women was strictly academic; domestic economy did not figure. It covered maths, science, Latin and Greek. Other universities – Oxford, London, Edinburgh and Durham – soon followed suit and allowed girls to sit their examinations.

The women's next campaign was to enable women to take degrees at university, starting with Oxford and Cambridge. Emily Davies argued that 'it is one of the greatest difficulties of female teachers that they are called upon to instruct others while being inadequately instructed themselves' (Zimmern, 1898, p. 104). The women had limited successes in this (and, indeed, it was not until 1948 that women were awarded the degree of Cambridge University). At first, only Cambridge again was at all interested. But it suggested, at the behest of almost 1,000 ladies from the North of England, the setting of special examinations for women. Here Emily Davies and Annie Clough parted company. The latter was willing to agree to this; Emily Davies favoured equality with men. Newnham College at Cambridge was therefore established, first as a boarding house in 1870, then in 1876 as a college, by Annie Clough and other non-conformist women mainly from the north of England 'to offer academic education on the lowest terms for women preparing to be teachers'. Emily Davies, with other Church of England women, started in 1869 a college at Hitchon 'designed to hold in relation to girls' schools and home teaching a position analogous to that occupied by the Universities towards the public schools for boys'. Davies's college moved in 1872 to Girton College, and its students started to take the Cambridge Tripos examinations. There was much opposition, since women were still not expected to earn a living. By 1880 both colleges were incorporated into Cambridge University, although in neither case did their women students actually receive official degrees until 1948.

Meanwhile, in 1870 University College, London, which had been established in 1840 on non-denominational lines, opened its ordinary classes to women. In 1869 Manchester and in 1871 Newcastle Colleges of Science both admitted women. This had been a result of the campaigns started in the north of England, in 1866 through the creation of local associations of schoolmistresses and in 1867 through the North of England Council for promoting the higher education of women. The Council's first success was in 1867 with the start of university extension lectures for women teachers and pupils, by professors mainly from Cambridge University. Oxford and Durham Universities followed suit in the early 1880s: and two women's colleges were established for London University – Westfield and Royal Holloway, in addition to Bedford College.

The third campaign was to extend girls' secondary education. The Taunton Commission was pressured to consider girls' education, and some of its major recommendations were about this. Fitch, a Commissioner, speaking of the prejudice against girls' education, said 'it is wonderful to see how common is the assumption that the repose and enjoyment of the home are in some way incompatible with intellectual education for women. It is true that no one seems able to point to any example in illustration . . .' (Burstall and Douglas, 1911, p. 7). The Commissioners argued that:

> if one looks to the enormous number of unmarried women in the middle class who have to earn their own bread, at the great drain of the male population of this country for the army, for India and for the colonies, at the expensiveness of living here and the consequent lateness of marriage it seems to me that the instruction of girls of a middle class family for anyone who thinks much of it, is important to the very last degree . . . There is weighty evidence to the effect that the essential capacity for learning is the same, or nearly the same, in the 2 sexes . . . Mr. Hammond reports that in mixed schools taught by masters he found no noticeable differences in the attainments in the two sexes . . . (ibid., p. 11).

The Taunton Commission recommended that old endowments, originally made for both boys' and girls' schooling but invariably used only for boys, be opened up for girls in every large town. This was written into the Endowed Schools Act of 1869. The Commissioners also suggested the extension of girls' secondary education, but not on boarding lines, and higher education especially for schoolmistresses.

> Assuming, as we may fairly do, that the homes of our middle class are commonly favourable to the growth and development of the female characteristics, we are ourselves inclined to the opinion, which also appears somewhat preponderate in the evidence, that in the case of girls more than in that of boys the combination of school teaching with home influence, such as day schools admit of, is the most promising arrangement (ibid., p. 10).

Developments from the 1860s

Two major developments grew out of the report of the Taunton Commission and the Endowed Schools Act of 1869. One was the opening up of endowments for girls' grammar schools. The other effect was the setting up of associations and, in 1871, of the National Union for the Improving of Education of Women of all classes above the lower. This particular 'Educational Charter for Women' had two aims – the creation of girls' public day high schools in every town where schools did not exist and the testing of teacher efficiency and subsequent registration of teachers which 'would make the schoolmistresses' profession as honourable and honoured as the schoolmasters' ' (Adamson, 1930, p. 334). In 1872 the Girls' Public Day School Company (GPDSC) was founded, after much public campaigning by the National Union for funds. The schools established would be modelled on the North London Collegiate School, which in 1871 became public and acquired a governing body of men and women and a new lower school known as Camden School. The GPDSC argued for women's education to counter traditional views such as that attacked by Maria Grey: 'there is a pretty theory abroad, which is always brought forward when women's education is talked about, that they are educated to be wives and mothers. I do not know a more fallacious one. They are *not* educated to be wives but to get husbands' (Kamm, 1971, p. 20).

The aims of the Company were not just instruction but that girls should learn to understand *relations* – whether to fellow-beings or to members of a family, country or race. Each school was therefore to have three departments (preparatory, junior and senior), with a head, a staff of trained teachers and a class of student teachers. To get trained teachers the GPDSC had to start its own scheme. The schools would provide a thoroughly academic curriculum achieving the university local examinations, but with extras such as piano and drawing in the afternoons, and time for 'home duties' (Zimmern, 1898, p. 62). The academic subjects included religious instruction, reading, writing, arithmetic, mathematics, bookkeeping, English grammar, composition and literature, history, geography, French, German, Latin, physical science, social economy, drawing class, singing and harmony, gymnastic exercises and needlework. Accomplishments were relegated to the background (Zimmern, 1898, p. 72). Games were used to improve the tone of the school and promote loyalty and public spirit. Lunch was *not* provided and girls were expected to return home for it. The schools also aimed to take in young children and teach them in small classes. So the GPDSC established a Froebel society in 1874, to develop methods of kindergarten teaching.

The teacher training scheme was begun by the Company but in 1873 the College of Preceptors established its own training scheme, with the encouragement of Sir James Kay-Shuttleworth. A year or two later, the National Union founded the Teacher Training and Registration Society. It aimed to attract both men and women, but women predominated, and its first teacher training college was for schoolmistresses from girls' middle and higher schools. The aim to have such training for one year after a university course took longer to be achieved, as men in the proprietary and endowed schools were not enthusiastic. A rival company, the Church Schools Company, was set up in 1883, to provide Church teaching and general education for girls at moderate cost.

A more general effect of the educational changes begun in the 1860s was the increasing concern of teachers with their own position. A variety of associations proliferated to safeguard the positions of various types of teacher but, because schools lacked any unity of purpose, so did the associations, Indeed, in the last quarter of the century the boys' public schools, according to Simon (1960), were influenced by the Headmasters' Conference (HMC) to become more independent and divorced from the rest of the system. The teachers retained their autonomy. Sir James Kay-Shuttleworth in 1875 tried to get the HMC to consider post-graduate training, but 'on the whole they seemed rather bored and were simply obstructive' (Gosden, 1972, p. 216). But the HMC in 1879 approached Oxford and Cambridge Universities to develop courses at post-graduate level. These were begun and were mainly attended by graduates from the women's colleges.

The boys' grammar and public schools developed rapidly after 1869, their popularity being based on perceived utility (Honey, 1977). Many of them grew in size and therefore required more than just a headmaster. By 1891 the Assistant Masters' Association had been formed to cater for the interests of such masters. The specific catalyst was yet another move to register teachers in Parliament. These teachers recognized their insecurity of tenure and grouped together to provide a Legal and Provident fund. They did not, at first, involve themselves in questions of curriculum.

The girls' public day schools also developed rapidly, partly through the efforts of the School Headmistresses' Association, founded in 1874 by Miss Buss. Ten years later their Assistant Mistresses organized themselves. The main development of these schools was in the numbers of students sitting for the Cambridge Local examinations. Throughout this period more girls than boys began to take these examinations. In December 1878, 6,435 candidates took the Senior and Junior Cambridge Locals, of whom 2,480 were girls. The senior girl candidates considerably outnumbered the boys (997 to 626) and the predominance of girls continued to grow. Indeed, the girls' schools gradually attracted more pupils because of their academic curriculum. The SHA also encouraged the training of women teachers, and set up its own training centres. For example, in 1885 Miss Beale set up a full training course for secondary school teachers which was subsequently linked with St. Hilda's College at Oxford. Both residential and day training colleges developed in the 1880s and 1890s.

The major association, however, to develop out of this period was the National Union of Elementary Teachers (NUET), founded in 1870 for certified teachers only. In 1889 it became the NUT. Its membership was always predominantly female; that is, over two-thirds were women (Gosden, 1972). It had dual aims of influencing education and advancing the position of its teachers, especially *against* the Teachers' Registration movement. It was to be a Benevolent and Friendly Society. It was not, according to Tropp (1957), very successful in its aims to win a measure of professional autonomy from the State and local school boards, because of various splits such as religious and sexual divisions. Women, although the majority in the NUET, were not active at first. Their position and pay in the profession were inferior to those of men, and they were treated, curiously, as a special class. Most women teachers were not trained or certificated. The problem, immediately after the 1870 Education Act, was to increase the supply of teachers for school board schools. Between 1870 and 1875 the number of pupil-teachers doubled from 14,600 to 29,200. But the NUET was not able to change the terms on which teachers worked. The Revised Code, for example, continued to dominate elementary teaching, merely with modifications in the standards, until 1895.

The developments in education during the last quarter of the century were set by 1870. The only major change which had not been presaged was the improvement in technical and vocational education, which was not initially the result of central initiative but came about through local involvement of employers and industrialists. During the 1870s and 1880s Britain's international competitive position declined, partly as a result of limited technical innovation. Attempts were therefore made to improve curricula. The only limited measure that the government had previously made was the creation of the Department of Science and Art in 1853, which provided grants for these subjects to individual schools. In the 1880s these grants were increased, as a result of another Royal Commission, chaired by Samuelson. In the larger industrial towns such as Manchester, Bradford and Birmingham the school boards began to develop special training schools, known as *higher grade schools*, which either taught the HMIs' standards in advanced terms or taught mainly technical subjects, including needlework and domestic science for girls, with grants supplied for work above the basic standards. Some schools also developed evening continuation classes. The government tried to encourage more technical education, first through the creation of county councils in 1888 and through the Technical Instruction Acts of 1889 and 1891, which supplied grants to the county councils who could use them for board schools and organized science day schools and technical institutions, scholarships or grants to the endowed, proprietary and evening schools. These latter Acts subsequently used money which had been acquired through a tax on the import of whiskey. Working-class girls' education, especially in domestic science, was specifically encouraged. Yet this could not be fully effective without more specific training for teachers.

The problem of training teachers for elementary schools was addressed in 1885 by the Cross Commission, although its main interests were religious teaching and the nature of the curriculum. The Commission argued (Elementary Education Acts, 1888, p. 201) that 'whilst there is a growing demand for fully qualified female teachers the supply of trained male teachers was somewhat in excess of the demand.' Nevertheless, the Cross Commissioners could not agree: the authors of the majority report did not want the extension of education for the working classes or the training of their teachers. They felt the existing pupil-teacher residential arrangements should be maintained, and were willing to encourage more untrained teachers and the reduction of higher grade schools. The authors of the minority report welcomed schools as 'laying the basis for a system of industrial, technical and commercial education'. They argued that grammar and secondary schools were, and should remain, the province of the middle classes and part of a ladder to university; only a few working-class children should be allowed access through scholarships. They criticized the pupil-teacher system, arguing that pupil-teachers were poorly instructed and bad teachers (Gosden, 1972, p. 197). Although there were such differences of opinion, the Cross Commissioners did alter teacher training, by suggesting the foundation of day training colleges.

In 1890, on the Cross Commission's recommendation, the Tory government proposed the setting up of day training colleges and extended the maximum length of course from two to three years to enable teachers in training to read for a degree. The course syllabus would be tied to a university college. In the Code of 1890, however, to facilitate the supply of teachers, a new category of teacher was created, subsequently known by the section of the code as Article 68ers. *Women* were to be allowed to teach *without any* qualifications save three – approval of an HMI, being over eighteen years old and having been vaccinated. Women, in any event, predominated. The Cross Commission had found that, of 42,212 certificated teachers, 16,805 were men and 25,407 women. But many were certificated by examination and not by teacher training. The change to female Article 68ers led to a decline in the overall professional qualifications of teachers. On the other hand, attempts were made to register teachers again but in 1891 Parliament rejected this registration.

Teachers' working conditions, however, improved. For the first time, in 1894, the government sought to regulate the size of classes. The new system of day teacher training also led to a rapid increase: by 1900 the new colleges had over 20,000 places, whereas in 1890 the 49 residential colleges had only 3,679 students. Another effect of the Cross Commission was the creation of a government departmental committee in 1896 to inspect the pupil-teacher system and the supply of teachers. Its report in 1898 had a major impact on the future of the system.

The Commission also modified the elementary school curriculum. Through the Codes of Regulations of 1871, 1872, 1875 and 1880 elementary schooling had become more diversified. The 1871 Code laid down a course in three primary studies, which was still divided into six standards. To pass the examination in the sixth, or highest, standard, pupils were required 'to read with fluency and expression, to write a short theme, or letter, or easy paraphrase and to work sums in proportion and vulgar or decimal fractions'. The Code also introduced more advanced studies and military drill such as squad and company drill. In the 1872 Code, singing became grant-earning. The Code of 1875 detailed a more systematically ordered course. In addition to the three Rs (and needlework for girls!) there were class and specific subjects. The former were for groups of children (covering grammar, geography, history and needlework), which under the 1880 Code could only be taught through reading books. Specific subjects were for individuals and included algebra, Euclid, mensuration, Latin, French, German, mechanics, animal physiology, physical geography, botany and domestic economy. In 1882 the Code was further extended but the three Rs, and needlework for girls, still remained obligatory. Elementary science and English were added.

The Cross Commission, in 1885, was divided on the extent to which these special subjects should be encouraged. Those writing the majority report did not want them to be. However, both the majority and minority Commissioners, under pressure from the NUT, deprecated the system of 'payment by results' which led to this rigid system of standards and examinations. They recommended (Elementary Education Acts, 1888, p. 183) that

> we are unanimously of the opinion that the present system of 'payment by results' is carried too far and is too rigidly applied, and that it ought to be modified and relaxed in the interests equally of the scholars, of the teachers and of education itself.

The Code of 1890 introduced by the Tories modified the system on the Commissioners' suggestion: the capitation grant was made a fixed one, determined by the average number of children in attendance at school. Examination in the obligatory subjects was confined to sample groups numbering not less than one-third of the school. In 1895 this plan was abandoned and examination was replaced by mere inspection. Two years later, payment for individual passes in specific subjects was ended. In 1900 a block grant was developed, *but* payment of grants for special subjects continued for cookery, laundry, gardening, dairy work and manual instruction. The Codes of 1890–4 also introduced new technical subjects such as shorthand, navigation and hygiene (Adamson, 1930, p. 374), since the middle classes objected to the heavy emphasis on training for 'black-coated' occupations.

The secondary schools were reconsidered by a Royal Commission set up in 1894. The Commissioners worked quickly, reporting in 1895 (the Bryce Report), and focused upon both the content of secondary education and the training of its teachers. They did not make any specific proposals for the latter although agreeing that it was 'generally desirable' (Gosden, 1972, p. 225). They supported one of the Commissioners' twenty-year campaign for university-based education. They also maintained the distinction between teaching in elementary and secondary schools. The report was concerned to make secondary education as a whole more harmonious and unified, although it stuck to the Taunton Commission's threefold classification of schools (Schools Inquiry Commission, 1868). The Bryce Royal Commission on secondary education deprecated the overlap of function of the various types of school and college, and recommended a central board and a register of teachers. The last term was unfortunate since majority preference was for a single register for masters and mistresses! Schoolmistresses at that time disdained the title of teacher. The Commissioners had little to say on the curriculum save that it should be left to local option but contain three elements – literary, scientific, technical – 'and the last of the three will thrive all the better if the two former receive their fitting need of recognition' (Royal Commission on Secondary Education, 1895, p. 285). They also claimed, 'we hold it unadvisable to attempt to fetter their discretion by any rigid rules; and we shall deplore as certain to be hurtful to educational progress the uniformity of system which such rules would tend to produce' (ibid., p. 284). They did try to distinguish technical instruction, claiming secondary schools should teach 'the practical arts such as the elements of applied mechanics and the subject connected with agriculture, as well as modern languages and the kinds of knowledge most useful to the merchant or trader' (ibid., p. 284). The Bryce Commissioners also considered the question of co-education (Adamson, 1930, p. 460), but did not make any judgment. Middle-class schooling therefore remained organized on a single-sex basis.

By the end of the century there had been a transformation in the educational system and the teachers who served it. Children were increasingly being taught about their position in adult life: boys especially to earn a living and girls as wives, mothers and workers. In 1911 Mrs Gilliland was to argue (Burstall and Douglas, 1911) that girls' 'schools that omit all instruction in the preparation for home life . . . are doing very little to help our national life, because they are doing nothing to make our girls builders of homes and makers of men'. To this end, curricula had become increasingly differentiated even in middle-class girls' schools. Teachers were trained for specific subjects to this purpose, but it was mainly women who trained. Male teachers, especially in the public and grammar schools, still disdained such involvement. Women, in an attempt to obtain gainful employment, were willing to train for it. Middle-class women were trained by the girls' schools and universities to be schoolmistresses (rather than teachers). Elementary teachers were trained through the pupil-teacher system and training colleges, where again women predominated.

By the end of the century, it was more common for women to earn a livelihood and various channels had been created to aid women's entrance to employment. At the same time, of course, men's employment opportunities had altered and become more differentiated. In particular, higher and vocational education served to increase the supply of skilled and professional men and women. At the turn of the century five new universities, in addition to Oxford, Cambridge, Durham and London, were given charters. They all provided access for women. Moreover, the existing universities had by now all allowed the admission of women and the creation of women's colleges as part of the university. Nevertheless, the major field of employment for women, save in one or two particular industries and domestic service, was teaching or being a schoolmistress. This occupation had been made available for middle-class women by the development of separate institutions for girls and for working-class women by the insistence on providing the working classes with only a limited amount of education. Women therefore would suffice as their teachers and, in particular, to care for young children (infant classes) and girls' departments. In the last half of the nineteenth century women moved out of the home into the field of employment, at least for a period in their adult lives. But that work closely paralleled the work of the home – caring for children. What girls learnt, too, by this time mirrored the work of the home, although for middle-class girls this was not a major emphasis. Nevertheless, girls of any social class were still not expected to be the equals of their brothers.

6

The rise of the 'homely arts' and the demise of the homely teacher

The nature of schooling and of the teachers who supplied the schools changed dramatically in the first forty years of this century. When the Second World War broke out, both the curricula of schools and the teaching profession had been transformed from their nineteenth-century origins, but the major reforms which achieved this transformation were initiated in the first two decades of the twentieth century. The inter-war years were, as described in chapter 3, lean years in terms of policy solutions and implementation, but they were years of substantial policy proposal. They were also years when the policies of the previous two decades were put into effect. The main trend of the 1920s and 1930s was to tie education more closely to the economy, in terms of the constituent occupations rather than merely its social divisions. Women, however, were increasingly excluded from the labour force, especially when married and mothers, and particularly during the Depression of the 1930s. This exclusion was reflected in what girls were taught at school and how their teachers were treated. Curricula became specialized not only for the economy as a whole but for the sexual division of labour in particular. The marriage bar was more stringently enforced in the teaching profession and arguments against some teachers' demands for equal pay were articulated on the grounds of women's prime responsibility being the home.

As schooling became more and more oriented to a differentiated labour market and as training for skills became a function of the education system, work-based training, or apprenticeships, declined in number. This characteristic of industry was mirrored for other occupations, in particular teaching. In the first two decades of the twentieth century the pupil-teacher system, for example, was replaced by an autonomous system of training, albeit within the education system. Moreover, the characteristics of teaching, exemplified by the sorts of people recruited to teaching, became more separated from the home. There were attempts to professionalize teaching as the distinctions between schooling for the working and middle classes changed: teachers' registration was a key issue. The curriculum also became more differentiated into separate subjects. Nevertheless, sexual divisions continued within the curriculum and it continued to be a major task of schools to prepare girls for their place within the home rather than the world of work; they were to be trained in what were known as the 'homely arts' – to be wives and mothers.

Teaching in the early twentieth century

When the twentieth century opened, the pupil-teacher system as a method of training teachers for elementary schools was under attack by the government. This was in line with the general attack upon elementary education and its political control (see ch. 3). A government departmental committee had been appointed in 1896, as a result of the majority report recommendations of the Royal Commission chaired by Cross which reported in 1888. The departmental committee's report, on the workings of the pupil-teacher system and the supply of teachers, caused particular offence to the NUT and yet was to change the basis of the whole elementary system. The committee argued (Gosden, 1972, p. 197) that:

> The traditions of primary teaching are still, through no fault of the teachers, narrower than is consistent with sound education; and we believe that better methods, greater spontaneity, a wider outlook . . . would result from the more frequent employment in primary schools of persons whose experience has not been exclusively or chiefly primary . . .

It argued that elementary teachers should be recruited from the secondary schools and be trained separately from the schools from which they were recruited.

Elementary education was to be reduced in scope because it competed with education for the middle classes. The elementary schools were to be controlled, not by their own representatives, but by representatives of the wider community, who were, in all probability, more middle class. The teachers in the elementary schools, as a corollary, were to be recruited from sections of the middle classes in that they were to come from secondary schools. At this time, only the lower-middle classes and above were able to attend such schools. The departmental committee report added (Gosden, 1972, p. 197) an explicit comment:

> We look forward to the ultimate conversion of those [pupil-teacher] centres which are well-staffed and properly equipped into real secondary schools, where, although perhaps intending teachers may be in the majority, they will have ample time for their studies and will be instructed side by side with pupils who have other careers in mind.

The 1902 Education Act transferred the political control of schools to LEAs, enhanced the distinction between elementary and secondary education and enabled changes to take place in the recruitment and training of teachers. It allowed LEAs to develop their own teacher training colleges alongside those of the religious bodies which already existed.

The pupil-teacher system had, in any event, already been breaking down for two reasons. One was the administrative change from residential to day training colleges (discussed in ch. 5). The other, more important, change was the impact on the supply of teachers of the increase in elementary schooling from the 1870s. The increase resulted from reductions in class size, as well as the introduction of compulsory schooling and the raising of school-leaving ages, in the 1890s. More teachers were needed than the pupil-teacher system was able to train. In 1900 nearly one-third of the certificated male teachers and over half of the certificated women teachers had never been to college. In 1899, for instance, about three-fifths (7,113 of 11,892) of those examined for the teaching certificates had no college training. In 1890 a new category of teacher had been introduced (Article 68ers) who were almost all women. Partington has argued (1976, p. 2) that they 'were married to headmasters: most were employed with the youngest children who were far more numerous in the schools then than later in the century.'

During the last quarter of the nineteenth century and up to 1914, the increase in elementary teachers was mainly amongst women. In that forty-year period the increase in male teachers was 291 per cent and that of women 862 per cent (Holcombe, 1973, p. 34). So by 1914 women constituted 75 per cent of the teaching profession in elementary schools. Nevertheless, they were not as well trained as men. In 1875, 70 per cent of the men were trained and certificated and 57 per cent of the women were. With the increase in teachers and the changes in training by 1914 only 66 per cent of the men were trained and certificated. The decline for women was even more dramatic – to 32 per cent. This was in part because of the category of supplementary teacher. In 1900 there were 20,000 of these. It was also because more women than men were assistant teachers. In fact, the changes in the training of elementary teachers attendant upon the 1902 Education Act and the 1903 Pupil-Teacher Regulations meant that yet more women entered teaching as an occupation. Many of these women were from the lower-middle classes.

The Regulations of 1903, and the explanatory circular from the Board of Education, spelled out the detail of the principles previously proposed. There were two main points: one was the raising of the minimum age for a pupil-teacher to sixteen (except in rural areas); the other was to insist on at least 300 hours of instruction in approved centres or classes of pupil-teachers. This latter requirement was translated into administrative practice by recognizing secondary schools for the purpose. The circular stated the aim of 'utilising the secondary schools to the fullest possible extent for preliminary training purposes' (Gosden, 1972, p. 201). He added that 'an increasing number of secondary schools became involved, so that by 1906–7, out of 694 secondary schools recognised for grants under the Secondary Schools Regulations, 357 were also recognised as pupil-teacher centres; at this time there remained 179 independent pupil-teacher centres in receipt of grant.'

In 1907 new regulations were introduced by the Liberals, which led to the further decline of the pupil-teacher system. Full-time secondary education was to continue to the age of eighteen and any attempt at gaining practical experience in the elementary schools was to be deferred until training college had been entered. They also introduced maintenance grants for students at training college. The NUT continued to express dissatisfaction with the government's policy changes. In particular, it was concerned that its members would be squeezed out of teaching through lack of adequate qualifications. Yet the government was implacable. The NUT recognized that this was an attempt to further downgrade the elementary schools and bolster up the new secondary schools. The *Schoolmaster*, the newspaper of the NUT, published in 1908 an article 'entitled "A Stolen Profession" alleging that the teaching profession was gradually becoming the preserve of children of middle-class parents' (Gosden, 1972, p. 204). It added (ibid.), 'a useful profession is being stolen from the child of the working man, and while he sleepeth an enemy hath removed his landmark.'

The other way in which the government attempted to emasculate elementary education and the pupil-teacher system was through the establishment of training colleges especially for teachers, which from 1904 no longer came under the elementary Code of Regulations. These were to be independent of the elementary schools and not connected with the day courses run by universities, but were to be run by the newly created larger, composite LEAs and under new Regulations, for Secondary Education. To this end, from 1905 special building grants were provided. Within ten years, twenty colleges catering for 4,000 students had been established. The curriculum of the colleges was narrowly defined and students were less likely to take university degrees than hitherto. In 1905 the *Schoolmaster* complained (ibid.) 'these movements are inspired by one unworthy and sinister purpose, which is to confine the elementary teacher, trained or untrained, graduate or non-graduate, to work of a purely elementary kind and to bring in persons of other antecedents for every kind of higher work and for every office of substantial emolument.'

Indeed, the policy changes had far-reaching consequences. Not only did they alter both the class and sex ratios of the elementary school teachers but also encouraged their organization in pursuit of control of the teaching profession. In 1915 Beatrice Webb (1915, pt. 1, p. 1) wrote of the teaching profession, 'it is predominantly feminine. Out of a quarter of a million persons in England and Wales claiming to be teachers at least 175,000 are women . . . out of the 250,000 teachers . . . at least 150,000 are known to be at work all day in the public elementary schools, and of these about 100,000 are organised.' She then went on to discuss the work of the NUT, having as members 37,496 men and 53,911 women. She pointed out that 'the proportion of men [was] considerably greater than the proportion among the whole body of such qualified teachers.' Moreover, 'the exclusion of nearly one-third of the total number of teachers in public elementary schools constitutes the most intractable problem in the professional organisation of the teaching world. They are deliberately excluded whom it regards as unqualified.' The split between qualified and unqualified was not the only problem: there were religious conflicts and conflicts between the recently created group of class teachers and headteachers and over the position of teachers and heads in central schools.

The most far-reaching problem, however, was the changing *position of women* within the profession. Their organization had an important impact upon the development of the teaching profession and resulted from specific policies towards women. As Webb (1915, pt. 1, p. 8) so succinctly argued:

> Down to the end of the 19th century the women elementary teachers seem to have acquiesced in the control of the profession

> by their male colleagues, and even to have accepted without complaint the lower scales of salaries and lesser opportunities of promotion that are afforded the female sex. But by 1900 the relative position of women and men had changed, both in the teaching profession and in the teachers' organisations. Women had long formed the majority of the teachers . . . they came to be a large majority in the NUT . . . Moreover, with the entry of middle-class women into elementary school teaching and the marked improvement in girls' schools, the relative quality, as well as the relative quantity, of the male and female teachers had been slowly changing. During the first decade of the twentieth century the growth of the suffrage agitation and the increasing demand of equal pay for equal work, inspired with missionary fervour those women teachers, still only a minority, who desired that women should take a full share in public affairs. Hence we find springing up between 1900 and 1910 various sectional organisations of women teachers having for their purpose the levelling up of the women's status to that of her male fellow-professionals and fellow citizens. The largest and most influential of these is the National Federation of Women Teachers . . . they are not merely satisfied with economic equality; they desire to obtain a greater share both in the control of their profession and in the government of the country.

During the early years of the twentieth century women, especially middle-class women, needed to find employment outside the home to maintain themselves economically. This employment was, to a large extent, now more acceptable than half a century earlier. In particular there were opportunities for women to join the teaching profession. They did so in ever increasing numbers in the years preceding the First World War. Nevertheless, they were in no sense seen or treated by the LEAs and government as equal to men. Indeed, the fact that women were allowed to teach in such numbers testified to the lack of status afforded elementary education. Within the teaching profession, women were not the peers of men.

There were three issues of conflict – *positions*, *pensions* and *pay*. Women had been given particular teaching positions (Partington, 1976, pp. 2–3):

> In elementary schools women taught in girls' and infant departments, which were under headmistresses. Women also usually taught in Standards I to III of boys' departments, although Standard IV and above were almost always taken by men. Mixed classes for older children were declining in numbers before 1914 mainly because it was widely believed that co-education created

unnecessary difficulties in the teaching of laundry work, carpentry and other skills thought suitable for one sex only. Work in special schools was very largely in the hands of women; men were normally brought in only to instruct older boys in manual work, games and drill. In the early years of this century, about 44 per cent of elementary headships were held by men, although they constituted only a quarter of the teaching force; indeed until 1905, there were more heads than assistants among certificated men teachers. Large mixed schools were exclusively a male preserve. Small rural mixed schools of about 60 or 70 pupils often had headmistresses for reasons of economy and because suitable men were difficult to attract to remote country areas.

Women were regarded as most capable of teaching young children, especially those in nursery and infant classes, as this was an extension of their maternal attributes. They could also teach older girls subjects which would fit them for life in the home or domestic work. Yet the women who were to do such teaching were usually single or widowed. The majority of LEAs dismissed women on marriage: they were not considered capable of combining two jobs. Teaching was thus a precursor to, or substitute for, a career in marriage. Curiously, parenthood was *not* the point at which women were considered to lose capability. One LEA was the exception. The London School Board, and subsequently the LCC, according to Webb (1915, pt. 2, p. 8) 'always employed them [married women] and made elaborate arrangements for special leave of absence.' The predominant ideology, however, made a distinction between teaching as paid employment and the home. It was only exceptionally, where the supply of teachers may have been at risk, that changes or modifications to this ideology were made.

The first organized political moves by women teachers were not to alter this position. They were over women's economic position within the profession. The NUT had first operated as a Benevolent and Friendly Society and had campaigned successfully for state-supported pensions. In 1899 the government had passed an Act to this effect. Contributions for all NUT members were the same but benefits differed for men and women. In 1903 the women were successful in their campaign to receive full benefits. As a result of this initial action, women began to organize for equal pay. Here they were not successful for over half a century! They were encouraged by the general climate of opinion for further changes in women's position. In 1904, after the defeat of equal pay motions at the NUT annual conference, the Equal Pay League was formed, with both men and women on the executive. In 1906, in order to broaden its base and recruit women to the NUT and its executive, the name was changed to the National Federation of Women Teachers, but it remained until after the First World War a pressure group within the NUT. Much of its work, in fact, was devoted to the female suffrage campaigns rather than equal pay. Both issues were vigorously and succcessfully opposed by the male members of the NUT. They even argued that the suffrage question was beyond the scope of the NUT. The equal pay question was opposed on the grounds that men and women not only had different work but had different commitments. Men had families to support, whereas women, because of the habitual exclusion of those who married, were only self-supporting. This ignored women's dependents such as elderly parents and relatives. Partly because of these arguments, the Association of London Married Women Teachers was formed in 1909, within the London Teachers' Association. Webb argued (1915, pt. 2, p. 8) that again it was a defensive measure, 'serious attacks having been made on the right of their members to employment'. This strategy did not gain wider national support.

By 1914, the character and organization of teaching had changed dramatically from the nineteenth century. This was in large part due to the campaigns and actions of the teacher organizations. Webb also commented on this (1915, pt. 2, p. 11):

> Smaller classes, really compulsory attendance, the better enforcement of the [1902] Education Act, the abolition of 'half-time', the prevention of the gainful employment of children after school hours, the raising of the age at which the child may leave school, the prevention of street trading by children, the enforcement of attendance at continuation schools, with the consequent reduction in the hours of labour of the adolescent, have all formed part of the permanent policy of the NUT. The adoption of medical inspection and treatment, the feeding of necessitous children, the general improvement of the conditions of working class life . . . in more ways than one the NUT has identified itself with the needs of the wage-earning class family and with the educational aspirations of the most enlightened of the manual workers . . . The perpetual insistence that 'teachers must be free to choose their own methods' . . . or, the teachers' 'right to a free hand to conduct their schools according to their own judgment' – are . . . manifestations of a professional egoism in the teacher which tends to impair the social value of his service.

The courses boys and girls should study

The changes in teaching were reflected in what and how children were taught. Although the Revised Code and 'payment by results' were effectively abolished by the twentieth century, the government continued to lay down Codes which defined the content of elementary schools' curricula. Immediately following the 1902 Act, a new code was issued for elementary schools in 1903. As Lowndes (1969, p. 109) has argued, it was radically different from previous codes because it defined the *purpose* of the elementary school. It was, however, the 1904 Code which was more significant since it did not have to help schools in the transition from one form of political control to another. It set out to define the purpose of the school in creating worthy members of the community through imbuing them with particular skills – 'for the work of life', 'habits of observation and clear reasoning', 'some familiarity with the literature and history of their own country', 'some power over language', 'natural activities of hand and eye by suitable forms of practical work and manual instruction', 'the workings of some of the simpler laws of health' and a 'strong respect for duty'.

The 1903 Code was a lengthy 76-page document detailing the differentiated curriculum, since children now spent more years in school. A yardstick was also included for the sufficient number of teachers (Lowndes, 1969, p. 123). The Code focused attention on the special subjects to be taught and the way to develop *interest* in children. These subjects had increasingly been encouraged under previous Codes. By 1902 special grants were being given for cookery, laundrywork, dairywork, household management, manual instruction, cottage gardening *and* cookery for boys in seaport towns (!). Between 1895 and 1902 (Lowndes, 1969, pp. 134–5), the number of departments taking gardening had increased sixteenfold, manual instruction sixfold and domestic subjects from 4,700 to 11,062. The new Code did not lay down any new subjects but tried to allow for the more flexible teaching of individual subjects. It included, in the general curriculum, English language and literature, history, geography, music, physical training, hygiene, nature study, and (for girls) cookery, laundry and housewifery. It encouraged *class* teaching rather than teaching *en masse*. But still the sexual division of labour was stressed and mirrored that within the teaching profession.

The main way in which curricula were distinguished for boys and girls was over the parts they would play in adult life. Increasing employment for women notwithstanding, the argument for specific education for girls was couched in terms of their adult job within the family. 'The education should be linked much more definitely and thoroughly to what will normally be the chief business of their lives' (Kamm, 1971, p. 16). Subjects were not to be taught separately for boys and girls. They were to continue to learn *different* subjects. 'Every school should have its own kitchen and laundry and girls should learn cookery, laundrywork and housewifery.' Boys, on the other hand, were to be taught manual instruction and cottage gardening. However, there were far fewer school departments financed for this in 1903 (about 2,000) than for cookery (3,744), laundry (783) and household management (173). There were in total 4,700 departments teaching specific women's subjects. Practical subjects for both boys and girls were to expand and change through the new elementary codes. They did not, though, allow for boys and girls to be taught together. Their adult lives would lead them in different directions and their school work should be a training for this (see also Dyhouse, 1977).

Another major change in schooling in the years before 1914 was the dramatic decline in provision for young children. As argued in chapter 3, the Boer War led to concern about the health of the nation. As a result, the first group of women HMIs were asked to report on the state of children under five in public elementary schools. The HMIs were influenced by the views of Froebel on child-centred education. They were horrified, therefore, by the large classes and lack of stimulation of pupils. Their report was such an indictment that it had to be suppressed. They recommended *nursery* schools rather than 'schools of instruction' where children learnt nothing. At that time nursery and infant children were taught together, and the HMIs recommended their separation. As a result of the HMIs' report, in the 1905 Code, LEAs were given discretion to exclude children younger than five. Thus most children of this age were no longer taught anything. Those left were treated in a less formal and more relaxed manner, and not expected to read or write. The Code also gave wider scope to the teaching of five- to seven-year-olds. Nevertheless, the Chief Inspector, as a result of the HMIs' report, was able to remark that 'it is desirable that there should be a special training for infant teachers, but under present circumstances might not 2 supplementary teachers of *good motherly instincts* be as good for 60 babies between the ages of 3 and 5 as one clever ex-collegian?' (Partington, 1976, p. 5) [my emphasis].

The curriculum of the higher elementary schools was also reviewed in the years following the 1902 Act. In the 1905 Code, the schools were defined as those for children over twelve. The LEA was allowed more freedom with the curriculum (Graves, 1943, p. 74) but

> this would not be approved by the Board of Education unless it

> provided for a progressive course of study in English language and literature, in elementary mathematics, and in history and geography, in addition to special instruction that would bear on the future occupations of the scholars. Drawing and manual work for the boys and domestic subjects for girls had in every case to be included as part of the general or special instruction.

In 1906 the Consultative Committee of the Board of Education, writing on the higher elementary schools, recommended a course fitted for livelihoods with three strands – humanistic and scientific for both boys and girls plus manual for boys or domestic for girls. But few such schools developed to take up the recommendations. Between 1905 and 1917 there were never more than 45 such schools or 10,000 pupils in them. Instead, central schools and technical schools replaced them, and these developed narrower curricula.

Thus, through changes in teacher employment, teachers were given more autonomy within the classroom and in how they taught. Indeed, they were also less subject to arbitrary dismissal or extraneous duties. Nevertheless, women and men teachers were not treated equally, in part because of the difference in how men and women were viewed but also because of the subjects they taught.

Secondary schools before 1918

Changes were also taking place within the teaching profession for secondary schools. Until 1902, few secondary schools were publicly assisted, except by grants for particular subjects from the Department of Art and Science or the Education Department. They also may have had children who were scholarship-holders. The 1902 Act changed the financial basis of many secondary schools. The LEAs were able to provide fee-paying secondary schools through the rates and with the addition of grants from the Board of Education. Through this Act and its subsequent regulations, more schools came under public control (see ch. 3). Many voluntary or endowed grammar schools opted for such State aid. Other schools agreed to grant aid from central or local government. By 1914 there were over 1,000 secondary schools on the grant list – with 668 headmasters and 349 headmistresses. The number of men and women assistants, however, was almost equal: 4,799 men to 5,028 women. These differing ratios were partly because the LEAs established some *mixed* secondary grammar schools and did not follow the example of the endowed grammar schools, which were traditionally single-sex. In the mixed schools women were virtually excluded from headships.

Many women teachers opposed these new mixed schools, first, because their own status suffered and, second, in the interests of girls, who, they argued, needed female care in their adolescence. The opposition was not very successful and co-educational schools were set up on grounds of economy, not pupils' needs! Moreover, many higher grade schools, established under the elementary regulations, came under the new secondary schools regulations after the Act. Thus the making available of public money from local sources for aiding, and later for the foundation, of secondary schools led to a rapid expansion in the size of the secondary school teaching force. But there was an initial problem with the supply of such teachers.

Early demands were made both by the LEAs, who were already training elementary teachers, and by the Board of Education to improve this teaching force through *training*. Until the turn of the century, because the characteristics of the secondary schools varied there had been no unanimity on training. Indeed, teachers in public schools for boys had disdained this, believing it would lower their status: they continued to do so. These varieties among employing authorities were paralleled by differences among the teachers employed. Webb (1915, pt. 2, p. 12) stated that:

> Out of 30,000 persons claiming to be secondary school teachers, perhaps one-half are still at work in definitely private schools carried on for profit by individual proprietors: whilst the other 15,000 are in the service of a miscellaneous array of governing committees of all sorts: trustees of educational endowments, the courts of livery Companies or Gilds, directors of joint stock companies, County Councils and Borough Councils and other Local Authorities.

However, the development of special subjects and special types of secondary schools had led to the recognition that such teaching required special training. A whole variety of professional associations, based on school subjects, began to spring up (Webb, 1915, pt. 2, p. 1).

By 1908 there was much more demand for the specialized training of such teachers: the Board of Education, therefore, issued its first set of regulations for the training of teachers for secondary schools. 'As well as recognising existing secondary training colleges or departments for grant purposes, the Regulations also offered recognition and grant-aid to the few specially organised secondary schools where "a great deal of excellent training work is being carried on" although the grant was only payable in cases where a minimum of 10 students could be trained in this way' (Gosden, 1972, p. 229). The grant regulations neatly distinguished elementary from secondary schools and required specific training in and for the latter. A mix of schools and universities, ten in all, first received the grant (Gosden, 1972, p. 203). But few students, especially men, were forthcoming and the Board had to try to issue further incentives. In 1910 maintenance grants were first offered for teaching training at university. In 1913 grants were offered to schools for individual students. The original plan was to encourage men only but, as a result of protest from both schoolmistresses and headmistresses, the plan was modified to encourage women.

By 1914 training for secondary schools had not advanced very far. It still remained a problem, in particular for boys' schools. The developments for elementary teachers retarded progress for secondary schools (Webb, 1915, pt. 1, p. 18). Secondary teachers therefore preferred to concern themselves with other methods of professionalization such as teacher registration, over which they disagreed especially with the NUT. Of 10,000 teachers in grant-aided secondary schools only 4,000 were trained and the majority of those were women. Gosden has provided Table 6.1 (1972, p. 215).

Table 6.1

	Graduates	*Non-graduates*	*Totals Men*	*Totals Women*
Trained Men	1,466	504	1,970	–
Women	1,534	915	–	2,449
Untrained Men	2,257	1,019	3,276	–
Women	1,186	1,523	–	2,709
Totals	–	–	5,246	5,158

The teachers' register, on the other hand, was an attempt to make teachers more autonomous. Initially, the campaigning was successful and a clause calling for a Registration Council was included in the Liberals' Education Act of 1907. But the Board of Education was hostile to the proposal and effectively quashed it administratively. It never allowed for the various teacher associations concerned to meet. This had the effect of driving the teacher associations closer together. As a result of conflicts over the definition of teachers embodied in the circular of 1910–11, the Board of Education conceded on the setting up of a Registration Council in 1912, but it could still not control entry to the profession: it merely would keep a register of teachers. At that time most teacher associations were delighted and did not forecast its demise. It ran into early major problems in defining who should be included as a teacher.

By the First World War, the secondary teaching profession had also moved towards establishing itself on a more professional footing. However, this was moved forward mainly by teachers in grant-aided or girls' schools. The boys' public schools still held aloof. The methods of this latter group were to distinguish themselves on a class basis from the elementary teachers. The differentiation of the school curriculum into specialized subjects formed the origin of the moves for more professionalism and also autonomy. But the methods chosen were not to recognize the authority of the State over their work.

The curriculum of secondary schools was also changing in the years before the First World War. Indeed, the publicly assisted secondary schools were first subject to curriculum control through the Secondary Schools Code of 1904. The first task was to define the schools subject to the regulations, since the word 'secondary' was not used in the 1902 Act (McClure, 1967, p. 156): 'It will be held to include any day or boarding school which offers to each of its scholars, up to and beyond the age of 16, a general education, physical, mental and moral given through a complete graded course of instruction of wider scope and more advanced degree than that in the elementary schools.' In fact, the Code modelled such schools on the old public and grammar schools, and it suggested three curricular elements: 'the instruction must be general, i.e. must be such as gives a reasonable degree of exercise and development to the whole of the faculties'; 'specialization . . . should only begin after the general education'; 'the course of instruction must be complete; i.e. must be so planned as to lead up to a definite standard of acquirement'. The Code also set out the subjects (ibid.):

> A certain minimum number of hours in each week must be given, in each year of the Course, to a group of subjects commonly classed as 'English' and including the English Language and Literature, Geography and History; to Languages, ancient or modern, other than the native language of the scholars; and to Mathematics and to Science. Ample time is left for a well planned curriculum to add considerably to this minimum in one or more of these groups of subjects as well as to include adequate provision for systematic Physical Exercises; for Drawing, Singing and Manual Training; for the instruction of girls in the elements of housewifery.

The regulations also spelled out the number of hours to be devoted to each subject, but these requirements were abandoned three years later. They were, however, narrow in that they did not cover the work that had been carried on in the higher grade schools or that which the teachers were capable of. They were to cover the work of intending teachers, replacing the old pupil-teacher centres. Although the curriculum was basically 'academic', girls were required to pursue a special course for life at home, in addition to the boys' subjects.

Under the Liberal government, the secondary school regulations were modified to allow for free places for children from elementary schools, in particular as intending teachers. This had the effect of regularizing entry to the secondary schools, which had hitherto been haphazard and varied. 'In order to ensure that the children were up to the ordinary standard, entrance examinations were instituted; but except in London no age limit was fixed for some time, and as late as 1910–11 only 26% of the total number of entrants were under 12, while 15% were over 14' (Graves, 1943, p. 68). It did not affect the content of the courses, except that in 1906 the Board of Education concerned itself with 'overpressure' on girls, through extraneous home duties and the inclusion of housewifery. A suggestion, never implemented, was that science 'might be wholly replaced by an approved Scheme of Instruction in Practical Housewifery for girls over 15 years of age.'

The Consultative Committee of the Board of Education also considered the curriculum of the secondary schools. Its concern was with the question of examinations. Its initial report in 1904 was ignored. In 1911 it recommended the setting up of an Examinations Council representative of the LEAs, the Board of Education and university examining bodies to exercise supervision over all external examinations and to lay down conditions. Having considered the merits and disadvantages of examinations on both pupils and teachers, they viewed some external examinations as desirable. These recommendations were subsequently put into effect. The curriculum of the public schools did not receive any public scrutiny at this point. Nevertheless, the schoolmistresses in the girls' public schools did give it constant attention. The Girls' Public Day School Company, because of its need and desire for more State grants and aid, in 1906 converted itself into a Trust and came under the rubric of the State's Secondary School Regulations, but it did not acquiesce with all the Board's regulations. It opposed strongly the demand for housewifery, arguing that its schools taught needlework in the lower forms. As a result, the Board dropped its stringent rules for these aspects of housewifery and the GPDST schools were willing to teach cookery and needlework. The HMIs, inspecting these schools for grants, still found the curriculum lacking. So the GPDST introduced a one-year post-scholastic course in domestic economy for girls aged seventeen to twenty-one. The emphasis was on 'household management', 'seeing that the students will probably become mistresses of households' (Kamm, 1971, p. 145).

The question of 'home arts' in girls' curricula and schools was central during these early years. The schoolmistresses were concerned about the curriculum. In 1911, at a national conference on public schools for girls, Sara Burstall argued that the public examination system had become too academic and limited. She added of the girls' schools (Burstall and Douglas, 1911, p. 20): 'it became a reproach that they modelled their systems too much on that for boys.' On the other hand, she argued that the State's influence had led to a too-differentiated separate education for boys and girls. The State planned girls' curricula for 'the special duties of girls and women, their place in the world and their work in the social order'. A colleague, M. Gilliland, also argued against this (ibid., p. 158): 'in recent years there has been a widespread movement to bring the education of our girls into relation with their work as homemakers. The old "blue-stocking" type . . . no longer appeals . . . But we no longer share the conception of a woman's whole duty held by our grandmothers.' But she did argue for the retention of *home arts* in the curriculum. 'We must never forget that they are women first, scholars afterwards; dutiful daughters and wise, sympathetic mothers, not only college lecturers and high school mistresses . . . It behoves the school to remember that the future of the race depends on the mothers of the coming generation.' Her recommended syllabus consisted of not only cookery and needlework but 'lectures and practical work in the chemistry of food and the house, in laundry, practical and scientific, in upholstery, in dressmaking and in nursing, in childstudy and household accounts and how to carry out economies.' Douglas (ibid.), looking at the whole aims of such schools, argued that if some of the girls were to become head-mistresses, the quality most needed was *'an all-embracing motherliness'* [my emphasis] . She added that for the majority two ideals of service were required – in the home and beyond the home: 'we can make girls understand the fundamental truth that a man is only enriched in so far as his sphere of interest is enlarged.' She, too, argued for more domestic arts training and single-sex schools: 'the motherly relationship of the big to the little girls; the sisterly relations of those on a level; all these things belong to school life and they also belong to the home or to the State or both.' Indeed, the schoolmistresses were moving to the position of arguing for both separate schools and separate curricula because of the division of labour in adult life.

The impact of the First World War

The First World War had a devastating impact upon the organization of schooling and teaching. Its primary impact, inevitably, was on the labour force as a whole but it also affected the educational labour market. Women entered the labour market in unprecedented numbers; and women were needed for teaching. About 22,000 men teachers joined the armed forces and about 13,000 women therefore returned to teaching. The recently introduced marriage bar had to be abandoned to ensure an adequate supply of teachers. Women's place in the home could, in such a situation, be combined with employment.

The effect of the increase in women's labour force participation was to encourage their demands for more political and economic control. The suffrage movement gained in strength and contained many women teachers. The equal pay lobby within teaching also gathered momentum. Indeed, salaries had been an increasingly pressing and vexed question amongst all teachers in the years immediately before the war, along with the more general question of conditions of service. The first teachers' strike took place in 1913, when the NUT opposed Herefordshire's rejection of a proposed salary scale. About fifty schools were closed. Until the war, few LEAs had a scale and there were no national scales. Although unemployment and falling incomes were predicted at the outbreak of the war and salary campaigns were halted, a boom occurred within two years (Gosden, 1972, p. 36). The NUT then reopened its salary campaign, as did the secondary teacher associations, seeking 'war bonuses'. The Board of Education in 1917 introduced higher grants to LEAs, but this did not resolve the issue at all. The government also passed the Superannuation Act to provide pensions for both elementary and secondary teachers.

In 1918 and 1919 the teachers became more militant, with strikers in thirty areas (Gosden, 1972, p. 38). The three local authority associations concerned with education – CCA, AMC and AEC – met to try to resolve the problem and establish common salary scales throughout the country. This induced the Board to establish standing Joint Committees on salaries to relieve the tensions within the profession and ensure a steady supply of teachers and that they work to implement the new Act. Separate committees, both chaired by Burnham and subsequently always called after him, were set up for elementary and secondary education, consisting of LEA and union or association representatives.

By 1920 national scales had been agreed, but they did not incorporate equal pay. This issue was raised unsatisfactorily. The men argued that equal pay could not be agreed until 'the State shall make adequate provision for wifehood and motherhood'. Women argued that their case did not warrant separate consideration since they had the same work, training and qualifications as men. But the issue was fought, not on their *work but on their worth*. Women teachers were easy to recruit and pay because there were still few alternative occupations. Men had to be given incentives to teach; they also had, supposedly, greater family obligations than women. The issue was so stormily debated within the NUT that it led to men's secession and the formation of the National Association of Schoolmasters (NAS) which was opposed to equal pay; 5,000 men joined in 1919! Militant women also formed a new association, but retained links with the NUT. This was the National Union of Women Teachers (NUWT). Meanwhile, a government departmental committee, chaired by Atkin, had been set up to look at the question of *Women in Industry*. Its report, in 1919, urged the principle of equal pay for teachers and the civil service. But 'it may be necessary to counteract the differences of attractiveness by the payment to married men of children's allowances' (Partington, 1976, p. 21). The Burnham Committee did not accept this view and applied instead a 5 to 4 salary ratio for men to women. By 1920 the economic climate was moving towards depression and moves to improve women's situation were quietly dropped. However, the franchise had been won for women over thirty by the Suffrage Act of 1918.

The war had an impact upon school curricula. The 1918 Education Act was debated and passed during the war (see ch. 3). Its main provisions were to tie education more clearly to work. Day and evening classes had been provided for vocational courses since the 1890s. Special regulations had been issued in 1903 and 1904. The Act sought to rationalize the system and ensure a national network of such continuation classes. These part-time courses would now be established for all who left school at fourteen. In addition the elementary curriculum was to be extended: 'for the purpose of supplementing and reinforcing the instruction and social and physical training provided by the public system of education'. Physical training was to be extended by the LEAs' provision of holiday or school camps, centres and equipment for physical training, playing fields, school baths, swimming baths and other facilities (Graves, 1943, p. 112). It also, by section (2)(a) of the Act, was to cover 'cookery, laundry work, housewifery, dairywork, handicrafts, and gardening' and be incorporated into the regular curriculum.

The wartime government also took measures to modify the curriculum of secondary schools. As a result of the Consultative Committee's recommendations, the Board of Education in June 1917 issued a circular defining two school-leaving examinations – the School Certificate and the Higher Certificate. The two examinations would be for school forms not pupils and 'the examination should follow the curriculum and not determine it.' To qualify for the School Certificate, a candidate had to pass in at least five subjects, with credit in one, and these had to include a subject from each of three groups. Group I was English subjects; II, ancient and modern languages; III, maths and various sciences. A fourth group, including music, drawing, manual work and housecraft, was recognized but the certificate was not dependent on success here. The main groups were clearly linked to a 'grammar' curriculum and special subjects for boys or girls were seen as marginal for the certificate. The Higher Certificate was for those who had studied for a further two years. A co-ordinating authority was set up to monitor the work of the seven bodies recognized for examining purposes. The Prime Minister also set up two wartime committees to inquire into the position of science and modern languages in the education system and, in 1919, two on Classics and English. The Board did not deal with the proposals until 1922. The teaching of English was pinpointed and made to appear more important than hitherto.

Policy developments in the 1920s

By the end of the First World War, teachers had achieved some of their aims of being recognized as having a professional status and women over 30 had been enfranchised. Teachers were no longer examined and certificated: they attended training colleges. The curricula had been rationalized so that they linked more clearly with the kinds of work that children would be expected to take on in adult life. However, many of the achievements of this period were dissipated by the economic depression of the 1920s. First, teachers' salaries did not rise but trailed behind the cost of living. In 1922 the Geddes Committee recommended a voluntary abatement of 5 per cent of their salaries for the fiscal year 1923–4. It also suggested raising the school entry age and cutting superannuation but neither suggestion was implemented. The NUT accepted the recommendation, hoping to preserve salary scales. But in 1925 and 1926 further reductions were not accepted. The Burnham Committee then gave a more generous settlement, a reduction of less than 1 per cent (Gosden, 1972, p. 52) but with heavier reductions for women.

Second, the equal pay issue was not resolved although women continued to campaign for it, along with equal opportunities and the full enfranchisement of women. But teachers were in the position of defending, not extending, the gains of the war years. Teacher unemployment grew in the early 1920s. The LEAs, rather than improving the position of women teachers, responded to the economic crises by retreating into a traditional view of the position of women. Married women were ousted in many areas. A teacher-training scheme for ex-servicemen produced 1,000 mature male entrants, since the profession appeared safe. Women attacked the NUT for accepting an unfavourable settlement in 1925 but were on difficult grounds because of the extent of unemployment. Men only accepted a drop of 4 per cent and women one of 7 per cent, although the cost of living had risen by one-third in six years. The marriage bar was also attacked in the courts but it was not found illegal. Attempts to introduce legislation also failed to outlaw the bar.

Many of the curricular changes planned by the 1918 Act were not introduced. The compulsory continuation classes did not get off the ground and the practical elementary classes such as cookery had to take place in old and inappropriate buildings. The 'Geddes axe' also involved a cutback in spending on schools. It meant that fewer children attended secondary grammar schools than hitherto. Instead, LEAs began to develop central elementary schools, having started immediately before the war. The changes in secondary curricula were introduced, and financial aid was provided to ensure satisfactory implementation. The new examining boards were allowed from 1920 to offer State scholarships to successful pupils, boys *and* girls, from grant-aided secondary schools to enable them to attend university. The grants were means-tested but could cover tuition fees and a maintenance grant of £80 for three or four years. Again, the cuts affected these. In 1922 and 1923 none was provided but in 1924 there were additional scholarships and the age limit was raised to twenty for girls because they had to avoid 'over-strain' (Graves, 1943, p. 117).

The Consultative Committee to the Board of Education had also been asked to consider boys' and girls' curricula in secondary schools. It reported in 1923. Its views on girls' futures mirrored those of the LEAs, that boys and girls had different social functions in adult life which must be mirrored in learning. Although many LEAs had been developing mixed rather than single-sex secondary schools, the question of co-education was relegated to an appendix. The main report focused on whether sex differences should have any implications for educational policy. The Committee argued (Board of Education, 1923, p. 47) that there should be less than recommended in the 1921 Secondary Regulations: 'it seems to be implicitly assumed that girls' schools in addition to giving their pupils a general education should also give them some training designed to fit them for the duties of home life and motherhood.' The Committee's argument rested on demographic evidence that married women barely outnumbered the unmarried and widowed, that girls (whether of the manual or middle class) did not give up wage-earning on marriage; that the average marriage age had gone up to twenty-five and the professions were opening up for women. It therefore set three aims for secondary school curricula: 'that they make children into useful citizens, able to earn their own living and that girls learn to be makers of homes – but the curricula should also teach boys to help share home-making' (ibid., p. 24). The Committee further argued that the determining voice in girls' curricula should rest with women themselves (ibid., p. 130). This might entail girls taking the School Certificate a year later than boys and that less pressure be put on the organization of the curriculum. They also recommended special curricula for non-academic pupils over fifteen and that domestic economy should not be left out of curricula 'because girls would not like it . . . it had a strong, natural appeal.' In the appendix to the report, the Committee argued against co-education from both the teachers' and pupils' points of view, using mainly evidence from headmistresses. Women teachers inevitably would be denied promotion (the evidence already existed) but men might gain. Girls would also be disadvantaged in mixed classes for they would be inhibited and overpressed and they needed the support of women teachers. Girls worked at a slower pace than boys. Headmasters were more in favour of co-education than the headmistresses who provided this evidence.

By 1924 the economic crisis seemed to have abated. A Labour government came to office and immediately commissioned the Consultative Committee to report on the organization of elementary education and the testing of the attainments of its pupils. The government also tried to reduce the size of classes further through its circular 1325 but was unable to effect its policy because of the lack of availability of buildings. The government was short-lived and fell, because of the General Strike, before it could implement any radical change of policy.

The recommendations of the second Hadow Consultative Committee, published in 1926, subsequently transformed the shape of the education system. Not only did it recommend the division into primary and secondary education and the raising of the school-leaving age: it also planned the curricula of the new type of school. It proposed that both primary and the new modern schools be co-educational. The modern schools were to have a three- to four-year course (Board of Education, 1926, p. 101), 'simpler and more limited in scope than those in grammar schools . . . more time and attention will be devoted to handwork . . . the courses of instruction, though not merely vocational or utilitarian, should be used to connect the school work with the interests arising from the social and industrial environment of the pupils . . . a new leaving examination should be framed' for these schools. The Committee also suggested less differentiation in curricula for boys and girls – it was important for girls, like boys, 'to develop while at school tastes for occupations that they can practise in their leisure time in later life' (ibid., p. 110). It did propose more housecraft 'to prevent the housewife sinking to a domestic drudge. It should include cookery, laundry, housewifery and some instruction in the use of tools and household repairs: first aid, home nursing and the care of children connected with elementary sciences and hygiene' (ibid., p. 234).

These proposals were not put into effect immediately, although a number of LEAs, individually, began to modify their central schools into new secondary modern schools. There was also from about 1924 a change in policy towards more technical education (Graves, 1943, p. 140). In 1922–3 there were 86 junior technical schools attended by 10,413 boys and 1,793 girls. By 1938 there were 223 such schools with 20,229 boys and 7,672 girls. For boys there were engineering and construction courses; for some boys and for girls mainly commercial courses. But until the 1938 Consultative Committee Report the technical schools fitted uneasily into the secondary system.

However, England experienced yet another economic crisis from 1929 which delayed the implementation of these changes in education. Furthermore, teachers were not adequately equipped for these new kinds of schools. In 1925 a departmental committee had reported on the training of teachers for public elementary schools. Unfortunately, it had to stick to the administrative distinction between elementary and secondary schools. It managed to point to the undesirability of this division and sought to develop a new system which would cater for the needs of both elementary and secondary schools. It recommended joint examination boards, from the training colleges and universities for the qualifying examination at the end of the training course, But training college courses were to remain of two years' duration only, whereas a degree and professional teacher training would continue to take four years. This system of training, which was put into effect in 1929, sought to fully professionalize teaching, divorce it from the elementary system and finally abolish the pupil-teacher method.

In 1918 there had been over 2,000 pupil-teachers, of whom 1,985 were women; in 1927 this had shrunk to 1,000, with 821 women. By 1938 there were less than 100 pupil-teachers, 77 women and 18 men. At the same time, though, the numbers of teachers with certification increased rapidly. Indeed, the government used the new system to regulate the supply of qualified teachers. Initially, because of the Labour government's moves to raise the school-leaving age and develop a network of nursery classes and schools, in 1929 more teachers were needed. But by 1931 the slump was such that these policies had to be postponed, and so fewer extra teachers were needed. On the other hand, the ratio of certificated to uncertificated teachers changed drastically in this period. In 1925 the ratio for men teachers was 4 to 1 and for women 5.5 to 3. In total, there were 2,500 men and 8,500 women. By 1938 the ratios were 20 to 1 and 6 to 1 respectively. There were fewer than 1,000 uncertificated and over 6,000 certificated teachers. The percentage of supplementaries in the teaching profession also declined from 7.3 per cent in 1921 to 3.2 per cent in 1938, and there were far fewer of these teachers: almost 6,000 less.

The same effects occurred within secondary teaching, although the associations were less militant than the NUT. In 1927 the male trained-to-untrained ratio was 5.3 to 3.4 and by 1938 3 to 2; for women teachers it was 3 to 2.5 in 1927 and by 1938, 5.4 to 2.4. It can be seen from these ratios that men still disdained training more than the women in secondary schools. The public school headmasters saw training as an apprenticeship or a method of learning to be a journeyman and were very scornful of this approach to the profession. Nevertheless, despite this opposition, in thirty years secondary teaching was transformed. In 1905, there were only 62.7 per cent graduate male teachers; in 1934, 85.5 per cent of male teachers were graduates. For women the actual increase was greater but the total proportion by 1934 was less: from 41.7 to 68.1 per cent.

The slump and educational initiatives

Throughout the 1930s, because of economic conditions, there were only abortive attempts to improve teaching and schooling. The teachers' salary position did not change and equal pay was not achieved, although all women achieved the same voting rights as men in 1928. Indeed, because of the recurring economic crises the position of women teachers worsened. Arguments for occupational family allowances, which the NUWT had opposed as a way of achieving equal pay, gained support. Women's disadvantageous position was affected by the implementation of the Hadow Report of 1926, even though it was not a central government policy. Many primary schools were amalgamated and became junior mixed and infant schools. In 1925 the Board of Education, in circular 1350, had recommended the virtues of mixed junior and infant departments. The NUWT opposed this policy on the grounds that women teachers would suffer. As a result of NUWT campaigning, the Board in 1928 stopped pressing for this, but continued to advocate senior mixed and junior mixed schools in place of separate boys' and girls' elementary schools (Gosden, 1972, p. 117). As a consequence, *and* as the NUWT had predicted, the proportion of women headteachers declined. In 1927 women headteachers constituted 87 per cent of the heads of junior mixed schools and by 1936 only 61 per cent, despite the fact that women in elementary teaching outnumbered men 3 to 1. The NAS exacerbated the friction over the policy, by campaigning both to refuse to work under women and against equal pay. This campaign was effective in a time of mass unemployment. Women found it especially difficult to counter these views and to argue for equal pay for themselves. The NAS argued that there were two separate markets for men and women in terms of supply and, therefore, pay. Yet in 1925, before the Hadow Committee reported, the Board of Education had stated it was 'strongly in favour of separate departments for senior boys and girls, where such an organisation is practicable.'

Two other Consultative Committee reports under the chairmanship of Hadow – in 1931 on junior and in 1933 on nursery and infant schools – had an impact upon elementary education. They both argued for smaller classes, rejecting the idea that age was relevant to class size, and they also proposed young classroom helpers – girls of fifteen to eighteen – in infant and nursery schools. The NUT regarded this suggestion as a blow to professionalism, but the Board of Education implemented it. The Hadow Committee on nursery schools also argued against universal nursery education: it stated that most children under five should be looked after at home, unless care was needed on health grounds (see ch. 3). The Hadow Committee on junior schools advocated a child-centred view of primary education, influenced by the American progressive movement and psychological theories. But neither of the two Hadow Reports could be implemented immediately, given the economic climate.

Although there were no major educational policy changes during the 1930s, the schools themselves did alter a great deal. Many LEAs began to establish modern schools; more and more children attended secondary grammar schools. In 1917 over 185,000 girls were being educated in recognized secondary schools. By 1936, the number had increased to 500,000. Nevertheless, boys continued to outnumber girls in such schools. The curricula of these schools became more differentiated into subject areas, although designed more flexibly by the teachers. Because of mass unemployment, the ideology of a woman's place in the home was applied with increasing force. Married women were barred from teaching and their spinster sisters were required to teach their girls detailed courses in housecraft and the other home arts, covering a whole range of topics that included elementary science and hygiene. Such courses were taught in varying degree in all types of secondary school and in senior elementary schools.

By the time the Consultative Committee's fourth report on secondary education was published (Board of Education, 1938), the political and economic situation had changed considerably. Some of the Hadow Committees' recommendations were in the process of implementation and the 1936 Education Act, specifying the raising of the school-leaving age, was to take effect from 1939. The new recommendations drew on those of the Hadow Committees but were based more exclusively on the notions of psychological ability and interest. The Spens Committee had investigated the possibility of multilateral schools but, on size and cost grounds, rejected them in favour of a system of selective schooling. It suggested three types of secondary school. The choice was based on the needs of boys and not girls, since the schools would in the later stages cater for pupils' vocational interests. In terms of curricula, the Spens Report concentrated most on the junior technical schools, which were now officially admired. These schools should be capable of educating boys for the engineering and building industries, and should also 'develop training of such a character as (a) to provide a good intellectual discipline, altogether apart from its technical value and (b) to have a technical value in relation not to one particular occupation but to a group of occupations' (ibid., p. 21). Although the Spens Report did not mention girls in particular, at the time of its publication the view was prevalent that girls' primary adult responsibility was not in paid employment but as a housewife and mother. The Committee did not suggest an alternative policy, but implicitly accepted the prevailing ideology: it did not suggest how technical schools should train girls.

By 1938 the international situation was beginning to threaten war, and most new educational policy was abandoned. The implementation of the 1936 Act was postponed, and the Spens Report was not discussed. The government's policy became oriented to coping with a warlike situation. Yet by 1939 schooling and teaching were virtually unrecognizable from that existing at the turn of the century. Most children now received both a primary and a secondary education, although they were not legally entitled to the latter free. By March 1938, 544,862 children were in secondary grammar schools, but many children were still educated in elementary schools only, which was the legal minimum requirement. Many of the secondary schools though were still privately financed and outside State control although State aided. Apart from one Board of Education report in 1932, they had not been investigated for seventy years. This departmental report had suggested a form of registration and inspection either by central or local government, but this had not yet been implemented. Teachers, on the other hand, had developed more professional autonomy. They were no longer subject to 'on-the-job' training but entitled to professional training in special colleges or universities and their departments of education. The effect of the educational and economic problems in the 1930s had been to reduce the proportion of women, and especially married women, in teaching.

When the Second World War broke out, the teaching profession in both elementary and secondary schools was more masculine than it it had ever been, although women remained the majority. Boys were increasingly being educated for a range of occupations, rather than merely for their position in the social order, and girls, perhaps more importantly, to be wives and mothers, although they could now contemplate an occupation for at least a short period of their adult lives, when they were single. During the first forty years of this century there had been an expansion of occupations, both professional services for social and domestic needs and in commerce and government, and yet, at the same time, the curriculum for girls had been reflecting a sexual division of labour in the home and the economy. Curiously, the teachers who would provide this knowledge of the adult world were not any longer especially qualified by their personal attributes to do so. A trained teaching profession had, by 1939, become the predominant form and with it came a reduction in the proportion of women as teachers, at all levels within the education system.

7

Professionalizing schools: maternalism in teaching and in the classroom

The foundations of the contemporary education system were laid down during the Second World War, when circumstances forced both a major review of schooling and relevant curricula and the recomposition of the teaching profession. This chapter surveys these events and their consequences over the following twenty-five years to 1970. The review of schooling culminated in the Education Act of 1944, but it did not end there: important government reports, the recommendations of which were not incorporated into the legislation, were produced around that time and had far-reaching curricular consequences. In particular, curricula of schools became more closely tied to specific aspects of the economy, especially to scientific and technocratic needs. Curiously, however, girls' curricula still placed a priority on their future roles as wives and mothers, although recognizing that women would participate in the labour force for at least a part of their adult lives. Not only were school curricula differentiated in this way, but also educational institutions became diversified in the 1950s and 1960s to take account of specialized economic needs.

During the war, too, because of problems of teacher supply, women teachers were encouraged back into the labour force but resistance was made to such teachers' attempts to make their new situation permanent and more palatably equal. Although equal pay was successfully circumvented, justifications for the employment of married women had to be found. Immediately after the war, in an effort to vitiate the wartime circumstances, these arguments were overturned, but a decade later, because of demographic trends which were in all probability a consequence of the war, the issue of teacher supply resurfaced as a critical problem and married women were once more encouraged to return to teaching. But the content of their teaching had barely changed: it was still mainly concerned with infants, young children and girls' courses, the latter of which were primarily oriented to women's future role in the sexual division of labour in the family.

The thirty-year period (1940–70) was characterized by attempts to restructure the education system and its teaching profession on a more professional, bureaucratic and technocratic basis. These attempts were justified not only by politicians but by the academic community which amassed evidence of the links between education and the economy. By the end of this period, the teaching profession had become one based upon high academic qualifications. Yet women teachers were still expected to use their maternal qualities in the classroom. By 1970 they had to be taught how to be maternal and how to convey maternalism through their classroom teaching.

The Second World War's impact on teachers and teaching

The war made for quite drastic changes in the composition of the teaching force. Women, in particular, were drafted into newly created nursery schools and centres. Many young women teachers worked in both primary and secondary education. However, although the demand for women teachers increased, the legal situation for married women initially continued as it had in peace-time. For example, in October 1939 the parliamentary secretary to the Board of Education refused to put an end to the marriage bar, even for women teachers with husbands away, on the grounds that it was in the LEAs' discretion to lift the restriction. The fall in the number of men teachers, as they were called up, was thus not at first fully compensated for by women teachers. Instead, in some areas the pupil-teacher ratios rose. However, the school population began to decline during the war and so fewer teacher replacements could be justified. In 1938 there were 6 million children in State-aided and maintained schools: this had dropped to just over 5 million in 1945. Women became as involved as men in schemes of evacuation and gradually, as the war continued, women were recruited to teaching.

The situation of women teachers, especially those married, was modified during the course of the war. In 1942, by the Board of Education's circular 1591, the marriage bar was lifted temporarily, since 'it cannot be justified in present circumstances and should be suspended at least for the war period.' Second, women were eventually encouraged not to leave teaching and join the services because they were needed in schools. Supply became a pressing concern in the early 1940s. Recruitment of part-time teachers, especially married women, was encouraged. Third, the evacuation pay of teachers was queried by the unions, and this had an impact on the pay of all teachers. The NUT campaigned for parity with evacuated civil servants. Eventually, as a result of NUT negotiations, men and single women teachers were given slightly less than the allowance to civil servants. Not all were householders, especially not the women. Married women, inevitably, were not covered, since 'the husband has the obligation to provide accommodation for his wife.' The assumption that men should be treated differently from married women also continued to be made for teachers' pay through the Burnham Committee. Because of pressure, in particular from the NAS, men continued to be regarded as householders and women were assumed to be single *or* dependent upon men.

This issue, of the type of men and women suitable for teaching, was a key factor in discussions on policy change. However, it was not directly addressed but arose from the struggles, especially from the NUWT, for changes in the legislative framework which were under consideration throughout the war. It was intimately related to the worrying question of the likely shortage of teachers after the war.

Before the public political debate on the education system reached its zenith, the NUWT started in 1942 campaigning again for equal pay. It asked LEAs to adopt the principle of equal pay for equal work. However, this was in a context where the Burnham Committee had just used the 5 to 4 (male-to-female) principle fixed in the 1920s for awarding the war bonus to low-paid teachers. The NUWT campaign did not meet with much success, but the NUT joined the campaign in 1943, being concerned not only with war bonuses but with pay after the war. Finally, this campaign was successfully dissipated by the government during the debate on the 1944 Education Act.

The campaign for equal pay was more extensive than it had been in previous decades because of the wartime composition of the teaching force. This was, in itself, a cause for concern. The government was not certain whether it should, or would, retain its women teachers, especially married ones, after the war. It was also concerned with the quality of the teaching force in terms of prior training. Training had always been a major educational question but in the war, when the uncertainty over future supply was more stark, the question became pressing. To this end, in 1943 the government established a departmental committee to inquire into the recruitment, training and supply of teachers. The committee, chaired by McNair, was also asked to inquire into the position of youth leaders, since the specific worry about the future of education was over the ways in which adolescents would be trained to be useful adults. The relationship between teaching and the youth service was seen to be close. The inquiries took place against a background of debate over the general organization and content of the education system.

Changes in the education system had been mooted in the 1930s (see ch. 3). The 1936 Education Act to raise the school-leaving age, scheduled for implementation on the day war broke out, was obviously not pursued. Consideration had also been given to the structure and organization of secondary education. The Spens Committee, reporting in 1938, had presented a critique of both the types of secondary school in existence and their curricula. The main theme had been the physical and mental development of pupils between the ages of eleven and sixteen. The Committee was, therefore, concerned with children's treatment in school, as well as their futures. Although it did not recommend a common secondary school, it did suggest common elements both to curricula and over the treatment of boys and girls. One of the reasons why the idea of a common school was not pursued was that the pattern of an academic course directed to university education (the grammar school model) would, in all probability, be followed in the new schools. This would not suit the needs of *all* boys and girls. It was argued (Board of Education, 1938, p. 107) that the aim should be to 'foster . . . the free growth of *individuality*'. Having said that, the Committee recommended a common core curriculum for eleven- and twelve-year-olds, consisting of English, scripture, history, geography, maths, science, music, art, physical education, one foreign language and handicrafts for boys *or* domestic science for girls. For older pupils, a smaller core of English, science and one foreign language was suggested. The distinction between types of secondary school was then to come into force: more academic curricula in grammar schools and more practical and vocational work in technical and trade schools. Boys, at these latter schools, should have more training in building and engineering; girls, in home management or commercial subjects. Indeed, the Spens Committee's argument about girls' training for future positions was based upon assumptions about existing practice. In their anxiety for girls' healthy physical development and lack of overstrain, they stated (ibid., p. 181) that 'we are strongly of the opinion that the parents of girls in secondary schools should not expect of them any undue amount of domestic work in the home.' They were, though also worried about the strains schools imposed and counselled against curricula being too closely linked to the School Certificate Examination (SCE).

The Spens Report, because of the war, was not implemented but its ideas formed the context in which further reports were written and eventually translated into the 1944 Act. For example, the concern with school-leaving examinations and their relationship to university education was quickly followed up. In 1939 the Secondary Schools Examination Council reported on the Higher School Certificate Examination in 1937, being the first investigation since 1926. The major problem identified was the subjects examined and their relationship to scholarships to attend university. The Committee recommended (Secondary Schools Examination Council, 1939, p. 49) that not all school subjects be examined:

> In many schools it is the practice to introduce into the timetables of sixth forms what are sometimes known as 'relief subjects' e.g. a classical sixth in a boys' school will devote two periods a week to science or to maths or in a girls' school to art or music or domestic science . . . the Investigators are of the opinion that they should not be examined.

Although it did not want all subjects to be examined and felt that examinable papers should only be academic subjects, it, too, did not view girls and boys as identical. This did not just refer to the subjects studied but also affected the distribution of university State Scholarships. These were introduced in 1920, for students from grant-aided schools wishing to attend university. In 1926 the age limit was raised from nineteen to twenty, initially for one year to cope with the economic recession. It was then kept at twenty for girls on the grounds that: 'Girls develop rather later than boys and a higher age limit would tend to relieve overstrain.' In 1930 the number of grants was increased but the ratio between boys and girls was made dependent upon numbers of candidates. This ratio was not altered, nor did the Committee suggest that it should be. There was an assumption of fairness, since an analysis of the careers of State Scholars showed only 1.5 per cent of the men were unemployed, whereas 5 per cent of the women were 'unemployed *or at home*' [my emphasis]. Moreover, 30 per cent of the men went into professions, 17 per cent to industry or commerce, 16 per cent to research and 34 per cent to teaching, but 70 per cent of employed women were teachers. Women's occupations, including of course teaching and being 'at home', were assumed to be less valuable than men's and therefore not to be as highly rewarded or encouraged.

This report, like the Spens Report, inevitably had very little immediate effect but was part of the context in which the debate about school changes took place. Prior to the drafting of any specific legislation, the Secondary Schools Examinations Council was re-appointed in 1941, chaired by Norwood, and reported again in 1943. A commission was also set up to investigate the public schools for the first time since the nineteenth century. Its report was published after the drafting in 1943 of the government's White Paper on education. The Norwood Report on *Curriculum and Examinations in Secondary Schools* (Secondary Schools Examination Council, 1943) was concerned with three issues – the organization of secondary schools, examinations and curriculum. It did not discuss the first issue fully but asserted that schools should be organized on tripartite lines (see ch. 4). The Report was also brief on the question of examinations, recommending two new examinations at sixteen and eighteen in place of the School Certificate Examinations. Little was said about their content, except that there should be more choice of subject. The Report claimed (ibid., ch. 1) to favour 'the child-centred conception of education'. The main curricular recommendations were for grammar schools (ibid., part III) and mirrored those of Spens. The *core* curriculum should include physical education, religious education, English, history, geography, maths, natural science, modern languages, Classics, art, music and humanities, domestic subjects, education for commerce and Welsh. Again the Committee suggested a *core* curriculum in all schools for all children only up to thirteen and differentiation, therefore, between types of secondary school. But it argued much more forcefully that 'education must prepare for life . . . [and] for citizenship . . . and, more importantly, for work.' This did not lead it to make new suggestions about subjects or specialisms but just about curricular balance. The three elements should be 'training of the body, character and habits of clear thought and expression in the English language'.

Although the Norwood Committee argued for child-centred education, it assumed a difference between boys and girls. Boys were to be prepared for an adult life at work, girls for one at home. The Report included a lengthy chapter (ibid., pp. 127 ff.) on *domestic subjects*. These only included needlework, cookery, laundry and housewifery; they did not cover hygiene and nursing. But the Norwood Committee had already suggested, as a specialism, pre-nursing studies for girls of sixth-form age and status. Three reasons were given for this choice of domestic subjects: first, 'a knowledge of such subjects is a necessary equipment for *all* girls as potential makers of homes'; second, it had 'the advantage of a practical approach to theoretical work'; and, third, 'for girls likely to go on to Domestic Science colleges it is necessary for a variety of posts'. So, it was assumed that girls' interests were as homemakers. Indeed, the Report added (ibid., p. 128), 'for many girls it is felt that domestic subjects provide a centre of interest natural and congenial to them . . . Further, the practical nature of domestic subjects evokes a ready response in girls whose abilities do not lie in the field of academic studies.' Nevertheless, the Report was not rigid. It proposed a minimum of needlework, cookery and laundry, and discretion about sixth-form subjects such as pre-nursing, that is, hygiene and parentcraft. In addition, because of the war, it was suggested that co-educational schools allow boys to do cookery and girls carpentry. This was not to be a long-term recommendation and it did not lead the Committee to make more specific recommendations about single-sex or co-educational schools. Indeed, it only argued for such temporary curricular changes in schools where it would be immediately feasible, because of facilities. Single-sex schools were not to be modified, and it was also assumed that they would be the model for the development of grammar schools, the main focus of the Committee's concern. These latter schools would continue to prepare pupils mainly for the learned professions. Yet, since such schools were oriented to 'learning for its own sake', provision should be made for girls, although their adult occupations were not important. Here their natural interests as homemakers took precedence.

The Norwood Report became the ideological basis for the government's White Paper *Educational Reconstruction*, in which secondary schools for all children over the age of eleven were proposed. They were to be organized on tripartite lines, that is, as grammar, technical and modern schools, but this system was not to be inflexible. Children were to be chosen for their schools on the basis of 'individual aptitudes . . . and the careers they have in mind' but the choice would 'be subject to review as the child's special gifts and capacities develop'. Individual, child-centred learning became the axiom, but tempered by the needs of a developing economy: 'If education is to serve the interests of the child and of the nation, some means must be found of . . . directing ability into the field where it will find its best realization.' The White Paper was more concerned with structure and organization – spelling out the three stages of education (primary, secondary and further), their internal organization and the school-leaving age – than with curricula. This primacy of concern was reflected in the Act itself. The other concern of the White Paper was the supply of teachers necessary to carry out the new system of education. On the whole, the drafters of legislation were willing to await the McNair Committee's findings but could not resist stating their own interim recommendations that the teaching profession should 'represent . . . a cross-section of the interests and experiences of society at large', but that it should be more highly professionalized. Old forms of teacher training were deemed inadequate, because they did not fit teachers for the task of education in a highly industrialized economy.

The White Paper, although mainly concerned with educational organization after the war, was quiet on the future of the public schools and the general place of boarding education versus day schools. This was mainly because the second committee of inquiry had not yet reported. The framers of legislation did assert that the benefits of boarding education should be made more widely available.

Before the White Paper was translated into law, both the Fleming and McNair Committees reported. They did not have equal influence on the course *or* content of legislation. The Fleming Report (Board of Education, 1943b) was a very controversial document and even the Labour Members of Parliament were loath to pursue its recommendations, which were to integrate the public schools, through two alternative schemes, into the State system of education. It was argued that day schools had three features which were not mirrored in boarding schools, the lack of which led to the latter's ability to teach a more classical and religious education. It was also argued that boarding schools developed a perspective wider than that found in day schools, which was based on home background. However, proposals foundered not on this but on the financial recommendations, which appeared to most political commentators to abolish parental freedom to pay for their children's education (see ch. 4).

The McNair Committee's report was less controversial. It was also equivocal about procedure but more certain about principle. It demonstrated, through an analysis of the recruitment statistics, the need to improve the future supply of teachers. It estimated that after the war there would be a shortfall of 15,000 teachers. This need to affect supply was the more urgent in view of the proposed changes to the three stages of education and the increase in provision of State secondary education. The McNair Committee also asserted that the provision of nursery education, in addition, was vital. The Committee, therefore, suggested three ways of improving future teacher supply – widening the field of recruitment, abolishing deterrent conditions of service and improving the standing of education. The main suggestion was about who should compose the teaching force. Past practice showed that women had always been crucial. In 1938, for instance, of 200,000 full-time teachers, women constituted 70 per cent, but the majority were in nursery, elementary or special schools for the physically and mentally handicapped. In addition, there was a high annual wastage of at least 8,000 per year, partly because of the marriage bar. The Committee urged the lifting of this ban and actually proposed a *marriage allowance* to encourage married *men and women* to teach. It would help teachers to keep their children at grant-aided schools: they would not withdraw for economic reasons. It would help men (especially if there were a wife and child allowance in addition) and 'women of maturer age who want to teach'. In support of this proposal, the Committee argued that (Board of Education, 1944,

p. 24):

> It is surely the height of irony to adopt a policy, which, in effect, rules that women with children of their own shall as a class be debarred from making any contribution in the school beyond that of sending their children to them.

The Report went on that the notion of resignation on marriage represented a narrow view of public life (ibid.).

> Children of all ages, and not only young children, benefit from the care and training of teachers with experience of home responsibilities, including the experience of marriage, and, perhaps, the care of children of their own. The influence of a *wise married* woman on adolescent boys and girls and on her colleagues, both men and women, is an advantage which the school ought not to have to forgo. The presence of married men on a staff is equally desirable and is almost universally secured . . . generally to debar married women from work in the school is patently contrary to common sense. No other criticism of school by mothers can compare in significance with their criticism (though it may not be formulated in these precise terms) that the staff of the school to which they entrust their children, fail, by design, to include a reasonable proportion of women with experience and responsibility like their own [my emphasis].

The Committee not only argued for the lifting of the marriage ban, but proposed some measures to encourage married women explicitly. It also argued that 'suitable arrangements should be made to meet the needs of married women, particularly for motherhood, and be national.' Married women returning to teaching should be given a 'period of preparation' and offered the possibility of part-time teaching.

Other ways to improve supply were through conditions such as salaries. The Report proposed a new method and criteria of establishing salary scales with one scale for qualified teachers. It also commented on the differences between men's and women's pay and argued that if family allowances were implemented as proposed, the argument for a differential was weakened.

Its main proposals were to increase teacher training from two to three years and link it more clearly with universities. Here two schemes were put forward. There was, however, agreement that single-sex colleges be reduced in number and more emphasis given to co-education. Because of this, much attention was paid to the teaching of specialist subjects and technical education. This latter was said to consist of industry, commerce and 'instruction in the personal and domestic arts necessary for achieving a satisfactory private, social or family life'. Here again women teachers would be needed.

In addition, the McNair Report contained an appendix on domestic subjects. This was in part to lend support to their argument about the marriage bar (ibid., p. 165): 'If it is generally unfortunate that there is a bar, it is doubly so for homemaking and management.'

The Committee wanted the integration of training colleges for domestic subjects with ordinary teacher training. The teaching of such subjects to girls only should link with the financial and social as well as other aspects of running a home. The schoolteacher of such subjects should make contact with the mothers of the girls she teaches. 'Every mother is a competitor with school authority.' This rather unguarded statement referred mainly to the question of girls.

The McNair Report was critically concerned with the position of women within the economy and thus in schooling. All the recommendations were related to the issue. Nevertheless, the Report was based upon a curious contradiction – that women should work as teachers, in order to teach girls how to be homemakers. This was assumed to be girls' major interest. Although adult employment was an important function of education, for girls, housework was still regarded as their major job in adult life, and it should be more professionally taught. Although married women could, arguably, work at least part-time as teachers, little consideration was given to their specific occupations. Indeed, in the training of teachers, emphasis was to be put on 'the need for teachers to appreciate the *home* circumstances of their pupils and the impact of social services on the lives of children and their parents.'

The framers of the Education Act did take some account of the McNair Report, whilst ignoring the Fleming Report. For instance, concern over teacher supply was so acute that the ban on the marriage bar was written into the Act. Improved teacher training was also included, and a method of arriving at teacher salaries and scales was adopted. But *equal pay* for men and women became the main controversial issue during the Bill's passage through the House of Commons. Given the political impetus of the McNair Report, the NUWT pressed its campaign for equal pay into the debate on the Bill. Several Conservative women MPs were recruited to push the issue and succeeded – narrowly – in getting an amendment written into the Bill. The issue was hotly debated, with the NAS whipping up counter-support. The Conservative coalition in the government was fervently opposed to equal pay and the Prime Minister (Churchill) saw the amendment as a vote of no confidence in his government and war policies. He, therefore, pressed for a vote of confidence and planned a major political speech to argue that the question was misplaced and not relevant to education alone. He was to have argued (Partington, 1976, p. 58) that it was like 'putting an elephant in a perambulator'. But the speech was not delivered, although the vote of confidence was taken and won overwhelmingly. Only twenty-three MPs supported the retention of the equal pay amendment.

The government could not allow this matter to be left. A month later, it announced the setting up of a Royal Commission to inquire into the broad issue of equal pay. The NUWT and NUT saw this not as a victory but a delaying tactic. Indeed it was. It took a long time for members to be appointed, the Commission took over two years to gather evidence, and it reported only in October 1946.

By the end of the war, the educational scene had changed dramatically. Both the composition of the teaching force and the organization of schooling had been transformed. Women teachers were in the overwhelming majority and in 1945 there were 33,159 married women in post. This was not to continue. The Education Act, passed in 1944, was about to alter the entire shape of the education system, extending opportunities both up and down the age scale (nursery education and raising the school-leaving age) and allowing for more State provision of education. Moreover, welfare became more clearly a function of the education system – school meals, milk, the health service and financial maintenance for certain services were introduced. The teachers' role in school was clearly extended – they became responsible for more than curricula or subject-teaching. Teachers were to be involved in welfare activities and improving home-school relations, as, for instance, advocated in the McNair Report. What they were to teach, however, was not laid down in the Act; the only curriculum restraint being the compulsory teaching of religious knowledge. Neither the Spens nor the Norwood curriculum prescriptions were written into the Act but it was thought necessary to review the curriculum after the war. Nor was any change made to the examinations system.

Early post-war developments – returning women to the home

The war had created an unusual economy and labour force. After the war, the composition of the teaching force changed drastically and suddenly. In 1943 the Wood Committee had been set up to recommend on emergency teacher training after the war. Its proposals for education were followed. One-year crash courses, or emergency training, were set up for teachers, along with other further education. In the five years to 1950, 85,000 grants were provided for such courses, and 35,000 male teachers were thus trained. Slowly, the balance between men and women began to alter. But, because of the extension of the education system, especially through the raising of the leaving age in 1947, the reorganization into primary and secondary education, and the attempt at parity between secondary schools, more teachers were needed. There continued to be a shortage in supply. However, the government did not pursue the McNair Committee's suggestion of positive efforts to enable married women to teach.

The Royal Commission on Equal Pay, 1944-1946 (1946) did not, in any event, lend support to giving teachers equal pay. The majority report did not favour equal pay in industry on empirical grounds – it argued that women did less-skilled work than men and tended to have a higher turnover. Social and economic consequences were used as the main criterion for rejecting equal pay. Three women wrote a memorandum of dissent, in which they argued that it was cultural factors which gave rise to unequal work and pay, and not the strengths and reliability of women. They did, however, think that men and women teachers, on the whole, did the same work (ibid., pp. 187–96) but 'the work of women teachers is mainly centred on the education of the younger classes of either sex and on that of the older girls, while that of the men is mainly centred on the education of the less young of either sex and on that of the older boys.' Nevertheless, their argument of equal pay for equal work was not followed. Instead, the Commissioners followed the evidence of the Treasury and Ministry of Education that equal pay, rather than encouraging the recruitment of women, as put forward by the NUT, would be detrimental to the recruitment of *men*. It would make teaching less attractive to men and, in times of economic stringency, might even depress money levels of salaries as compared with employment outside teaching. They also argued against its introduction on cost grounds: '£14,500,000 for England and Wales and about £2,000,000 for Scotland.' In addition, equal pay would bring about demands for a family allowance scheme and thus further increase the cost to the government. Yet existing family allowance schemes, either for all the population or members of particular occupational groups, were arguably inadequate recompense compared with actual salaries.

In sum, the Commission argued against the introduction of equal pay on the grounds of lack of feasibility rather than fairness. By the time the Report appeared, there was a Labour government in office: it had not pressed forward on equal pay, awaiting the Report. It then took a long time to consider the recommendations. The Labour Party Conference in 1947 voted in favour of the introduction of equal pay in the public services. The government was forced to respond and neatly side-stepped the issue by accepting the principle but arguing that it could not implement it at that time. The cost was now estimated at nearly three times as much and furthermore would also affect the size of family allowances which had just been introduced. The situation remained one of stalemate. The TUC's support for equal pay in 1950 did not move the government. In 1951, as a result (according to some commentators) of Labour's lack of support for equal pay, the Labour Party lost office at the general election and the Conservatives returned to power.

Although Labour did not introduce equal pay, it continued to concern itself with teacher supply. In 1949, for instance, a working party was set up within the Ministry of Education, chaired by an HMI, Roseveare, to reconsider the question of the supply of women teachers. Its Report reaffirmed the McNair Report's commitment to married women and suggested methods to encourage their recruitment, such as adequate maintenance grants to help them at training college. It argued on ideological grounds in favour of married women (Ministry of Education, 1950, p. 5):

> Quite apart from the numerical increase in the profession which married women can provide, we believe that they can bring a particularly *valuable* contribution to the schools, especially those who have brought up, or are bringing up, children of their own. Every encouragement should be offered to married women to return to teaching, whether full or part-time [my emphasis].

The Roseveare Report also suggested modifications to facilities for teacher training to help women become students (ibid., p. 7):

> Students should be treated as adults and not adolescents. Young women students, in particular, like to make a *home* of their college and use it as a house . . . Until all colleges provide, as far as they can, something like the conditions of a *good home* – a home in the making of which students play a large part – and give their students a wide measure of freedom as responsible people, training for teaching will lack the full attractiveness which it could have [my italics].

Again, the Report assumed that women's natural interests lay in home-making. On the other hand, it contradicted itself about treating students as adults, when suggesting that LEAs help new recruits (ibid., p. 8): 'LEAs will do well, too, to make special provisions for those teachers appointed straight from training college . . . by keeping a *fatherly* eye on their welfare and progress' [my italics]. The Report was silent on equal pay, although it did propose changes in the ratio of male to female headteachers. No specific action was taken on this.

The first report of the National Advisory Council on Teachers, set up under the 1944 Education Act, appeared shortly afterwards in February 1951. It was also devoted to the question of the training and supply of teachers. It was, again, particularly keen to encourage women teachers, both for infant schools and so as not to imperil 'the efficiency of the education service'. The emergency training scheme had brought about an increase in male teachers. The report stated, 'nevertheless the infants' schools and classes must be taught by female teachers and will be under quite extraordinary pressure during the next few years as a result of the high birth rate of 1946 and 1947.' It proposed the use of quotas of women teachers on a regional basis. The other concern was with the quality of training for types of schoolteaching – in the grammar schools and in certain subjects, that is, maths and science. It suggested encouraging more graduates into teaching. Again, this report was not explicitly followed through.

The immediate post-war period was one of immense educational concern. Much attention was paid to the curriculum and its relevance to an advanced industrial economy. Two Committees of Enquiry, set up towards the end of the war, reported on the organization of technological and scientific education. Both commented on the inadequacy of provision in Britain for training scientists and technologists. The Percy Report of 1945 (Ministry of Education, 1945) recommended the establishment of a small number of colleges of technology to train students to the equivalent of degree-level courses, acquiring a new qualification. It was equivocal about whether this should be a degree or a diploma. The Barlow Report (Lord President of the Council, 1946) recommended the expansion of university education and doubling the output of scientists. It calculated that there were many capable individuals who were not receiving the benefits of such an education. In addition, it was keen to press the claims not merely of science but also of the humanities, and argued for an overall expansion.

Neither of the two reports was implemented instantly and completely. The Percy Report foundered on the problem of the type of qualification. The numbers of university students slowly began to expand and in 1949, at the Barlow Report's request, a new university was established at Keele. In general, the early post-war thrust was to make higher education more relevant to the considered needs of the economy. This was also the case with compulsory education. In 1947 the Secondary Schools Examinations Council reported on the existing system. It recommended the *abolition* of the School Certificate and its replacement by two types of examination. First, schools should develop their own internal examinations and improve their records of individual pupils. Second, there should be external examinations only for entry to universities and further education. This should also be a more flexible system than School Certificate, with *all* subjects as optional. Two tiers to the examination were to remain, a five-year course for the ordinary ('O' level) General Certificate of Education (GCE) and a further two years in the sixth form for advanced and scholarship work. It was felt that this system would lead to less premature specialization to allow for more choice in further and higher education. This approach to education had been gaining acceptance since before the war and the Labour government was therefore prepared for the change. From 1951 the new system of GCEs was enforced to replace SCEs.

The concern about the links between education and the economy was not restricted to the upper echelons of schools. The first report of the newly established Central Advisory Council for Education to the Ministry of Education, published in 1947 and entitled *School and Life*, was about the transition from school to independent life. Two issues were at the heart of the report: one was the relationships of home and school and the other was school and employment. For the former, it presented a new view of home life – it was concerned that mothers were still working although the war had ended and that childrer at school had too many household duties, so that 'they were frequently too tired to benefit from their life at school.' It suggested closer home-school liaison and that teachers encourage parents to the school to learn about appropriate parenthood.

In discussing school and employment, it distinguished between boys and girls, arguing that employment was important only for boys. It therefore suggested new curricula for girls in the final stages of school and in further education, which it called social and health education, to enable pupils to learn about the life of the future citizen and provide a technology of living in the home and the community. Courses would consist of hygiene, homemaking, mothercraft and sex education and rely on the use of educational films.

The post-war society was thus to be based on a clear sexual division of labour, with men in employment and women, on the whole, returned to the home. Men's education for employment was to be linked to an advanced industrial and technological society. Women, however, would have to be employed in education to provide valuable evidence of their experiences in the home.

The 1950s: teaching and classroom problems

The problems of how to achieve these developments in education continued to dominate policy discussions in the 1950s. The first pressing policy problem was still teacher supply, now, in part, because of the increase in size of the school population through the post-war baby boom. For example, 'between October 1945 and January 1951 teacher numbers rose from 173,501 to 216,000 but men teachers more than doubled from 40,223 to 83,000 whereas the number of women remained stable at just above 133,000' (Partington, 1976, p. 76). But by March 1952 one-third of all women teachers in service were *married* as opposed to 10 per cent in 1931. The Conservative government, elected to office in 1951, was no more willing than Labour to attract women back into the profession by providing equal pay. The Conservatives expanded supply first by increasing the numbers of teachers in training and this was mainly of advantage to men teachers. By 1955 the proportion of men to women was 37 to 63, as opposed to 32 to 68 in 1938. Equal pay, however, was soon put on the Conservatives' agenda. In 1952 a Labour MP moved an adjournment motion on equal pay, this time with the backing of a large number of Labour MPs. The NUT also stepped up its campaign and the NAS, overawed by the support for equal pay in principle, by the two major political parties, began to retreat.

In early 1954, two petitions – one from the Equal Pay Campaign Committee and the other from the Co-ordinating Committee on Equal Pay – were presented to Parliament. As a result, the Conservative Chancellor of the Exchequer pledged to introduce equal pay by stages to the civil service. In the summer of 1954, the Burnham agreement gave equal increases to men and women headteachers in the same group, adding support for equal pay if the government provided it for the Civil Service. In January 1955, equal pay by successive stages was introduced for the non-industrial Civil Service, so that by 1961 it would be fully achieved. The Burnham Committee quickly followed suit, and on 4 March 1955 the same type of scheme was agreed, to start on 1 May 1955 and to be completed on 1 April 1961. This agreement was not unanimously approved of. The NUWT was angered by the transitional arrangements and demanded immediate provision. The NAS, on the other hand, tried to resist all implementation.

The achievement of equal pay did not solve the problems of teacher supply. This problem was now acute for both secondary and primary education, since in 1955 and 1956 the birth rate again reached the 1949 peak. One reason for the lack of married women returners in the the second half of the 1950s was the declining average age of marriage and timing of children. The government gave further consideration to the training of teachers. In 1957 the National Advisory Committee on the Training and Supply of Teachers resuscitated the idea of extending training to three years, along with an expansion in the number of places. This plan, scheduled for implementation in 1960, was accepted in 1957, before the acute shortage was recognized. This shortage was occasioned by the steadily increasing birth rate. The government had to find new measures to encourage more married women into teaching. In fact, by 1960, 42 per cent of all women teachers were married. This was not sufficient and in 1961 a special campaign to encourage married women returners was mounted. A circular was sent to all LEAs. The number of part-time posts was increased in the last years of the 1950s and the LEA quotas on women dropped. A side-effect of this was a cutback in nursery school provision in 1960 to enable nursery teachers to teach in primary schools. By circular 10/60, LEAs were enjoined not to extend nursery provision except for the children of married women teachers who agreed to return to teaching.

The campaign to recruit married women was thus purely opportunist. It was not linked to wider encouragement to working women. Indeed, the opportunities to continue in employment whilst raising a family were severely curtailed generally through the axe on nursery schools.

The concern with *male employment* dominated the curricular discussions of the 1950s. First, it was evident through the Central Advisory Council for Education's 1954 report on *Early Leaving*, which argued for more grammar school places, to improve skilled manpower.

The emphasis on the skills necessary for the labour market was even more evident in the 1956 White Paper on technical education, which urged the expansion of technical education at all levels to ensure international competitiveness. Some of the colleges of technology were to become colleges of *advanced* technology (CATs), run by the LEAs and providing diplomas in technology, ratified by a new National Council for Technological Awards. Although the numbers of university students in science and technology had doubled between 1938 and 1955, this was not sufficient to supply new recruits to industry. Nevertheless, increases should be based on 'versatility' and not be narrowly vocational. 'A wide treatment of scientific and technical subjects is essential if students who are to occupy responsible positions in industry are to emerge from their education with a broad outlook. We cannot afford to fall behind in technical accomplishments or to neglect spiritual and human values' (Ministry of Education, 1956, p. 5). The White Paper sought to double again the output of scientists and technologists.

The Conservative government, however, continued not to be satisfied with the way in which the education system contributed to the economy. In 1956 it asked the Central Advisory Council (CACE) to report on the education of boys and girls between the ages of fifteen and eighteen. In 1958 the Beloe Committee was set up to investigate school-leaving examinations other than GCEs.

The spate of reports on class, educational achievement and women

In 1959 the CACE produced the Crowther Report, entitled *15 to 18* (see ch. 4 for full details). Basically, the report argued (CACE, 1959, ch. 1) that there was a great wastage of talent especially of men and they added, in parentheses, 'presumably of women' since most of the age group were not being educated. Again, it demonstrated the association between social class and educational achievement and between parents' educational achievement and that of their children Its solution was to raise the school-leaving age to sixteen as soon as possible. The main reason, it argued, for the extension of education for all classes of the population was changes in the economy; namely, a decline in unskilled jobs and an increase in jobs demanding some skill as a result of technological development. This led the Committee to show concern for further, as well as compulsory, education. These courses were, in fact, more clearly oriented to industry and mainly established at industry's behest. Here the Committee was quick to point to the discrepancy between boys and girls, especially in pursuing part-time further education. About 25 per cent of boys aged fifteen to eighteen, but only 6 per cent of girls, were in further education and the girls were all doing secretarial courses whose educational value, the Crowther Committee felt, was 'distinctly limited'. The reason for the lack of girls on courses was partly the fault of employers, who either refused day release to girls or employed them in very menial jobs requiring no technical knowledge.

However, the Crowther Committee's remedies for girls' lack of education were very limited. Following the tradition of child-centred education, the Committee believed that most girls' interests would be marriage first and career second, contrasted with boys' interests which were the reverse. The evidence it used was the age and rate of marriage: the former had been rapidly decreasing and the latter increasing. It only cursorily glanced at the work that women did as adults. For higher-ability girls, it felt that the schools were neglecting their careers and, for lower-ability girls, it felt that they could be given more choice. Girls' careers could also be in the fields of teaching, social work, health services, clothing trades and commerce. All these would be pursued after marriage but the Committee did not provide a programme for the education system to achieve such aims. Thus it relegated girls to a secondary position in the labour market. Moreover, it argued for a professionalization of housework (ibid., p. 34, para. 52): 'The prospect of courtship and marriage should rightly influence the education of the adolescent girl . . . her direct interest in dress, personal experience and in problems of human relations should be given a central place in her education.' The Report's concern was 'with the school's role in the preparation for family life and adulthood' (Lawson and Silver, 1973, p. 426). It was also to make boys' education more fitted to new technical skills and girls' to take up the slack and be concerned with the growing importance of the home. Since boys' and girls' adult lives were to be very different, the question of co-education did not seem very important. The Committee reported on the facts of co-education and single-sex education but did not make any proposals.

As soon as the Committee had reported, the government requested a second report from the Central Advisory Council on the thirteen-to-sixteen age group, of *below average* ability. Meanwhile, it received in 1960 the report of the departmental committee chaired by Beloe, which recommended the development of school-leaving examinations for children of average ability. These examinations were to supplement GCEs and provide employers with a guide to such pupils. Basic to its recommendations (Ministry of Education, 1960, p. 31) was the idea that 'the teachers in the schools using the examinations must have a major role in operating them and shaping policy.' This proposal was pursued but took five years to implement. In 1965 the Certificate in Secondary Education (CSE) was introduced, with three methods (modes) of setting the examinations.

The report of CACE chaired by Newsom and published in 1963 was equally concerned with the match between education and industry. Its key issue was with the new problem of automation, raised in part because of the economic crises of the late 1950s. The Newsom Committee recognized, more clearly than Crowther's, that women would be affected by these changes as much as men. Nevertheless, it did not prescribe how the occupational changes would affect girls' education, although it accepted women's participation in the labour force. It mentioned women's work in offices, shops, catering work, the clothing industry and other manufacturing trades. The courses in schools and further education were not, however, to be directed at these occupations but rather at girls' perennial interest in marriage and motherhood. The suggested changes in the curriculum were mainly related to this latter and, therefore, to sustaining a sexual division of labour.

At the same time as consideration was being given to the school curriculum, there was much concern with higher education and, in particular, teacher training. Here, too, the idea that more of the population should be professionally trained (and, indeed, be graduates) was being widely canvassed and gaining wide acceptance. One approach, tentatively suggested by the government in 1960, was that there should be an increase in primary teacher training in the colleges and 'that more graduates should be recruited to secondary schools' (Gosden, 1972, p. 300). This dichotomy was seen by most teacher unions to be divisive for the teaching profession. However, it continued as an issue throughout the 1960s. Some of the heat was taken out of the issue with the establishment in 1960, by the Tory Prime Minister, of a Committee of Enquiry chaired by Lord Robbins into all full-time higher education. This was occasioned by the expansion of teacher training, the CATs and the growth of school sixth forms with which the universities were not keeping pace. The report of the Robbins Committee was published some two years later (Committee on Higher Education, 1963) and argued the case for a massive expansion of higher education. Its case was similar to Crowther's and Newsom's: that there was a wastage of talent on social, not genetic, grounds. This had to be remedied to ensure Britain's position in the international economic market-place. It therefore recommended that the total percentage of eighteen- to twenty-one-year-olds receiving higher education be increased from 8 to 17 per cent (or over half a million places) by 1980 and that the distribution be 12 per cent for girls and 22 per cent for boys. Although concerned with education's links with the economy, it did not take a narrow view of the advances in technology and suggested expansion in all aspects of universities, in teacher training and the creation of new technological universities out of the CATs, but with the balance in favour of universities. It also proposed the setting up of five special technological institutes to be called SISTERS and that teacher training colleges be upgraded by a change of name and status to colleges of education, with removal from LEA control and the awarding of degrees, not diplomas. Admission to university or CAT was to be based not upon manpower criteria but student choice, given students' achievement of minimum entry criteria (specified as two 'A' level GCEs). The Report did not envisage the directing of students into particular courses, professions or occupations.

One special concern was the wastage of female talent. A part of the Report was devoted to this problem, on the efficiency grounds of 'making better use of what must be the *greatest source of unused talent*' [my italics]. It was argued that able women should be encouraged into careers. First, the Committee concerned itself with teacher training, adopting a pragmatic view (ibid., p. 107):

> For example, a young woman with no desire to take a degree in psychology but with a genuine interest in children may study their psychological development with an enhanced sense of relevance when it is combined with observation of children in school and practice in her future vocation.

However, unlike Crowther and Newsom, it did not only point women to female-type activities, but took a more eclectic view of women's careers, stating that (ibid., pp. 126–7):

> means must therefore be found to attract more of the ablest students of technology. In particular, it is desirable to encourage more girls to read applied science. At present, very few girls in this country seem to be attracted to a career in applied science, and the contrast with some other countries, notably the Soviet Union, is very striking.

In addition, it suggested positive methods to attract women, especially after marriage and raising a family, into higher education, stating categorically that 'higher education is not a one-and-for-all process'. Unfortunately, all the estimates of numbers and places in higher education were based on the assumption of entry at eighteen years old. Still it made some policy proposals to modify the situation: first, that 'there are far too few students taking refresher courses and courses of further training. This is not because of the dearth of courses . . . but partly because of inadequate support from employers and partly because of a lack of awareness of the opportunities that exist.' In this, it echoed the Crowther Report, and yet its prescriptions went very much further (ibid., p. 167, para. 514):

> It is particularly important that such courses should be made available to married women. Before the war over three-quarters of the women in employment were unmarried: now more than half of them are married. Many more go out to work (over $^1/_3$ now compared to $^1/_4$ in 1951 and $^1/_{10}$ in 1921). At the same time the age of marriage has fallen and the expectation of working life lengthened. As a result a new career pattern has emerged: a short period of work before marriage and a second period of work starting perhaps 15 years later and continuing for 20 years or more; the indications are that this pattern will become increasingly common. The prospects of early marriage leads girls capable of work in the professions to leave school before they have entered the sixth form and, even after sixth form studies, too many girls go straight into employment instead of higher education. When their family responsibilities have lessened many of them will desire opportunities for higher education. And many, if not most, married women who have already enjoyed higher education will need refresher courses before they can return effectively to professional employment. This will be particularly true of doctors, teachers and social workers but there will also be a need in other fields such as commerce and languages. There is here a considerable reserve of unused ability, which must be mobilized if the critical shortages in many professions are to be

> met . . . It is important that the arrangements should be both flexible and variable to suit varying needs. Not all the education of married women need be on a full-time basis: it may often be easier to arrange part-time courses and more convenient for married women to attend them.

The Robbins Committee also discussed the financial maintenance problems that women in higher education might encounter. On grounds of expediency – empirical changes in the labour market and female employment – it argued for changes in women's position in higher education, as well as major changes for men. The Conservative government accepted most of its proposals and immediately moved to implement them. It did not, though, create SISTERS or remove training colleges from LEAs, although the names of the latter were changed to colleges of education and they were empowered to give degrees. CATs did become universities. This enhanced the status of both aspects of the traditional non-university sector of higher education.

Social democracy and women's place in education

The Labour Party's accession to government in 1964 meant major political changes in educational policy. In its rhetoric, the Labour government was more committed to a policy of equality of opportunity (Benton, 1974; Finn *et al.*, 1977). However, it did not make a dramatic impact upon either the role of the teacher or the sex balance of the curriculum. One of its first moves was to follow through the Robbins Report, which the Conservatives had started to implement, but Labour's strategy was different. In 1965 the (newly titled) Secretary of State for Education* announced a new binary policy for providing higher education: in the universities and in a set of institutions not hitherto included – polytechnics. These latter would have parity with the universities but would be oriented more to industry and vocationalism and would be created out of colleges of technology which had not become universities in 1963. They would remain in LEA control, as would the new colleges of education. So the institutions of higher education would reflect developments in the economy – where there remained a clear division of labour. And importantly, teacher training, albeit now of a graduate kind, also reflected that division,

*The Labour government reorganized government departments and elevated the Ministry of Education to the Department of Education and Science. The minister in charge was renamed Secretary of State for Education and acquired two junior ministers to help carry out all the responsibilities (David, 1977, ch. 1).

with some post-graduate training still within the university sector.

Even though the training of teachers had been improved in status, supply remained a problem in the 1960s. The Labour government proposed a new category of ancillary school help, some outside the classroom (for example, clerical help and library assistants), but also teaching auxiliaries. The teaching unions resisted the use of auxiliaries, having just managed to rid the profession of supplementaries but supported the idea of ancillary help external to the classroom. The NUT specified four such categories – clerical, school meals duties, welfare assistants and laboratory assistants or technicians. The NAS also supported this. It was in this area that help to schools increased in the 1960s. In addition, as a result of moves to professionalize teaching, the NUT began to campaign *against* the employment of unqualified teachers. It was not until 1967 that any government action was taken. A working party was set up to consider the position. It reported in May 1968 and proposed that no unqualified, temporary teachers should be appointed after September 1970. These proposals, for further upgrading the teaching profession, were implemented from 1969.

A year later, similar proposals were pursued for *graduate* entry into teaching. No one graduating after January 1970 would be accepted as a teacher in a maintained primary school without a course of professional training, and the same would apply to secondary schools after January 1974. These proposals could be effective since the Robbins Committee's estimates for expansion in teacher training had already been well exceeded. By 1967 there were over 100,000 students in colleges of education; in 1968 the first Bachelor of Education degrees were awarded and over 2,000 graduates were studying at colleges of education. Moreover, there were twenty-eight university departments of education, with over 5,000 students. One of the most spectacular changes was 'the breakdown of the traditional single-sex structure' (Lawson and Silver, 1973, p. 436). Even by 1963 the number of all-female colleges had decreased by 22 and this trend continued. But, in 1967, 20 per cent of all non-graduates entering teacher training were aged twenty-five and over, and were mainly women (ibid.). 'Special colleges and courses for mature women students with families were now being opened.' The teaching labour market was changing considerably. By 1970 about one-third of all women still teaching at the age of sixty were married women returners (Partington, 1976, p. 96). This meant a change not only in the sex and family-status composition of teachers but also in their class backgrounds. More women than men teachers were recruited from stable middle-class origins (ibid.).

The Labour government was still concerned about the connection between education and the economy and pursued this by developing educational provision in several areas. One interest was in further education, which was regularized with the development of polytechnics (Burgess and Pratt, 1974). A further component was the expansion of day-release courses in colleges of further education, initiated by the creation in 1964 of industrial training boards for different industries to develop training. These courses, however, developed locally and haphazardly, with little central government control. The government did try to control the number of science and technology students in higher education. To this end, the Dainton Committee was set up in 1965. It analysed 'the swing from science in schools', since, in the two years after the Robbins Committee reported, a large number of science and technology places at universities were unfilled. The Dainton Report was published in 1968 and proposed major changes in the structure of school science courses, since they appeared to influence choice of science. Sixth-form studies would be broadened (Council for Scientific Policy, 1968, pp. 87–90) to postpone 'irreversible decisions for or against science, engineering or technology . . . as late as possible.' Science courses and teaching should be made up-to-date and maths should be a compulsory subject until pupils left school.

By the time the Dainton Report appeared, there had been attempts at major changes in the secondary school curriculum. One was the creation, from 1965, of comprehensive secondary schools by the Labour government, in which curricular changes were not of paramount importance, but teaching organization was. In trying to break the association between type of school and social privilege or inequality, the streaming and setting of pupils by academic ability came under question. A number of comprehensive schools adopted the approach of mixed-ability teaching, at least for the younger pupils. However, flexibility and variety were the hallmark of the comprehensive school schemes proposed and adopted after 1965. The Labour government proposed, in circular 10/65, various patterns of secondary school reorganization and all of these were adopted by different LEAs up and down the country (David, 1977).

Curriculum development was an important feature of the 1960s. In 1962 the Nuffield Foundation launched what was called the Science Teaching Project, to design materials for use in both junior and secondary schools. Teachers worked to produce new approaches to science teaching, and these projects inspired further changes. In 1964 the Schools Council was set up, virtually replacing the Secondary Schools Examination Council and emerging out of a Ministry of Education curriculum study group. It set out 'to secure a happier marriage than in the past between the actual work of the schools . . . and the examinations which . . . can all too easily stand in the way of necessary innovation' (Schools Council, 1965, p. 21). It launched a number of projects on teaching method and also mooted the changes in examination structure originally proposed by the Beloe Committee. The main distinctive feature of the new CSE was the contribution of teachers to the actual examinations. Indeed, the role of the teacher was vital to all these changes. LEAs began to establish teachers' centres as discussion units on teaching methods and materials.

Another major concern of the 1960s was primary education. In 1963 the Tory government asked the Central Advisory Committee 'to consider primary education in all its aspects, and the transition to secondary education'. The impetus for this request was the evidence of three prior committees – Crowther, Newsom and Robbins – about the influence of home background on children's performance. The report, under the chairwomanship of Lady Plowden, was published in 1967 and followed the themes of the previous reports, suggesting a number of policy remedies. The Plowden Report put much stress on the relations between home and school and therefore suggested new methods of liaison between school and home (CACE, 1967, p. 48, para. 129): 'It has long been recognised that education is concerned with the whole family.' This led the Committee to suggest more parent participation in school activities, including the classroom. The major concern, however, was with children growing up in poor environments. To remedy that, the Plowden Committee suggested a policy of positive discrimination – identifying the children through the designation of educational priority areas (EPAs). These schools would receive more teachers, more salary allowances, more equipment and building renovations. In addition, to counteract the effects of poor home circumstances, it suggested a new programme of nursery education, starting in the priority areas, with the deployment of more staff, including nursery aides. The Committee was also concerned about teaching organization and method and, over the transition to secondary education, suggested flexibility. Twelve should be the age of transfer to secondary education but middle schools could be created for eight- to twelve-year-olds, and opportunities for starting school should be made more flexible. It also argued against dogmatic teaching methods and put the case against streaming.

The Plowden Report was the first attempt to divert resources towards the deprived and disadvantaged. Nevertheless, in so doing it 'blamed the victim' for the problems (Ryan, 1973). In particular, mothers were condemned for their inadequacies and recommended to return to school to make up for them. Indeed, much hinged on 'the efficiency of the mother' (CACE, 1967, pp. 64–5). Schools were to compensate for inadequate mothering. Not all of the Report was implemented. The major aspects implemented were the creation of EPAs in 1968, at local choice, the setting up of a research monitoring project, an Urban Aid programme in 1969 which incorporated Plowden's nursery prescriptions and encouragement to progressive methods of primary teaching.

A further attempt of the Labour government to divert educational resources from the traditional class system was the setting up of a Public Schools Commission. This was to try to integrate such schools into the State-maintained sector of education. Its first report, in 1968, on public schools did try to provide methods of integration, especially by redefining the criteria of boarding need and by eliminating the schools' charitable status. The second report, in 1970, concerned the direct grant and independent day schools. The proposal here was to establish a School Grants Committee which would help finance those schools wishing to become part of the maintained sector. Neither report was implemented during the Labour government's period of office.

In sum, the main thrust of the post-war period up to 1970 was to professionalize teaching and to make educational curricula more fitted to the demands of the economy, especially the needs of manufacturing industry and technology. Little account was taken of the changing rate of participation in the labour force of women, especially married women, except as it affected teaching itself. The school curriculum became narrowly, and explicitly, oriented to employment possibilities and not to the broader aspects of adult life. Class differences in education were barely altered. In the process, children were to be slotted more exactly and efficiently into the occupational positions provided rather than learning to deal with a range of skills and posts. The intention was overwhelmingly technocratic. The main contradiction, during this period, was that girls would continue to be taught that their major occupation and career was to be marriage and motherhood. Only limited recognition was made of the fact that women could, and did, contribute to the economy through their involvement in the labour force. Yet, at the same time, women were increasingly encouraged into a rapidly professionalizing educational labour market, on the grounds that they were needed to teach girls, in a professional way, to prepare for their role in the sexual division of labour in the family.

Part III

Contemporary issues in the family–education couple

Introduction

In this, the last part of the book, contemporary debates about educational policy are examined. The two themes that underpinned the organization of the first two parts of the book are used as a basis for the analysis of policy issues in the 1970s. The emphasis is still on the ways in which the State has tried to regulate relationships between the family (particularly parents) and the education system and familial relationships within schooling. However, some current struggles to modify the organization of education are also examined, as examples of the ways in which changes are being demanded.

The decade of the 1970s was chosen advisedly. It is a period which was clearly distinct from the earlier post-war era. The 1970s were characterized by a severe economic recession, with financial crises on an unprecedented scale. Education, along with other public and social services which had enjoyed expansion in the 1950s and 1960s, came under political scrutiny and, eventually, attack and financial reduction. Indeed, for much of the decade education was made a scapegoat by both major political parties as being, not the product, but the cause of Britain's ills (see also Silver, 1978b). Education was constantly high on the political agenda, but it was, in fact, treated in common with other public services. In the first place, attempts were made to make the machinery of the government more efficient, through the application of management techniques. The main tool of such efficient management was cost effectiveness, which was but another term for budgetary reductions (Glennerster, 1975). These techniques were applied across the whole of the public sector and hence affected education, including its system of control. Here parents were critically involved. The second set of efforts was to make the whole economy operate more efficiently, and education was to play a major part in this endeavour. Parents, teachers and curricula were all implicated: parents were afforded rights to their adolescent and infant children but limited in the extent of State sharing of child-care responsibilities; teachers were to be trained to a graduate level, to be more professional; and curricula for adolescents were more clearly tied to the needs of industry, especially manufacturing industry. Differences between boys and girls were maintained, although rather less explicitly than hitherto. By the end of the decade, much of the education system had been tightly reorganized and economies effected. Indeed, economy was perhaps the hallmark of the whole decade.

Chapter 8 examines the policy debates and prescriptions affecting the relations between education, parents and the economy. The major educational changes occurred in the second half of the decade, under a Labour government, but they were presaged by the earlier Tory administration. Labour's policies were in line with those of the Tories and not at all oriented to achieving equity within education, a former Labour ideology. The resolution of two major struggles – at the William Tyndale school in the Inner London Education Authority and in the Tameside LEA – has indicated the extent to which middle-class parents have been able to preserve the education system for their own ends, rather than for changing social relationships. This is borne out to an even greater extent by the influence that a right-wing pressure group – the Black Paperites – has been able to exert in the polity, which has affected the development of educational legislation, especially Labour's 1978 Education Bill and the Tory Education Act of 1979. Finally, the ways in which adolescents and preschoolers have been treated, through policy prescriptions such as EMAs, Youth Opportunity schemes, and the type of preschool provision, have indicated attempts to tie educational solutions to the vagaries of the economy.

Little has been written on the politics of educational issues in the 1970s, although during this decade there have been major developments in the sociology of education and attempts to understand, theoretically, the relationships between the State, education and the economy (see especially Young and Whitty, 1977). The most important studies, albeit brief on the links between education and the family, have been those emanating from the Centre for Contemporary Cultural Studies in Birmingham. The two papers that have informed this chapter are by Finn *et al.* (1977) and Hall (1979). Benton's (1974) study of post-war Labour governments' attitudes to education was also of use. Much has been written about the period by journalists, among them Adam

Hopkins (1978), who tries to summarize and characterize the Great Debate, and Devlin and Warnock (1977), who try to provide a prescription for the education system. Wright's (1977) attempt to evaluate the evidence about the extent of progress and progressivism in education is the most sober, scholarly and readable account of developments in schooling and a critique of their critics, especially the Black Paperites. Although both youth unemployment and preschool provisions have received much political attention, little analysis has been undertaken of the major contours of the issues. One unpublished paper by McClure (1979) has pinpointed the key features of the former issue; government and other quasi-official publications are mainly the relevant material on the question of preschoolers and their mothers, apart from Tizard *et al.* (1976) and a series of conference papers edited by Fonda and Moss (1976). As regards the two educational struggles (Tyndale and Tameside), much has been made of them by journalists or, tangentially, by academics. I have elsewhere tried to study the former (David, 1978a). Griffith (1976 and 1977) has used the latter in his study of the judiciary.

In chapter 9, attention is focused upon contemporary developments in teaching and what is taught. It is argued that the period has been characterized by attempts to professionalize *all* teachers, largely by converting training into a graduate qualification. No justifications have been made in this decade for the continuance or the encouragement of the employment of women, especially married women. On the contrary, the types of changes implied a reduction in the ratio of women in the profession. Equally, in terms of the curriculum, the trend has been towards the less explicit recognition of the differences between boys and girls as adolescents and possibly as adults. However, this trend was a result of two external factors – the impact of legislation for sex equality, fought for by women outside the education system, and the need to tie education more clearly to the economy. The main policy thrust has been for vocational courses, linked especially to industry, for adolescents and, at the younger age ranges, the designation of the necessary or 'core' minimum curriculum, which would provide for a more adequately educated labour force. Nevertheless, given these trends, sex differences in the curriculum have not been eliminated. Indeed, in the one LEA studied since the Sex Discrimination Act of 1975 by the Equal Opportunities Commission – Tameside – it was impossible to find grounds for disapproval of its discriminatory actions. But differences between adolescent boys and girls in terms of curricular offerings are no longer as blatant as they used to be and, if they are, may be subject to judicial intervention. What happens to boys and girls in the education system is still, however, based upon traditional ideological notions.

Again little has been written of substance about the period under review. Lord James's (1973) own analysis of the report he chaired is instructive; the education journals, especially *Education*, were also critical in their appraisals of the James Report. On the other hand, there is little published material on the subsequent events, except again for journalistic accounts such as Hopkins (1978) and Devlin and Warnock (1977).

As regards the curriculum, much commentary has been provided on the Great Debate but the most accessible studies are by Hopkins (1978) and Wright (1977). As far as girls' schooling is concerned, there is now a wealth of literature, although little of it analyses the political debates surrounding its development. The two most pertinent works are Deem (1978) and Byrne (1978), both of which try to locate, at different levels of analysis, the current dilemmas of provision. Sharpe (1976) provides the most readable analysis of working-class girls' position *vis-á-vis* schooling; Blackstone (1976b), in a short article, tries to summarize the present state of educational opportunities for girls. The survey which has most informed policy development was that of the HMIs in 1975, entitled *Curricular Differences for Boys and Girls* (DES, 1975b). It showed the persistence of the familial emphasis in secondary schooling. And there is no further evidence, in policy rhetoric, prescription or research, to suggest that by the end of the decade girls were no longer taught that their adult lives would consist of two activities, one of which would be the care of the home and children.

In the final chapter of the book, the argument is both reviewed and summarized. It is concluded that, at the end of thc 1970s, the prospects for a radical transformation of the education system, in its relationships with and to the family, look distinctly bleak. Rather the trend has been towards the consolidation and reaffirmation of the social and sexual division of labour through schooling. Any struggles developed to counter the *status quo*, as illustrated by instances such as the William Tyndale dispute or the Tameside legal battles, have been settled against the working classes rather than for them. Schooling can be still seen to reinforce and reflect the prevailing socio-economic system rather than in any way counter it.

8

Reasserting parental rights to achieve economic efficiency

The early 1970s in Britain witnessed an economic crisis of unprecedented proportions since the 1930s. This crisis, which led into a deepening economic recession, has continued throughout the 1970s. Its effects have, therefore, been manifold. On the one hand, the deliberate attempts both by private capital and industry and by the State to deal with economic problems have included a restructuring of the education industry. Indeed, in this respect education has frequently been used as a scapegoat for the economic ills that have befallen Britain. Silver argued in *New Society* (1978b): 'Education was brought into the discussion of every conceivable problem.' Even when education has not been thus stigmatized, it has, almost inevitably, been affected by economic remedies. On the other hand, the effects of the recession have been such as to stimulate groups and classes to action in pursuit of changes in their situation. Thus, the 1970s have been characterized by much educational rhetoric and activity. Whether this has resulted in a fundamental restructuring of the whole system is a much more open question. The core of the discussion has been the relationship between the family and the education system. In particular, the emphasis towards the end of the decade was on establishing and redefining *parental rights* rather than further imposing parental duties, by applying the State's standards. In this chapter, I examine the ways in which, first, the State and, second, struggles by different groups have attempted to change the characteristics of parental involvement in the education system. In particular, it is important to look at the redefinition, through action and edict, of the division of responsibility between parents for their children's schooling and the attempts to change parental relationships within the education system.

As shown in chapters 2, 3 and 4, changes in the organization of the education system usually followed from major economic events. In the 1970s, it was certainly the case that both the Tory and Labour administrations tried to revamp the education system. The most important concern has been with the purposes of the education system and how to restructure education to make it both more efficient and more readily serve economic ends. This latter objective emerged only slowly out of the economic depression and became explicit in Labour proposals in the second half of the decade. Hall (1979) has referred to the Labour period of office as 'the Great Moving Right Show'. Labour did not any longer even pay lip-service to its traditional ideology and the principle of equality of educational opportunity.

The Tories' treatment of education and economy

Initial Tory concerns, when they were in office from July 1970, were with the fabric of education and the links with broader social policy. First, they laid an emphasis on strengthening and improving school buildings and sought to abolish all primary schools built before 1903, before the passing of the 1902 Education Act. This drive for improvement did not last long: in actual fact few of the primary school buildings were replaced and, more important, the Tories launched a number of initiatives which were concerned with reducing the costs of the education system. One such policy was that of withdrawing free school milk from all children over the age of seven. This action was deliberately taken because of the financial strains the government was beginning to experience.

The second, and most important, educational initiative of the Tory administration was its White Paper, produced at the end of 1972, which attempted to set out a thorough reorientation of the education system. Entitled *Education: a Framework for Expansion* (DES, 1972a), it was, in fact, a recipe for retrenchment. Byrne (1978, p. 203) has stated that it was 'oddly named . . . (since when we have seen the worst planned, and unplanned, recession and cuts since the 1922 Geddes axe).' The main impetus for the White Paper was the introduction of new techniques of government which affected the ways in which each policy department of central government operated. The techniques were drawn from both American government and private industry and have been variously named as 'managerialism' or 'corporatism' (Smith, 1972; Cockburn, 1977; Glennerster, 1975). The Tory government adopted a variety of methods in an effort to improve the decision-making process. The particular method that underlay the White Paper was called programme analysis review (PAR) and was first explained in an earlier White Paper (1970) on the machinery of government in late 1970. Essentially a simple method, it has often been argued that it was technically very complex. It merely required the setting out of the programmes financed by each government spending department and the cost implications of their development (Glennerster, 1975).

The Education White Paper, therefore, was in one sense a very comprehensive document, for it covered all aspects of the education system from nursery schools to universities. However, it did not set out the ways in which all sectors would expand and indeed was only slightly concerned with compulsory education by making brief mention of improving the pupil-teacher ratio. Almost inevitably, the main areas of expansion anticipated were non-compulsory – nursery and higher education. There was no suggestion of extending compulsory schooling. Detailed plans to 1981–2 were presented, and shortly afterwards explanatory and explicit circulars were produced. But the focus was on resource allocation. For instance, circular 2/73 on nursery education, published only weeks after the White Paper, was a very expansionist document in financial terms. It argued for the achievement of the Plowden Committee's proposals (CACE, 1967) for numbers in nursery education (75 per cent of three-year-olds and 90 per cent of four-year-olds) by 1981. This was, though, not to be. The recession began to bite and although for two successive years the DES announced possible programmes for nursery building, few LEAs took up the offers. Then, in a series of public expenditure revisions, the expansion of nursery provision was reduced. Equally the proposed developments in higher education did not take place.

The only other initiative embarked upon by the Tory administration was concerned with maintaining educational standards. In response to alarm expressed by both academics and right-wing pressure groups about standards in school, and especially reading ability (Hopkins, 1978, p. 89), the Secretary of State set up a committee of inquiry in 1972 (chaired by Sir Alan Bullock) to investigate language standards in school. The Committee acted with due speed and the results were published as *A Language for Life* in 1975 (DES Committee of Enquiry, 1975). The Tory administration was unable to act upon the recommendations since they appeared after the Tories had been voted out of office.

In sum, Tory proposals for a reorganization of education concentrated on non-compulsory education, for apparent expansionism with little financial commitment or inducement. The overriding concern was not with improvements to education but with the adequacy of spending on it. So the Tory attitude was one of fitting education, along with other public services, into a new system of economic management. Underlying this, however, was an ethic of individualism, as evinced by the approach to comprehensive education. One of the first actions of the Tory government in 1970 was to change, by what appeared to be minor amendments, the pattern of comprehensive education. This dramatically altered the relationship between parents and the State. The government rescinded circular 10/65 and replaced it with circular 10/70, which set out the new procedures for the approval of plans for the reorganization of secondary education. The basic change was that plans would not be considered LEA by LEA but school by school (Saran, 1973). Objections to a plan previously were only considered if they focused on the balance between schools. By circular 10/70, objections could be raised about changes to one school, which would, in effect, allow for objections to the reorganization of grammar schools. The main objectors probably would be parents, if the legal evidence of the previous five years were an indication. There had been three major court cases over these issues (Fowler *et al.*, 1973). This Tory change of procedure, therefore, allowed for parents to compete with each other over the system of local schooling. A grammar school parents' association, or PTA, could effectively put an end to plans for a fully, that is, LEA-wide, comprehensive system of secondary education. Thus some parents – those with children currently in grammar schools – would have a greater role in educational decision-making. The *status quo* of a tri- or bipartite system of education was deemed to carry more weight than an educational change. And, indeed, this proved to be the case. A section of the 1944 Act was invoked to prevent Surrey County Council from disallowing pupils in one comprehensive school catchment area from taking the 11-plus examination. Section 68 allowed the Minister to prevent the 'unreasonable' exercise of powers by LEAs. Thus the parents of some pupils were allowed to opt for selective education. Indeed, the whole thrust of this Tory administration was to support a selective group of parents and only allow LEAs to act against parental wishes (Section 76) if unreasonable public expense would be incurred.

Indirectly, in another sense, too, some parents were afforded more responsibilities and influence in the early 1970s. This was because the Tory administration allowed for the raising of the school-leaving age to sixteen in 1972–3; a measure promised almost thirty years earlier and postponed several times in the 1960s (see ch. 4). Extending the years of schooling inevitably extended the time that children would be dependent upon their parents and, therefore, the amount of influence that parents could exert over them. With this raising of the school-leaving age, there was a good deal less consensus of opinion about its obvious benefits than with previous compulsory extensions of education. In particular, the schoolchildren affected did not appreciate the purpose of such a measure and were unable to accommodate themselves to the notion of long-term benefits. Nor did they, as a whole, appear to appreciate the short-run gains (see White and Brockington, 1978).

Equality of educational opportunity: the early Labour approach

On the whole, educational policy was not of great moment to the Tory government. Initially, the first Labour government of 1974 was far more concerned with pursuing specific educational objectives. However, these were very soon followed by a period of severe economic retrenchment out of which a policy of educational curtailment and reduction appeared. Labour's ideological stance, as a result, was completely modified, to one of supporting parental rights rather than achieving equity between parents. In the first two years of Labour being in office attention reverted to the restructuring of secondary education, with the avowed aim of using education to achieve equality in adult life. Three different policy instruments were used with this object. First, circular 10/70 concerning approval of comprehensive schemes was replaced by circular 4/74, which merely reverted to the *status quo ante* (i.e., circular 10/65). This was seen to be a holding measure pending more drastic statutory action. Legislation did not occur until 1976. In the interim, steps were taken to extend the scope of the comprehensive principle from the maintained sector of schooling to the wider reaches of the public sector. The second policy change was that the government took up some of the recommendations of the two Public School Commissions that its Labour predecessor had appointed (see ch. 4). Its policy initiatives were but a pale reflection of the Commissions' far-reaching proposals. The only schools that the government took action over were the direct-grant schools (176 in total). Together, the Commissions had been concerned with all public and independent schools (over 2,000 in all) (Public Schools Commission, 1968). The reasons for Labour's caution were its slender parliamentary majority, the obvious Tory opposition, and the fact that this policy did not require any legislative change which might have provoked political controversy. All that the Labour government did was to withdraw, on a staggered basis, aid to those schools receiving grants both for individual pupils and for buildings direct from central rather than local government. The purpose of this action was to clarify the status of the public and private sectors in education and to ensure local (rather than diffuse central) control over public sector secondary education. The stated aim was to reduce privilege and ensure more equality in State education. In fact, the 176 schools were given a choice over their future position in the educational structure – without a grant, either to enter the LEA system or to become independent of direct State aid. The latter still implied some measure of indirect State subsidy, in the fact that the schools all had charitable status and were exempt from certain taxes (a point which both Commissions had made much of) and that they had to be registered with the DES. The majority of the schools chose independence; only the Roman Catholic schools, which constituted slightly less than one-third of all the schools (Glennerster and Wilson, 1971), chose to come under LEA administration. Indeed, many of the other schools could not have come under LEA control had they wished to do so, for often the LEAs in whose areas they were located found their buildings inadequate and decrepit and their secondary school places superfluous to need. This was a portent for the future.

The effect of the measure was limited. It had been intended to stop LEAs selecting pupils for such schools. Nevertheless, some LEAs, particularly Tory-dominated ones, continued to use their powers under the Local Government Act (Hopkins, 1978, p. 30) and the London Government Act 1963 (Sofer, 1978) to pay to send some able pupils to independent schools. The aim of the measure, to reduce distinctions between schools and pupils on the basis of academic ability, was not very effective.

In 1975 the government took a further step in this direction of reducing parental choice and privilege by drafting a Bill to legislate for comprehensive education and the banning of academic selection for secondary schools. The Bill itself was extremely brief but was one of the most contentious pieces of legislation in a highly controversial year. It was a year in which the House of Lords took the unprecedented step of trying to hold up six items of legislation, using this Bill as the scapegoat. They did not succeed, but three amendments allowing some measure of selection – for the artistically gifted, for the 'handicapped' and to ensure academic balance by means of banding – were included. So the notion of equal education on social grounds was once again watered down and confused with the notion of 'comprehensive' as a spread across ability ranges. The issue of what constituted comprehensive education clearly was not resolved through the Act, and, although progress towards comprehensive education throughout the 1970s has been inexorable, if terminology only is any guide it is not on any one common basis. Moreover, the Education Act of 1976 was mainly concerned with the maintained sector and not with the independent and private sector of education. It did, however, include clauses to prevent LEAs selecting pupils and paying for their attendance at independent schools, without permission from the Secretary of State for Education. Although the latter do not touch on the lives of the vast majority of children (95 per cent of all schoolchildren are in maintained schools), those children in private schools will thereby have access to the privileged jobs and become part of the ruling classes.

In its early years of office the Labour government's concentration in education was on secondary schooling. It did little for nursery, primary or higher education. If anything, LEA programmes for nursery education were reduced. The only change in higher education was in terms not of structure but access. Amendments, which did not require legislative endorsement, were made to the rules governing the distribution of maintenance allowances to students in higher education. Previously, only grants to students in higher education, not to those on advanced further education courses, had been mandatory. Grants for students in polytechnics and colleges of higher education now became mandatory, no longer discretionary. However, most grants to students in further education remained discretionary (a point to which I return). The other development was in terms of the procedures for handling educational disadvantage: the government expanded and reorganized the administrative units in the DES to deal with this problem, partly as a response to the Bullock Report. Here, it concerned itself rather more with the question of the status of immigrants as disadvantaged and sought to devise methods to detect underachievement. The thrust of the Tory concern had been with educational standards. Labour took this forward and, in the context of the increasingly sophisticated managerial techniques being used in government, tried to develop a network of agencies concerned with ensuring the adequacy of all school performance, not only that of immigrant groups.

Labour's concern with education and efficiency

Indeed, as the decade wore on, official concern with the effectiveness of the education system became more and more strident. The Tories had made the first step in the direction of mounting systems of administration that would ensure the adequacy of education. Labour carried this forward, at first tentatively and then, as the economic recession began to bite, more vigorously. Concern with educational standards and the nature of education became paramount. Pressure had been mounting from extra-Parliamentary groups, especially ones loosely affiliated with the Tories, for example, those grouped around the Black Papers (Hopkins, 1978). Hall (1979) has argued that the Tories here 'gained territory if not power'. By 1976, the concern of the Labour government to use education as a panacea for social and economic ills began to dominate the political agenda. Initially, a team of HMIs was commissioned to review educational standards in schools. Before their report was ready for publication it was leaked to the press and later became known, infamously, as the 'Yellow Paper'. Since this documented considerable school difficulties, the need for an official public statement on the state of schools became vital. Less than a month later, in early October 1976, the Prime Minister, James Callaghan, in a speech at Ruskin College, Oxford, launched what he called The Great Debate on Education. This was to be a public (never well-defined) discussion of the purposes of education and the relationship between education and the economy. In particular, there was to be debate over the ways in which education prepared children for the labour market and for jobs. The debate, however, was not only to concern itself with the aims but also to consider the nature of educational control. In stating the contours of the debate Callaghan promised, 'There will be discussion . . . I repeat that parents, teachers, learned and professional bodies, representatives of higher education, on both sides of industry, together with the government, have an important part to play . . .' In this proposal (see David, 1978b) the control of education was modified. Until this point (see chs. 2–4) neither parents nor teachers had been included separately in the traditional educational discourse. More important, perhaps, was the inclusion of industrialists. This pointed up the concern to make the links between education and industry much more explicit. This became more obvious as the wheels of the debate were set in motion. First, the debate was never really what it purported to be. It eventually consisted of six regional, invited-audience discussions of a rigidly defined, prepared agenda. DES officials were common to all six debates; so, too, were some of the invited audiences. All categories of participant mentioned by Callaghan contributed but only by invitation. Second, and at this juncture more important, the discussions were limited to the issue of the relationship between education and industry. Published agenda were the basis.

The Great Debate was mainly concerned with aspects of compulsory schooling. There was little thought given to nursery or higher education, save in so far as they were implicated by the issue of compulsion. For instance, the whole question of the nature of teacher training was raised in connection with improvements in the curriculum (I return to this in ch. 9). Mainly the focus was on what children should be taught and to what end. The five areas spelt out were: curriculum and teaching method, school and work, assessment of standards, education and training of teachers. The formal debate lasted for about six months, after which the government undertook to prepare policy proposals. The object of the proposals was to reorient the direction of education and create a new constituency of control. This, of course, was along-side the normal running of the schools. The regional discussions did not resolve all the issues and a number of circulars and discussion documents were prepared for LEAs early in 1977. For instance, the question of what information schools should prepare for parents was the subject of one exploratory circular. The HMIs were also requested to spell out good school practices and did so in a pamphlet entitled *Ten Good Schools* (DES, 1977c). This detailed school organization and systems of control as well as curricula.

By mid-1977 the government felt able to put out a Green Paper for further discussion, summarizing the points made in the Great Debate and pointing towards a reconstruction of education (DES, 1977a). Indeed, there was little new in *Education in Schools: A Consultative Document*. It was essentially a restatement and extension of the Great Debate, but focused partly on parental involvement and educational efficiency. It pointed to Labour's concern with both the need to ensure the accountability and efficacy of the education system and the satisfaction of parents. Parents were mentioned in the introduction, where it was argued that 'parents should be given much more information about schools and should be consulted more widely' but discussion was deferred until the publication of the Taylor Committee's findings. But, in the body of the Green Paper, special attention was given to parents. It was stated (ibid., p. 28) that:

> The group most deeply involved with the school must always be the parents . . . *Parents* – and the pupils themselves – *have a right to know* how well the pupils are doing in different parts of their school work, and to have information on their conduct, attendance and application. Parents for their part *should have the opportunity to comment* on how their children are developing and to make any observations they wish about the school . . . There is also a *place* in the system for *parents collectively* [my italics].

In fact, Labour never acted upon two of these three principles. The 'right to know' was embodied in a circular, and subsequently in the ill-fated Bill; 'the opportunity to comment' was not elaborated; 'a place . . . collectively' was put into the Bill, if by that was meant parent representation on governing bodies, but this was never clarified.

Much of this was left in abeyance pending the publication of the Committee of Inquiry report on governors and managers (DES and Welsh Office, 1977). Several discussion papers and circulars later and over a year after the Green Paper, in the autumn of 1978, the government finally drafted a Bill which would give some substance to the debate and to the Committee of Inquiry's proposals. By now the country was definitely in a period of severe economic retrenchment, and the Bill did not envisage any extensions to education. Moreover, the debate over control had been something of a 'charade' – parents were vouchsafed little more than a nominal say, and only as individuals. No new mechanisms were devised to allow for the collective representation of parents. The Bill never reached the statute-books.

Involving parents in the control of education

The Committee of Inquiry, chaired by Taylor, which dealt with the question of how individual schools should be governed, was formed before the Great Debate was set in motion: in the spring of 1975. In one sense it had a narrow remit – to consider the management and government of maintained primary and secondary schools. The pressure for such a consideration had been steadily mounting from the 1960s onwards, when participation had been a key political slogan for the left, especially for those who felt excluded from traditional political discourse (David, 1975; 1978a and b). The main pressure – to ensure more adequate representation in the running of schools – was somewhat divided between the demand for more parental involvement and that of making schools more relevant to the needs of the community and the labour force in particular. Among the specific grievances to be considered was the fact that local government reorganization had distanced schools from their main locus of control, the LEA. In that process both teachers and educational professionals had been given less say, along with the community of which the school was a part. Middle-class parents, and mothers in particular, wanted to express their concern for the direction of school policy as well as for their individual rights over their own children. The economic crisis had exacerbated parental concern for individual children's success, especially in a rapidly shrinking labour market, and non-working middle-class mothers were more available to articulate their worries.

The Taylor Committee had been set up to solve the conflicting problems of lay, parental and professional control over aspects of education. By 1975, the demands for some new organization of school management could not easily be ignored. The terms of reference of the Taylor Committee were therefore not as narrow as they appeared to be, for it had to consider the relationship between the community, the LEA, teachers and parents. Nevertheless, it was not given any power to consider a changed form of LEA control. Moreover, the selection of the twenty-four members of the Committee demonstrated that the government expected a report which balanced the demands for involvement of a number of competing and conflicting groups and interests. Three mothers were appointed as the parent members, all of them professional, middle-class women.

(It is significant that no fathers were chosen to represent parents *per se.*) Five teachers were appointed, three of whom were headteachers and one a deputy. Only one was a classroom teacher.

The report which ensued from the Committee's two years of deliberation was balanced (DES and Welsh Office, 1977). It covered specifically the composition and functions of governing bodies. The majority of the Committee wished to stick closely to its remit and *reform* rather than retain (or, more dramatically, replace or rescind) the existing system of managing and governing bodies. One member of the Committee opposed the proposals and wrote a separate, brief, minority report. Other members added what they termed 'a note of extension' in which they argued for a clearer definition of parental rights.

The main theme was that there should be 'a clear line of delegated power running from the LEA through the governing body to the head and staff of the school'. Every school required a body to manage its own affairs. Because of past confusion over titles and types of organization, the Committee proposed one kind of body, with one distinctive name – governing body. The composition and functions of the body were also clearly designated.

The Committee was faithful to its terms of reference on composition. The four sets of people mentioned in the terms of reference were to make up the governing body. These were representatives of LEAs, the local community, *parents* and teachers. In defining how these groups should compose the governing body, the Committee relied on the practice of one LEA whose chief education officer happened to be a member of the Committee. The novel proposal was that there should be equal proportions of each group on the governing body. This is what Taylor himself subsequently called 'power sharing'. The Committee did not consider the different proportions or balances of each group within the educational process. It assumed that each group should be given equal weight in decision-making.

The Committee did, however, consider that each group was not homogeneous and was difficult to define. First, it believed that parents were to be represented on the governing body as proxies for their own children, who were the actual consumers of education. The age at which children could make their own judgments about their educational fare exercised the Committee. The DES tried to block the idea that children should participate in the governing body by arguing, in its evidence, that the question was not valid: children were not entitled to hold public office until they reached eighteen years, the legal age of majority. Schoolchildren would have to be excluded from the governing body. The Committee was not content with this advice and proposed that pupils over the age of sixteen should either be able to serve as governors, if the law could easily be changed, or, failing that, be observers. If children over sixteen became governors, they would replace some parental representatives.

The Committee suggested ways in which the representatives of the four groups might be selected for the governing body. Two sets were to be elected on a regular basis from, respectively, the current body of parents and teaching staff in the school. Pupils and ancillary staff, where needed, would be chosen in the same way, but only in large schools. The LEA and community representatives would be appointed. The method for appointing LEA representatives was not to be changed from existing practice.

In the process of clarifying the work of governing bodies, the Committee tried to modify the existing power relationships. In particular, it sought to delegate from LEAs to governing bodies some of the responsibility for teacher appointments, admissions policy, pupil treatment and some financial control, especially over buildings. The change in power here was to be slight. The Committee wanted the governing body to be consulted but not to have the power of ultimate decision. What Fulton, the dissenter, regarded as the essential object of existing policy, 'a restoration of confidence in our schools by parents and the community', could be achieved only if the following aims were fulfilled (ibid., p. 126):

> Firstly, that there is a good return on the massive investment in education. Secondly, that the people in the education service are competent to identify and provide for the needs of children to fit them for life after school. Thirdly, that the schools can be made more accountable.

None of these goals, according to Fulton, would be achieved by the insertion of this tier of government. He therefore did not want any change in power relationships. Parents' interests were, for him, not about control but (ibid., p. 128) 'very much more immediate and personal and it all boils down to how the school affects their child.'

The seven members who wrote a note of extension would concur with this last point. Their aim was to give individual parents more information about each school. To this end, they asked (ibid., p. 121) that there be a further change in the law to give 'each individual parent the right in law to the information relevant to the performance of his legal duty'. They added that this access to information should not be construed as 'access to classrooms, teachers or written material except in accordance with the arrangements made by the school and approved by the governors'. They also did not want a further change in power relationships but merely that the schools be more explicitly accountable, especially to parents.

In fact, the Taylor Committee did not establish the case for parental involvement in the control of schools. It argued that the 'consumer' had a right to have a say but this did not necessarily mean that the 'consumer' should work alongside the 'producer' – the LEA and its teachers – in the running of schools. The Committee did not consider that it might be inappropriate to combine these groups into a single body to run the schools. It might be more appropriate to create two bodies to give advice to the LEAs, who are ultimately legally responsible one composed of teachers (an academic board) and one of consumers, who would be able to act merely as a sounding-board of parental feeling. It was another Taylor (1972) who originally sounded the first warning note on joint bodies. In addition, the case was not made convincingly that parents were the legitimate consumers. Indeed, the Committee did argue, confusingly, that so too were pupils and the local community, composed variously of employers, industrialists and trade unionists. The Committee did not establish the relative claims of parents and the community over the lives of the pupils in schools. If anything, it confused the previous, relatively clear view that children in the State sector of education were, for educational purposes, more the property of the State than of their parents.

However, the Taylor Committee's deliberations were rather overtaken by the pace of events: and yet more strident public pressure for a clear parental role in education, linked with the demands for a clearer system of educational public accountability. Thus, whilst the government was formulating legislative action on both the Taylor Committee's recommendations and the Great Debate, it issued new regulations concerning schools' relationships with parents. Two circulars were published in late 1977. One formalized the information that schools were expected to give to both prospective and participating parents: what might be termed a prospectus. It was explicit in its concern to satisfy parents, although the draft circular of July 1977 listed items which should '*normally* be made available to parents' [my italics]. The actual circular repeated that phrase and asked LEAs to draw up twenty items of *written* information about its individual schools for public consumption. The other (circular 14/77) retreated on the likely commitment to parental participation in schools, arguing that

> the proper functioning of the educational system in England and Wales depends on the effective cooperation of the schools, their teachers and their governors and managers; the local education authorities; and the Secretaries of State with their departments and HM Inspectorate. The Secretaries of State have no intention of changing this position which reflects the provisions of the

> Education Acts. At the same time they recognise the legitimate interests of others – *parents*, industry and commerce, for example – in the work of schools [my emphasis].

However, it required LEAs to provide

> systematic information about curricular arrangements in local authority areas throughout England and Wales. This will enable the Secretaries of State to assess how far the practice of local education authorities meets national needs and will assist in the preparation of future educational plans, particularly for the training, recruitment and employment of teachers. The information collected will also be of value to their partners in the education system and to the Schools Council.

Legislative action on the policy debates and discussions was a long time in the making because of internal Cabinet disagreement over the extent of parental control and choice in secondary schooling. This was also confounded by the political objective of using education as a panacea for youth employment problems.

Labour's approach to education and the economy

As has already been argued, the Great Debate attempted to clarify and develop the relationship between education and the economy. However, the discussion here was in terms of a long-term strategy. At the same time, concern was expressed for a much more immediate problem – that of dealing with youth unemployment, in particular, the growing army of unemployed school-leavers. Initial solutions to the problem of unemployment had been based within the Department of Employment and schemes such as the Job Creation Programme had been devised. Although in some instances new jobs or created jobs might rely on the LEAs, as with other departments of the local authority, LEAs were not directly implicated in solutions. As the problem did not abate but became increasingly large, further consideration was given to it. In the first instance, the Manpower Services Commission (MSC) set up a review body to consider the parameters of the issue. The DES and representatives of the LEAs were involved in this review. The Holland Committee (Manpower Services Commission, 1977) considered the various ramifications of the problem and suggested several additions to the existing solutions of 'on-the-job' training. First, it proposed to separate two groups of young people – the sixteen- to nineteen-year-olds and those twenty and older – for whom two different programmes were to be developed. One package for the sixteen- to nineteen-year-olds would involve special job-training schemes, which could and might be conducted under the auspices of the education service, especially in colleges of further education. Those attending such courses would be entitled to a flat-rate maintenance grant from the MSC. This would also apply to the jobs created under the Youth Opportunities Programme and to those in the STEP schemes.

This proposal raised problems of equity with provisions within the education system. Different grant schemes existed for children who remained at school past the statutory school-leaving age and for those attending courses in the further education sector. However, neither the Educational Maintenance Allowance (EMA) scheme for school pupils nor the grants for further education were either automatic or at the level of subsistence. EMAs were discretionary awards and subject to a test of parental means (see ch. 4). The intention was very explicitly and well expressed by the parliamentary Expenditure Committee (1974, p. 5) which investigated EMAs in 1974:

> 16 to 18 year olds today make many more decisions about their ways of life than they once did . . . but we do not regard them as having the right of independent choice where their education is concerned any more than they enjoy, as minors, independence in the eyes of the law; nor should they look upon the E.M.A. as a substitute for wages.
>
> We are equally sure that nothing we recommend should tend to undermine the responsibility of parents for bringing up their children . . . We endorse the words of the 1944 Act: the purpose of E.M.A.s is 'to enable pupils to take advantage without hardship to themselves or their parents of any educational facilities available to them.'

In fact, the level of allowance, even without regard to parental means, varied enormously throughout the country. The same was true of awards to study in further education: both the level and the granting of the award itself varied throughout the country. Again, this award was based upon a system of partial help to enable a student to continue in education, regardless of parental means or circumstances. It was not intended that the grant would be equivalent to a living (if minimum) wage. This differed enormously from the objectives of the MSC grant, which was, in any case, never aimed at the same target group of sixteen- to eighteen-year-olds.

The DES and LEAs were willing to co-operate with the MSC and its plans to solve the youth unemployment problem, but at the same time they began to consider ways of incorporating job training into the education system and, moreover, of allowing for automatic entitlement to both courses and grant aid. Thus, the educational politicians tried to get onto the agenda a scheme of EMAs for *all* sixteen- to nineteen-year-olds who chose to stay within the education system. However, the proposed level of EMA was to be lower than the award offered by the MSC and was to be subject to a test of parental means. In other words, the scheme was a plan to increase the years of dependency on both education and parents, rather than to provide a system of early help with work. So far, the scheme has foundered on bureaucratic grounds – the conflict between the DES and the Department of Employment (DE) for resources to finance the scheme. The implications of the EMA scheme are that it would extend the powers of education, and commensurably reduce the powers of the DE. At the same time it would also increase parental influence and parental responsibilities.

Labour's attempt at educational legislation

The 1978 Education Bill, which never reached the statute-books because of the general election in May 1979, was the culmination of Labour's educational initiatives. It brought together the twin concerns of the four years of Labour administration – parental involvement in education and the links between education and the economy. The emphasis, however, was on the former rather than the latter. It did not even consider the question of equality but focused on how to achieve economic efficiency. The Bill related to three issues of parental involvement: school government, school admissions and school attendance. As regards education and the economy it only sought to legislate for EMAs for sixteen- to nineteen-year-olds and, initially, only on the basis of a pilot scheme. The details of the proposed legislation were as follows. The clauses on school government took up the Taylor Committee's proposals in a modified fashion. They only related to the composition and type of governors. They did not concern the functions or the workings of governing bodies. In respect of composition, the Bill proposed that each governing body (and this was to become the generic term for such bodies for primary and secondary schools) would include representatives of the LEA, teachers and parents. The LEA representatives were to be appointed by the LEA (in the traditional manner), the teacher representatives to be elected by the teachers in the school and the parents to be elected by the parents of children currently in the school. Four other *types* of governor were also mentioned: representatives of the voluntary foundation if that were the kind of school; representatives of the minor authority for a primary school if it existed in such a situation; for secondary schools only, appointed members of the community; and the fourth type was a major official concession – the possibility of pupil governors, but only of those pupils aged sixteen or over. The Bill stressed that the future usual practice would be for *every* school to have its own governing body but LEAs could apply to the Secretary of State for Education for special dispensation to group governing bodies. The clauses on school government therefore showed a major shift in Labour principles towards the sharing of school control with teachers and parents. The most important change was the incorporation of parent representatives into school government. This was at least an indication of how Labour had reneged on the principle of equality of educational opportunity, in that they now allowed some parental voice in decisions about education. However, traditional governors have had few real controlling powers and have acted rather as a system of support for the school and a mediator between school and LEA. Since the functions of governors were not to change it may be that the Labour government regarded the inclusion of parents as a concession to the growing parental lobby and more as a symbol than a real sharing of power.

The other main parental issue included in this proposed piece of legislation was over the admission of pupils to particular schools. As regards secondary schools, the Tories have always made much political capital out of whether sufficient parental 'choice' is provided, especially in a system of comprehensive schooling. Under the existing legislation (the 1944 Education Act), schools – either primary or secondary – were to be provided in accordance with parental 'wishes', and yet with regard to the principle of 'the avoidance of unreasonable public expenditure'. It was this latter, more general issue that the Labour government sought to clarify in the proposed legislation, rather than the more specific question of the distribution of particular kinds of secondary school. The Bill suggested new terminology – parental 'wishes' were to be replaced by parental 'preferences' and 'unreasonable expenditure' became 'efficient use of financial resources' or simply 'efficient education'. To elaborate, the Bill required each school to be clearer about the numbers of pupils to be admitted each year and, crucially, how that complement should be chosen. The main new criterion of admission was to be *parental preference*, the clause expressing it as follows: 'Every LEA shall make arrangements for enabling the *parent* of a child to *express a preference* as to the school at which *he* wishes education to be provided for his child in the exercise of the authority's functions and to give reasons for his preference' [my italics]. In essence, this clause merely restated the existing legal principle, except that, instead of parental wishes *en masse* being regarded, *each individual parent* was now to be vouchsafed a *say* in *his* child's schooling. So a new right was to be created. But, unfortunately, the rest of the legislative draft detracted from that principle. The LEAs' responsibilities to comply were hedged around with modifying conditions, which again, in essence, were the same as hitherto, namely 'the avoidance of unreasonable public expenditure'. There were to be four conditions for non-compliance:

(i) if the LEA believed the preference to be contrary to the interests of the child;

(ii) if the preference *either* prejudiced the provision of *efficient education* in the preferred school,
or prejudiced the provisions of *efficient education* in the area of the LEA,
or the preference prejudiced the *efficient use of financial* resources available to the LEA [my italics];

(iii) if the child was from outside the LEA and prejudiced one inside the LEA;

(iv) if the school operated selection of pupils according to the principles of the 1976 Education Act and the child was incompatible with them.

In other words, the LEA was afforded *discretion* to evaluate parental preferences either according to the criterion of efficiency (financial or educational) or according to the status or needs of the child. Point (ii) might be as vague as the old principle had been, but points (i), (iii) and (iv) allowed the LEA even more 'let-outs' than hitherto. However, under another sub-clause, parents were given the *right of appeal* [my emphasis] against an adverse decision on the part of the school governors or LEA, first to the LEA and ultimately to the Secretary of State for Education. And LEAs were required to ensure that parents did not express their preferences in ignorance of the schools available. LEAs were to be required to publish annual information about their own maintained schools and those schools they used which were either maintained by another LEA or were voluntary schools. This information was to be extensive – on the size limits of the school, the admissions policy and role of the governors and LEA and the circumstances under which out-county pupils would be admitted. In addition, the terms under which school attendance orders were to be issued were to be modified according to parental preference. Again, this set of clauses appeared to be creating new individual parental rights, but they were to be severely limited and restricted and in all probability would not alter the real situation drastically. The main change would be that all parents would be given a *say* over the school to which they would send their children!

The third set of clauses bearing on parental rights were somewhat more indirect, relating to financial awards and grants. The Labour government proposed, first, to introduce a *pilot scheme* to provide educational maintenance allowances (EMAs) to all sixteen- to eighteen-year-olds continuing in, or resuming, full-time education and, second, to extend the list of courses in higher education. Although no date was set for the commencement of the schemes and no details of the level of award set, both impinged upon parental rights. In particular, the introduction of EMAs purportedly allowed pupils to remain in, or resume, schooling or further education regardless of parental financial conditions. But EMAs did not provide pupils with the right to a 'wage'. They allowed each parent the right not to prevent his child from benefiting from the education system – by providing a small grant which would be varied according to parental financial means. In other words, financial hardship should no longer dissuade pupils from extending their education. Again, this parental right was neither absolute nor generous. According to the discussions prior to the drafting of the Bill, the grant would only allow parents to avoid dire pecuniary stress: it would not be large, or near subsistence level. For example, it would not compare with either the level of Supplementary Benefit for that age group or the awards provided through the Manpower Services Commission for young people undergoing courses of basic skills while technically unemployed.

The Bill was also used in an attempt to tidy up other aspects of educational legislation and here, too, it indicated a changed direction of educational aims. First, it allowed for nursery school-teachers to work in nurseries provided through the DHSS and yet remain in the education service. This enabling clause was important for the new direction of preschool provisions (a point to which I return). Second, provision was made for advanced further education to be under central direction, through the establishment of a Council for England and one for Wales. Indeed, Welsh education was to be enhanced by yet another provision, the payment of grants for courses taught in the Welsh language. This would allow for the separate development of Wales and Welsh education. Finally, the Bill reiterated the fact that the Sex Discrimination and Race Relations Acts applied to the education service, including the provisions of the Bill.

Parental rights in education: the Tory view

Thus, by 1979 the issues of concern to both Tory and Labour administrations had been brought together, if briefly, in one major Education

Bill. Although the Tories, in opposition, voiced objections to specific aspects of the Bill, its concerns were in general those that the Tories had put onto the political agenda.* They certainly were not traditional Labour objectives. In fact, the Tories, on regaining power in the general election of 1979, acted very swiftly to develop their own educational legislation, claiming it to be a reversal of all that Labour had stood for. The 1979 Education Act, passed into law in July 1979, was, as the new Secretary of State for Education, Mark Carlisle, himself argued in Parliament, 'simple in scope . . . its sole purpose is to remove the compulsion placed on local authorities and governors of voluntary schools to reorganise their schools on comprehensive lines.' It aimed to rescind the Labour Government's 1976 Education Act, which required LEAs to reorganize their secondary schools on comprehensive lines.

The arguments in the Act's favour were neither simple nor lacking in contradiction. The reason for repealing Labour measures was that they were 'solely about compulsion . . . not about the quality of education or standards . . . Parents – not politicians – should be given the opportunity to choose schools best suited to their children.' He then added:

> Above all, those areas which have fought hard to retain their grammar schools should be allowed to do so. We are not prepared to stand by and allow the destruction of schools which have proved their worth against the wishes of local people.

He was thus making it clear that the Act was not a charter for *all* parents but for those parents whose children proved academically able to attend grammar schools – traditionally, 20 per cent at most of the relevant age group. Moreover, those LEAs who chose to 'go comprehensive' would not be afforded the same 'freedom of choice' as those reintroducing selection at eleven: curiously (given the principle of parental choice), their plans would have to be vetted both by politicians *and* at central government level, i.e., by the Secretary of State for Education. In addition, however, he said that he would introduce another Bill, 'in which choice of parents and the needs of their children will be a central feature.' The contents of this Bill were to be revealed at the end of October 1979, and were likely, save for the question of comprehensive schools, to mirror those of the Labour Bill. For a new government the issue of parental rights in

*Since this was written, the new Tory administration has reintroduced this Bill in only a slightly modified form. The wording of the majority of clauses remains identical to the Labour Bill.

education had at least a prompt preliminary resolution.

Although the Tories here appear to be *the* advocates of parental rights, this was not the complete picture. The Labour government, while in office from 1974 to 1979, also did much to legislate for parental rights in education. It, too, was sectarian in its choice of which parents to favour, while, like the Tories in political rhetoric appearing to favour *all* parents. Labour's policies were a good deal more extensive although ultimately not so legally effective. At least five policy prescriptions, at different levels of legislative effect, had had a bearing on the issue.

The context for educational revision

What was the context in which these new policy objectives developed? At the beginning of the 1970s, public discussion, as expressed in the media, was focused upon the question of educational direction and educational standards. These topics were raised not by politicians of either political party but by intellectuals and academics outside the traditional political arena. In a series of pamphlets, of which the first two appeared in 1969, they argued that standards in school were falling: there was increased violence, truancy and indiscipline and progressive methods were the root cause of the problems. Why the pamphlets, called Black Papers, should have received so much media attention is a question that is still being asked and still requires an adequate answer. One set of explanations is to be found in Adam Hopkins' *The School Debate* (1978). He argued that, first, according to Cox, one of the main pamphleteers, many teachers 'secretly, almost guiltily . . . knew that informal methods were not working' (ibid., p. 85). The implication was that they supported the fears about educational decline expressed in the pamphlets. Second, the articles in the pamphlets were written by entertaining writers. Third, their alarmist facts and figures attracted much attention and enabled people's positions to be polarized into traditional or progressive. The fourth, and most important, reason was that the then Secretary of State for Education, Edward Short, a former Headmaster, allowed the first Black Paper to become 'an educational best-seller' by stating to the NUT that its publication day was 'one of the blackest days for education in the past one hundred years' and that the backlash against progressive education had created 'the crisis of the century'. Nigel Wright in *Progress in Education*, although reviewing the evidence of the Black Papers, did not attempt to explain why that evidence, which he claimed 'reveals a staggering number of errors, inaccuracies and misrepresentations' (1977, p. 140), became the talking point of the decade.

Other explanations for the popularity of the ideas and their later political acceptance may be found in the changing economic climate. From the Second World War on, there had been a steady improvement in living standards and changes in the composition of the labour force. In particular, the service sector of the economy began to expand and jobs became increasingly available. Women, and especially married women, began to be employed in the organized labour force in increasing numbers. By the early 1970s, however, this trend to improvement was slowing down and an economic crisis was beginning to be felt: jobs were scarcer and the unemployment rate rose dramatically throughout the 1970s. A concomitance of the rising standards of living in the 1950s and 1960s was rising expectations and aspirations, generated through increased educational opportunities. By the end of the 1960s it was clear that not everyone's aspirations would be fulfilled. Many of the aspirations were for parents to provide equivalent educational opportunities for their children. The frustrations of potentially blocked aspirations began to find political expression in the field of education – and this may go some way to explaining the popularity of the Black Paper critique, confused though it was.

The discussion of declining standards and the consequences of progressivism in education was certainly not an isolated incident in the early 1970s. The Black Papers sparked off a considerable backlash of criticism of the educational *status quo*. Two other major events illustrate the impact that such ideas were beginning to have in educational politics. One was the fight, with the Inner London Education Authority (ILEA), at the William Tyndale Junior School. The other was the controversy over comprehensive schooling in the Tameside LEA. Both events were about standards, direction and also control in education, and both took as a basic assumption parental involvement in schooling. Indeed, both events and the Black Paper controversies illustrated the increasing parental lobby in educational politics: but this lobby was not one of all parents, merely some middle-class parents. The events at the William Tyndale Junior School have been well researched elsewhere (see Auld, 1976; Ellis *et al.*, 1976; Gretton and Jackson 1976). The remarkable point, which has not been very well documented elsewhere, was that the fight over standards, progressivism and indiscipline was initiated not by officials or school managers but by *parents* and most especially mothers, concerned solely about their own children's schooling. I have discussed this issue at length (see David, 1978a). It signalled a new, and what was now considered legitimate, involvement of mothers in the running of schools. Hitherto, as Baron and Howell showed (1974), parents were not even regularly given a say on governing or managing bodies. The parents of some children at the William Tyndale school not only were able, without the traditional political means or channels, to raise the issue to hysterical proportions but got a public inquiry and, far more important, had the teachers sacked for indiscipline. (Of course, the mothers were initially fighting about pupil rather than teacher indiscipline.) The dispute brought together two of the three major concerns of the 1970s – standards and control. It also, as Roger Dale (1979a, p. 1) has argued, 'was not the cause but merely the occasion of the major changes in the English education system – the current restructuring and redirection.' Indeed, it was around the time of the setting up of the public inquiry into the William Tyndale dispute (Auld, 1976) that the Taylor Committee was established. The 'Yellow Paper' on standards was leaked to the press at the same time as the Auld Report was published. Both government initiatives were justified in terms of wishing to respond to the educational crisis provoked and to prevent further Tyndale-like problems. Taylor himself claimed that, with his proposals, 'another Tyndale situation could not arise.'

The first Tameside incident (the second is discussed in ch. 9) was also an escalation of the issues raised in the Black Papers. This event, too, has been discussed fully in other literature (Griffith, 1976 and 1977). The Tory councillors' reversal in 1976 of local Labour policies to achieve comprehensive education in the Tameside LEA was both a reaction to the restructuring of education and a reinforcement of the increasingly overt Tory policy of supporting parental involvement in education. The opposition to comprehensive education was justified on the grounds that parents would be denied freedom of choice in education. In this incident, as in all similar anti-comprehensive schooling cases, and as Nigel Wright has so eloquently argued, the concern was never with all parents, or, for that matter, all children. It was to preserve parental choice for, at most, 20 per cent of parents of eleven-year-olds in the LEA. Wright has stated (1977, p. 83), 'the paradox of this [Tameside] exercise in freedom of parental choice was that 560 families had their choice rejected, while 240 were accepted.' He added in criticism of the general Tory position about problems created by comprehensive schools 'to disappoint 5% is better than to disappoint 70%, but have we the right to disappoint any parent?' In fact, he argued that the figures of disappointment in Tameside were an underestimate since, first, only 800 parents applied for grammar school places and, second, 'all the researches indicated that a majority of parents would have liked their child to go to a grammar school – not surprisingly.' In a footnote, he cited a *New Society* survey of 1967, which 'found that only 10% of parents would choose a secondary modern school for their child.' So, presumably, even those parents in Tameside who did not apply for a grammar school place were to some extent disappointed: hardly an indication of parental choice and satisfaction with a bipartite system of education. Nevertheless, the issue raised in the media was Labour's dogmatism and Tory fairness with regard to educational provision. Comprehensive schools were attacked, of course, not only because they prohibited parental choice but also because they perpetrated a decline in standards and indiscipline. The comparison was always between grammar schools and comprehensives and not between comprehensives and secondary modern schools. In fact, as Wright has convincingly demonstrated, comprehensive schools, for all their faults, have not contributed to a decline in standards; nor, of course, have they been any more than marginally the reason for the improvement in standards (measured by examination results) that has occurred in the last two decades.

The resolution of the Tameside dispute in the courts in August 1976, in favour of the Tories, provided an occasion for Labour response. Indeed, the Secretary of State for Education was replaced in the summer of 1976, perhaps as a result of the government's defeat, and the Yellow Paper was leaked to the press shortly after the House of Lords pronounced on the Tameside appeal.

The other underlying contextual factor throughout the 1970s was the rapidly escalating economic crisis which created rising unemployment. As the decade wore on, unemployment became more and more concentrated amongst one sector of the population – school-leavers, especially (but not only) those leaving at the statutory age of sixteen. This required a government response! The first sets of responses were in terms of cutbacks in public expenditure, particularly spending on education. These cuts inevitably provoked a massive and angry response especially in terms of local campaigns but no reduction in impact was planned by the government. It was only later in the decade that the response was positive and in terms of a restructuring and redirection of educational provision (discussed above).

Although the decade was characterized by unemployment, women's employment prospects did not fare as badly as men's, mainly because of the rigid sexual division of labour in the economy. In other words, women's jobs did not suffer the same vagaries of the economy. The main beneficiaries were mothers of school-age, but also of preschool, children. This change had an important impact on maternal or parental exercise of responsibilities, but there was no government initiative to modify maternal responsibilities. Indeed, working mothers were accused by the right-wing protesters of being responsible for the indiscipline in schools, because of their neglect of their children (see, for example, a circular sent to all parents in Avon in 1977 (County of Avon, 1977)).

Working mothers began to organize, demanding changes in the daily organization of schooling and in the nature of preschool provision. The impact of this movement was manifold: between 1976 and 1978 there was a flood of official documents suggesting changes in preschool provision and the hours of schooling. However, most of the discussion went on outside the formal system of education. The DHSS was, in fact, the first body to respond officially to the demands for day-care and government involvement in preschool provision. Its response was tempered – a preliminary survey (Office of Population Censuses and Surveys, 1977) and a conference to discuss 'low-cost day-care' in 1975. Out of this conference came some minimal DHSS and DES co-operation and a joint circular to local authorities recommending local co-operation between education and social services and with voluntary organizations. No money was proffered to make co-operation viable: the emphasis was placed on involvement of the voluntary sector. This initiative prompted more official proposals for extending preschool provision, but all these official reports were from only quasi-governmental organizations and as yet (1979) have had little impact on policy change. The TUC set up a working party to consider provision for the under-fives from the point of view of working mothers. It came up with some imaginative and important suggestions, such as work-based, government-sponsored facilities and local authority-employed child-minders. There has been no public debate about the proposals. The government's think-tank – the Central Policy Review Staff (CPRS) – also considered the question of day-care for the children of working mothers. It recommended, above all, greater co-ordination and information exchange between government departments, especially the DHSS and DES. The Equal Opportunities Commission (EOC), established in 1976 as a result of the Sex Discrimination Act of 1975, also considered the issue of day-care. First, it set up an investigation into the running of ten existing nurseries with a variety of controls. The report showed the feasibility of several different types of scheme. Second, the EOC published in autumn 1978 a small, vibrant pamphlet entitled, *I Want to Work, but What about the Kids?* (EOC, 1978b). These recommendations went further than the others in linking preschool provision with after-school and holiday facilities. The report recognized the necessity of continuity in child-care responsibilities from preschool to school days. It highlighted the problems that ensue from school activities which affect mothers' involvement in the labour force, especially full-time work.

Although there has been a slow but steady build-up of recognition of the lacunae in day-care facilities, there has been little official development or response. The only minor step, from the point of view of the education service, was the legal recognition of the relationship between nurseries and nursery schools. A brief clause was inserted in the 1978 Education Bill to ensure that nursery-school teachers working in LA social services nurseries would not suffer any loss of status and would remain employees of LEAs (and therefore on teaching salary scales, which were higher than those for nursery nurses).

The traditional arrangements for schooling – hours of the day and school holidays – were not considered for amendment by the government despite demands to alter the nature of maternal responsibilities for schooling. On the contrary, as the economic crisis deepened, mothers' daily responsibilities for ensuring their children's schooling increased in a variety of ways. For example, working mothers were under attack for some of the problems of the educational system. Some LEAs actually formalized this attack. For instance, Avon LEA developed a 'contract' with parents to ensure that school problems would be reduced. There was an implicit assumption of constant maternal availability. Second, during strike action by low-paid workers such as school caretakers, which closed schools for days and weeks, mothers were forced to take as their first priority looking after their children. They were therefore unable to continue their employment satisfactorily.

Third, some official responses to the problems of schooling have been to increase daily maternal responsibility rather than to modify the education system around the needs of working mothers. For example, the original schemes for the extension of nursery education in the early 1970s, embodied in circular 2/73, recommended parental participation as a key to the success of preschool education. This was based on the research findings that the 'home' was a more important influence on learning than the school. It was also assumed that mothers could be taught, through helping with their children at school, better standards of child-care. This direct involvement of mothers in the classroom has also begun to occur increasingly in primary schools, too.

As the 1970s began to draw to a close, educational debate moved into a further mood of pessimism. This was occasioned by the accumulation of startling demographic evidence of a rapid decline in the future numbers of schoolchildren, with the effects already being felt in some regions and some schools in the country (Mack, 1979). Instead of this being an occasion for the introduction of new educational schemes such as the extension of preschool facilities in the emptying primary schools, the development of community facilities in school buildings or a move towards recurrent rather than rigid education, it has been characterized by a traditionalist mood. This was summed up in February 1979 by the head of one comprehensive school arguing informally about 'how to save our curriculum, how to save our teachers and how to save our head-teachers'. In sum, the 1970s have been notable for moves to reinforce the notion that children are the private property of their parents and yet of utilitarian value to the wider society.

It is still necessary to ask why Labour acceded to the right-wing pressures and went so far as to modify legislation to create new, individualistic parental rights. It must be pointed out that Labour, whatever its political rhetoric, has never been unequivocally the party of the working class or one espousing the principle of equality. Indeed, as was most cogently pointed out by Finn *et al.* (1977), there has been since the 1920s a duality in Labour ideology between efficiency and equality. For this reason Labour has always had an uneasy relationship with the working class and, in the field of education, with teachers. In previous decades, but especially in the 1960s, the path steered between these two poles has always been uneven. In the 1960s the party veered towards the goal of efficiency rather than that of equality (see ch. 4). Labour educational policies in the 1970s may be seen as an extension, and reassertion, of the efficiency principle. Parents have been given the semblance of rights in the 1970s, not for their own sakes but because it was felt that they would then, in their own interests, encourage the development of improved educational standards and would help to lift the economy out of the recession. In other words, parents were to help reform the education system by pressing for better school standards. This, Labour believed, would contribute to stemming the economic recession. Attempting to legislate for parental rights in education was not without reason and was not blind reassertion of right-wing political ideas. It was because Labour believed that the involvement of parents in their own children's schooling would provide the solution to the economic crises of the past decade. In effect, parents were to be made individually responsible for the future of both their children and the economy. The State would be absolved from the full responsibility of the fiscal crises. So, by the end of the 1970s, ensuring the efficiency of the education system and the economy became both a parental right and a maternal duty.

9

Sex discrimination in teaching and the curriculum?

The structure of the teaching profession and the curriculum were both under frequent consideration throughout the 1970s. There were two tendencies that concerned the supply of teachers, the consequences of which affected the status of women within the profession. The curriculum discussions also focused upon the relationship between boys and girls, particularly as adults, but within the context of a concern for the general relationship between education and the wider society, especially the economy. In both areas, the pressure was towards a more rigid specification of the nature of the activity – in teaching towards the creation of a graduate profession and in the curriculum towards the designation of 'core' or 'basic' elements – and yet, at the same time, with a concern for the needs of the child. Curiously, and yet coincidentally, the decade culminated with the International Year of the Child in 1979.

The Tories and teacher training

The 1970s opened with a Tory government which was not overly committed to the cause of education. As we have seen (ch. 8), its main interest was in questions of the application of management (of the economy) to education. New structures were developed in government to provide a more efficient infrastructure for policy-making. These ideas were extended, subsequently, to aspects of the social services and, in particular, the education service. At that time, it was believed that there was a superabundance of teachers, especially as the birth rate, projected for secondary school places, did not match potential teacher supply. The training of teachers, which had hitherto been closely linked to the issue of supply, was called into question (see ch. 7). The Secretary of State for Education therefore established a departmental Committee of Enquiry into the nature of 'teacher education and training'. Its terms of reference were (DES, 1972c, p. iii):

> to enquire into the present arrangements for the education, training and probation of teachers in England and Wales and in particular to examine:
> (i) what should be the content and organisation of courses to be provided;
> (ii) whether a larger proportion of intending teachers should be educated with students who have not chosen their careers or chosen other careers;
> (iii) what, in the context of (i) and (ii) above, should be the role of the maintained and voluntary colleges of education, the polytechnics and other further education institutions maintained by LEAs and the universities and to make recommendations.

The terms of reference themselves signified a change in the government's attitude towards teachers and their training. What was particularly important here was paragraph (ii), which implied that teaching might no longer require specialist and separate training. Teaching was now clearly regarded as a professional career and not merely a job, thus improving its status. The suggestion, however, that it might be seen only to require training along with other careers, as implied by the link with paragraph (iii), also implied dramatic changes in the characteristics of teacher training and hence the profession itself. Since men predominated in courses in polytechnics, further education and the universities (EOC, 1978a, pp. 63–7), the possibility that female predominance in teaching would be reduced was on the political agenda. At that time, too, this might have been seen as one of several ways of reducing potential teacher supply – by making other careers more attractive.

The Committee was set up and appointments made promptly at the beginning of 1971. Lord James (1973, p. 54) has stated that:

> It was unusual in 3 ways. It was small in number – 7 members with one assessor: all but 2 of its members were seconded from their posts to give full-time service; finally it was made clear that the committee should report as quickly as possible.

The hope was expressed that it would report within the year. In this case, the expectation of an early completion was fulfilled. The Report was completed by December 1971.

The recommendations followed the implications of the terms of reference. In particular, the Committee argued that teaching should become a graduate profession and that teacher education should be reorganized accordingly. This view was guided by one of the two principles underpinning the report (James, 1973, p. 7):

> The proposals should reflect and help to enhance the status and independence of the teaching profession and of the institutions in which many teachers are educated and trained. For too long the teaching profession has been denied a proper degree of responsibility for its own professional affairs. For too long the colleges of education have been treated as junior partners in the system of higher education. It is hoped that the implementation of this report would do much to encourage both the profession and the colleges to move forward to a new degree of independence and self-determination.

This, then, was an attempt to make a hundred-year-old aim of teachers become a reality. The specific way to achieve such status was that teacher education should be reorganized into three separate stages, or what the James Committee chose to call 'cycles' so as not to imply any degree of hierarchy between stages (DES, 1972c, p. 107), viz. 'the first, personal education, the second, pre-service training and induction, the third, in-service education and training'. The first stage was no longer to be linked directly with the teaching profession, or rather with training. Instead, students were to be provided, in colleges of education or polytechnics, with a broad general education over *two* years, at the end of which they would qualify for a Diploma in Higher Education. Such courses could be extended to a third year, to enable students to earn a degree. Even here, the courses were to be of a general nature.

Training for teaching would begin only in the second 'cycle' and be continued throughout the third 'cycle'. The second cycle, also made up basically of a two-year 'course', would provide students after the first year with a licence to teach and after the second year (which would be spent in teaching) with a teaching qualification, viz. B.A. (Ed.). The third cycle would also provide forms of training for teachers – those in post – on the basis of 'sabbatical' courses, and the result of certain courses would be the award of a degree, B.Ed. This was deemed, by the Committee, to be one of its most important recommendations.

The James Report proposed numerous organizational changes to the institutions involved in teacher training. The colleges of education, especially, would be transformed and become a more integrated part of the higher education system, providing general as well as specialist courses and awarding degrees. Equally, polytechnics, colleges of further education and universities were to be involved in the provision of courses for intending and incumbent teachers and the system of ratification of courses was to be organized under a new umbrella, rather than the Area Training Organisation – regional joint committees, independent of the universities.

Although women then constituted more than two-thirds of the teaching profession, this was nowhere noted in the Report. (Indeed, neither 'women' nor 'sex' was listed as a category in the index.) Yet the implications of the recommendations appeared to be that teaching, although requiring graduate qualifications, would move away from its narrow training emphasis. The attempt was to rid teaching of its low status. This in part had been attributed to its high female complement. By making courses of initial education and training longer – from three to four years – there was a distinct possibility that women would be less attracted to the profession. In addition, the proportion of women to men graduates had traditionally been very low; to make teaching an all-graduate profession would very likely, therefore, move it away from women and more towards men.

The only concession that the Report made towards the problematic position of women in the profession was with regard to re-entrants and their needs for 'in-service' training in the third cycle. The Report argued (DES, 1972c, pp. 8–9):

> More substantial problems are involved in the induction into the profession of re-entrants, perhaps after an absence of several years. Re-entrants of this kind should have a high claim on in-service training facilities – preferably before, or very soon after, their return to teaching. The largest group of re-entrants consists of *married women*, whose absence to have children of their own has left them out of practice and out of touch with developments in curriculum and method. A period of part-time teaching can do a great deal to help such teachers and part-time re-training, side by side with part-time experience can be at least as valuable as, and often more convenient than, full-time secondment to training courses [my italics].

Unlike the McNair Report (see ch. 7), this Report did not accept that looking after children at home constituted valuable experience for teaching, especially of young children. Such women returners would therefore have to be eased into the profession gently, through part-time teaching and part-time retraining. It seemed clear from this kind of statement that teacher supply was no longer to be viewed as a problem and few incentives were to be offered to married women to remain in, or return to, teaching.

Unusually for a Committee of Enquiry Report, these recommendations were incorporated, albeit in very modified form, into the package of educational proposals that the Tory government put forward only a year later, at the end of 1972. However, they were rather changed, not at all expansionary, although the title of the White Paper in which they were included had a visionary title: *Education: A Framework for Expansion* (DES, 1972a). The government did not accept the extension of educational training to two cycles of two years. It preferred to opt for a three-year course, providing a degree at the end and retaining the probationary first year of teaching in that form, but with rather more of an in-service training component. To this end, it proposed pilot schemes in four LEAs to test the efficacy of the proposals, since it assumed that they would require substantial numbers of additional teachers and extra resources. It was forecast that, by 1981, 20,000 more teachers would be needed, costing annually £55 million at 1972 prices. Although 'the Government [had] no truck with the consecutive course, nor with the two-plus-two pattern' (*Education*, 1972, p. ii), it did accept a modified version of the Dip. H.E., 'with a wider purpose', suitable for students not intending to teach. In addition, however, the existing certificate courses at colleges of education were to be retained, as were postgraduate training courses but these were a subtle change of emphasis (DES, 1972a): 'As competition for places increases, the training institutions should give preference to applicants who have followed a broad rather than a specialized undergraduate course.' This was meant to cover sandwich courses.

The government also rejected the proposal to abolish the ATOs and create new bodies independent of the universities. Rather it proposed modified ATOs on a regional basis, with academic validation of courses remaining the responsibility of universities, polytechnics, colleges of education *and* the CNAA. Nevertheless, an advisory committee to comment on both the supply and training of teachers was to be set up, rather than the teaching council proposed by the James Committee.

The net effect of the Tory proposals was to reduce the independence and potentially enhanced professional status of teaching, as specified by the James Report. Teacher education (and hence the teaching profession) was to remain controlled from without rather than within. Teacher education, although somewhat widened, was to remain separate from other forms of academic education and therefore the possibility of male dilution was lessened.

The government's White Paper plans did not go ahead without

further modification. The White Paper was written in an apparent mood of expansion and this could not easily be sustained. The economic recession began to bite more severely in 1973. By the summer, all hopes of expansion had faded. The first signs of contraction in education, as was habitual, took place within teaching itself. In July 1973 the government's *Report on Education* (DES, 1973) put forward its justification for beginning to contract the teaching profession. The argument was not couched in terms of an economic rationale but used demographic reasons. The factors giving rise to the need for a reduction in teacher supply were given as, first, a lower birth rate (p. 2: 'it seems almost certain that the trend in the number of births will lead to any revisions of the prospective pupil numbers in 1981 being downwards'), second, already established satisfactory pupil/teacher ratios,* third, a lower wastage rate of teachers leaving the profession than hitherto (ibid., p. 3):

> The wastage rates of several important categories of teachers have been tending to decline, a factor which has contributed to the buoyancy of teacher supply in the last two or three years. Wastage is not uniform. It tends to be higher for young teachers than for middle-aged ones, for women and for graduates.

This latter factor was apparently accepted without undue concern that the balance between men and women teachers might be altered. Furthermore, the specific proposals for achieving a reduced supply of teachers by 1981 were to further modify that ratio, at least implicitly. The emphasis was placed on attracting more graduates to teaching. The Secretary of State told the House of Commons, '. . . the proportion of one-year trained graduates in the whole teaching force would increase from about 14% to about 21% – a substantial increase – between 1971 and 1981. This is part of the qualitative improvement in the teaching force.' In order, therefore, to achieve this changed balance *and* reduction in numbers, the DES proposed to reduce drastically (but phased over several years) the numbers of entrants to colleges of education. However, the reduction was to be more sharp in some categories than others, since the colleges were then instructed to maintain their existing level of recruitment to nursery and infant training. Since this was traditionally a female teaching preserve, female recruitment to teaching was not to be heavily reduced. The reduction in teacher supply, begun in 1973, continued apace. Labour, returning to office early in

*Although, of course, this was not based upon any profound evidence about appropriate ratios for academic or emotional satisfaction, but merely on acceptance of the tenet that smaller classes are inevitably better than larger (for a discussion of the complexities of these issues, see David, 1976).

1974, was even more drastic to education as a whole (a point to which I return below) and to teaching in particular. In 1975 a plan to 'rationalize' teacher training – to close the majority of colleges of education and to amalgamate the rest with either the polytechnics or each other or colleges of further education, creating in the latter cases colleges of higher education – was put in train. Although teacher education would now be more integrated with other forms of academic education, as envisaged by the James Report, this change was to be on totally different lines: parsimony rather than improvements in teacher education was the order of the day.

Tory notions of teacher effectiveness

The Tory administration of 1970–74 was far more concerned about the role of teacher education and training than the position of the teacher in the classroom and in relation to the wider education system. However, as a result of pressure from groups such as the Black Paper authors about teacher effectiveness and accountability, the Tory government set up an inquiry into one aspect of the problem, reading and language standards in school (see ch. 8). The impetus for such an inquiry was an academic survey, carried out by the National Foundation for Educational Research, into the performance in the basic skills of 7,000 secondary schoolchildren. Its results seemed to show, as Devlin and Warnock (1977, p. 50) argued: 'that the steady progress of reading improvement maintained between 1948 and 1964 had been checked and that there were in 1971 more illiterate schoolchildren than there had been in 1964.' The terms of reference to the committee (DES Committee of Enquiry, 1975, p. 5) were set broadly as:

> To consider in relation to schools:
> (a) all aspects of teaching the use of English, including reading, writing and speech;
> (b) how present practice might be improved and the role that initial and in-service training might play;
> (c) to what extent arrangements for monitoring the general level of attainment in these skills can be introduced or improved;
> and to make recommendations.

What was significant was that the aims, as set out in (a), were wide and not confined only to the question of reading standards, that in (b), although teacher training had just been reviewed, it was to be reconsidered in the light of this issue and that in (c) management and accountability in the education system should assume an important position. This last topic was clearly in line with the government's general thinking and policy emphasis. However, the report was not received by the government that had initiated it.

Unlike the James Committee, the Bullock Committee sat for a long time, outliving the government that commissioned it by two years, and its report was not published until 1975.

The Tory government also fostered discussions that related to another aspect of teacher conditions, the issue of school-leaving examinations. These debates had begun in the 1960s and were taken forward in the early 1970s by the Schools Council, but no agreement could be reached with the universities on the specific nature of the proposals. During the Tory administration no changes in the examination system were mooted.

Finally, a Committee of Enquiry, which had been set up in February 1969 by the Labour government under the chairmanship of Sir Lionel Russell, reported in early 1973. Its terms of reference had been (DES Committee of Enquiry, 1973, p. v):

> To assess the need for and to review the provision of non-vocational adult education in England and Wales; to consider the appropriateness of existing educational, administrative and financial policies; and to make recommendations with a view to obtaining the most effective and economical deployment of available resources to enable adult education to make its proper contribution to the national system of education conceived of *as a process continuing through life* [my emphasis] .

The Committee did not recommend any changes in the organization of adult education. As the summary report in *Education* (30 March 1973, p. i) argued, it 'decided that what is needed is new spirit rather than new management.' However, it did not feel that adult education was perfectly adequate. It argued rather that three sets of needs should be met, which were not currently well dealt with. These were:

(i) Adult education, as a continuation of formal education throughout life, to cover remedial education, second-chance education and updating. Through it each individual should achieve true equality of opportunity instead of simply the chance to compete for the benefits of the education system.

(ii) Courses which relate to self-fulfilment of a personal kind, and centre on creative and artistic expression, physical or intellectual activity.

(iii) Provision which has to do with the individual's place in society

> and which helps him to contribute more fully in the life of the community, whether as voluntary worker, consumer, shop steward or local government officer.

In order to meet these needs for what has subsequently become known as recurrent or continuing education, the Russell Committee suggested some new structures, professional developments for teachers in adult education and ways of broadening courses and attracting students. Its main emphasis was on making such education more relevant and in places it envisaged closer links with industry. The Report, however, ignored the different needs of men and women. Although noting that 'the overall proportion of men to women in 1968–69 adult education was about one to three, with a much lower participation of men in the north of England as compared with the east and south-east' (ibid.) it did not attempt to explain the reasons for this discrepancy. Nor did it see this form of education as a unique avenue for women to achieve some modest form of equality of opportunity in educational provision. The recommendations were 'sex-blind' and, in fact, tended towards encouraging men, rather than women, to pursue such forms of education. The Report tried to conceive of adult education as remedial or second-chance, but this seemed to be to make up the lacunae for men rather than women. A chance to modify sex differences in educational opportunity was lost in this otherwise bold endeavour.

The Tory government did not initiate any changes in the compulsory school curriculum that would have a bearing on the sexual division of labour. In 1973 it put forward proposals in a Green Paper to combat sex discrimination in public life, goaded into this first by a Private Member's Bill and second by a Bill in the House of Lords, followed by a Select Committee, but the Tory plan was narrow and excluded educational provisions. Of course, it also excluded several other social policy areas, such as housing.

Labour's policies for teachers

During the Labour period of office, from February 1974 to April 1979 (which covered two Labour administrations), educational debate assumed a position of much greater political significance than it had under the Tories. The two issues that were constantly under review were the role of the teacher and the nature of the curriculum, both compulsory and non-compulsory aspects of it. Both were discussed in the context of the need to manage the economy more efficiently and to effect economies in public spending. Hence the concern was with how to reorganize the education system to make it more cost-effective. Neither of the issues was addressed in an expansionist frame of mind or in terms of increasing educational opportunities. Although sex differences in educational opportunities were the topic of much official concern, the orientation of the policy solutions was in terms of how to make better (i.e., more efficient) use of female labour-power. Indeed, as we have seen from the previous chapter, the whole focus was on how to tie the education system more clearly to the needs of the economy.

The first steps that the Labour government took in this area were with respect to the position of teachers, although the question of an aspect of the curriculum was addressed in the first few months of Labour office. The Secretary of State for Education rescinded, through circular 4/74, the Tory approach to secondary education and reinstated the Labour view, as enunciated in circular 10/65. The new circular was, however, merely a return to the *status quo ante* and did not state the precise nature of the curriculum to be used in the reorganized secondary schools, except that it should be on comprehensive, not selective, lines.

In June 1974 the government took an initiative in reorganizing the structure of higher education, following on from the system begun by the Tories. In circular 6/74, entitled *The Development of Higher Education in the Non-University Sector: Interim Arrangements for the Control of Advanced Courses*, two new proposals were mooted – one that the courses leading to the Diploma of Higher Education, as recommended by the James Report, be commenced and, second, that colleges of education, in which such courses were to be taught, be represented on the regional advisory councils (RACs) for further education. Thus, moves were being made to integrate teacher training into the local authority system of further and higher education, with all that that entailed for the future status of the teacher. Further to that end, the grants system for students 'attending approved courses of teacher training' was modified in September 1974, to take account of some of the reorganization. Only two months later, the Secretary of State for Education presented a much more far-reaching reorganization of the grants system to Parliament in the form of a Bill to modify the 1962 Education Act on grants for higher education. The aim of the Bill was to simplify the criteria for the award of mandatory, as opposed to discretionary, grants. In future, all courses 'comparable to first degree courses' (see circular 11/75) for students over the age of eighteen and deemed to be advanced further education would be recognized for the purposes of mandatory awards. Thus awards for university courses, courses of advanced further education, including Ordinary National Diploma (OND) and the Diploma of Higher Education and teacher training courses would be eligible for the same type of grant. What the Bill did not alter were the conditions for the grant, such as parental or spouses' contributions, residence requirements, etc. Indeed, these terms were more firmly articulated in the regulations that followed on the passage of the Act in early 1975, which constituted an amendment to the Education Act of 1962.

These changes did not finalize the new system of further and higher education. In 1975, as a result of the deepening economic recession, the government took a much tougher step to modify the system of teacher training and proposed the closure of some colleges of education and the merger of others into the colleges of further education or polytechnics. Two policy documents were produced to clarify the situation. One was a statutory instrument revising the further education regulations and the other an explanatory circular. In the latter it was stated (DES, 1975c, para. 2) that 'the new regulations reflect the policy that, outside universities, teacher education and higher and further education should be assimilated into a common system.' It added the rationale for the earlier changes to the grants system (ibid.):

> The legal foundations for this reform will be further extended by the new Awards Regulations made under the 1975 Education Act, which will provide for a common system of awards to students, including those following courses of teacher education.

In fact, although a 'common system' had been the objective of the James Committee, the Labour government's approach was rather different. The point of the new system was to *reduce* the numbers trained to be teachers and to close or merge institutions on the assumption of economies of scale. These views, of course, were not stated explicitly in the policy documents. Indeed, the one document that dealt with the financial implications of this reorganization implied that the costs could be enormous. This was the *Colleges of Education (Compensation) Regulations*, which laid out the various sets of conditions under which teachers in such colleges would be compensated for loss or change of status or job. Also what was never stated was the impact that this change would have not only on the trainers of teachers but on the pattern of recruitment to teaching qualifications, and hence to the profession. Given the reduction in the number of places, it was likely that female students, in particular those entering the system as mature students, would be penalized. The system of personal education followed by specific training, as envisaged by the James Committee, was likely to limit female prospects, since a longer than traditional course might act as a disincentive. Apparently, these issues were not considered since the paramount concern was to reduce the costs of the education system.

This concern was almost immediately made explicit with the

publication of a joint, interdepartmental circular on how to tackle the problems of inflation. Here it was argued that there was 'no scope for the improvement of educational standards and only for strict economy and planning or there would be a reduction of standards' (circular 9/75). Furthermore, it argued for a tightening of the student-teacher ratios in higher education. Thus it became clear that public economy, at least with regard to teachers, was to be the order of the day. The closures and mergers were set in train. By the end of the Labour period of office, the system of LEA higher education had been transformed.

The concern about the future of the teaching profession extended not just to future teachers but also to the characteristics of the teachers in post. This issue, which had been surfacing quietly for several years, began to assume greater proportions. One way was through the recommendations of the Bullock Committee, which was published in 1975. Another was the way in which teaching methods began to be evaluated and, in particular, became the focus of attention in the dispute at the William Tyndale Junior School in the Inner London Education Authority. The latter issue never became the subject of national official discussion but had widespread currency in the national media. As I have shown in the previous chapter (ch. 8), the main issue was about standards and control, whereas the media characterization of the dispute was that it was about teaching method. Teachers apparently had too much autonomy and exercised it, in this case, in ways which were detrimental to their pupils. The teachers at the school themselves admitted that they did not pursue traditional methods. They stated (Ellis *et al.*, 1976, p. 44) that 'the teacher, who had been the strict parent, now becomes the occasionally severe aunt or uncle.' They, too, relied on traditional systems of authority – in particular, patriarchal forms – to justify their activities. They merely became avuncular rather than paternal. The result of the dispute (which itself has been very well documented elsewhere) was that the teachers were disciplined (and ultimately sacked) for their attempts to change the approach to teaching and that the teaching profession, as a whole, would be more monitored than before. In fact, no general, national rules have emerged from the dispute. However, the general question of progressivism in teaching has been much more discussed in the media than hitherto. One very small research project at Lancaster University, which was published in 1976, 'got enormous publicity' (Wright, 1977, p. 40) because it apparently supported the view that 'old fashioned teaching is best' (ibid.). No criticisms were levelled at the report's methodology in the press, although this was criticized in the academic journals. Instead, 'it became a major political knock-about' (ibid., p. 41) in which teachers' techniques were vilified. Claims that teachers were 'to blame' for poor academic standards were frequently made in the media. As Wright argued cogently, no evidence of either teachers' inadequacies or a decline in standards was presented but the 'facts' were merely asserted. These 'facts' did create the climate for further political incursions on the organization and control of education: teachers, in particular, were implicated. Before discussing the new contours of the debate about education initiated in late 1976, it is necessary to sketch in the other issues relating to the curriculum that were mooted prior to the debate.

Curriculum control

In 1975 a number of varied moves were made by the government to exercise more control over State education and the curriculum in particular. The most important, but least discussed, was the initiative taken in the DES as a result of a report of the Select Committee on Race Relations published in 1974. This recommended that ways be developed to identify educational disadvantage and prevent its extension. In a White Paper in August 1974, entitled *Educational Disadvantage and the Educational Needs of Immigrants*, the government set out its strategy. The method that it chose was well in line with its new managerial philosophy. Three administrative units were established to check on the problem: one was to be an information centre, independent of government, to identify the scope of the problem, called the Centre for Educational Disadvantage and located in Manchester; the second was the Educational Disadvantage Unit within the DES, to detail the administrative problems; and the third, and most significant, was the Assessment of Performance Unit set up as a branch of HMIs in the DES. The terms of reference for the EDU (DES, 1974b, p. 3) were

> to serve as a focal point for consideration of matters, at all stages of education, connected with educational disadvantage and the education of immigrants; to influence the allocation of resources in the interests of immigrants and those identified, on the best currently available criteria, as suffering educational disadvantage; to develop with the APU such criteria, to establish arrangements for good practice.

The APU's task was set (ibid.) as: 'To promote the development of methods of assessing and monitoring the achievement of children at school and to seek to identify the incidence of under-achievement.' This latter unit was to develop techniques to monitor and assess pupil progress, initially to investigate performance at the individual rather than group level and to ensure that ethnic and other disadvantaged groups were not getting short shrift from the education system. From the outset, however, the APU exceeded its brief and tried to develop general techniques for testing the standards of all kinds and level of pupil. Its methods were certainly not perfected by the end of the Labour period of office. Wright (1977, p. 29) commented apropos of the issue of basic skills:

> So what have we? A dearth of evidence, certainly. One day this may be put right by the Assessment of Performance Unit (APU) currently being set up in the Department of Education and Science, though many people have their doubts.

From a totally different perspective, Devlin and Warnock (1977, p. 101) were equally sceptical of its potential effects:

> The connexion between curriculum control and testing on a national basis is of crucial importance . . . It is not enough for central or local government to monitor the system as a whole through such machinery as the Assessment of Performance Unit . . .

In fact, the APU was but one of many Labour strategies directed towards the objective of curriculum control. A second move, begun in 1975, was to tighten up the system of school examinations. A tentative measure (embodied in an administrative memorandum (5/75)) was to establish public grades for GCE 'O' level and to reiterate the relationship between CSE and GCE, namely, that CSE Grade 1 was equivalent to GCE 'O' level pass. In addition, the DES urged the Schools Council to continue its discussions on a new system and level of public school-leaving examinations. Pending a transformation, they set up, in 1976, a departmental Committee of Enquiry into the current system of examining boards, to try to rationalize the relationship between GCE and CSE. This Committee did not report until 1978.

The major public discussion of the curriculum occurred with the publication of the Bullock Committee's 609-page report *A Language for Life* (DES Committee of Enquiry, 1975), which Devlin and Warnock (1977, p. 51) characterized as 'long and, for a report on language skills, not itself very engagingly written'. The main contribution of the Report was to argue that the assessment of reading and language standards was an extremely complicated problem and not easily reducible to platitudes about decline or improvement. In addition, it was argued that there were no simple policy solutions in this complex area (ibid., p. 513):

> The solution does not lie in a few neat administrative strokes, nor in the adoption of one set of teaching methods to the exclusion of another. Improvement will come about only from a thorough understanding of the many complexities, and from action on a broad front . . .
>
> If there is one general summarizing conclusion we offer it is that there is nothing to equal in importance the quality and achievement of the individual teacher, to whom most of our suggestions are addressed. All our recommendations are designed to support and strengthen the teachers in the schools, for it is with them that improvements in standards of reading and language most assuredly lie.

Although the Committee had claimed that no easy solutions to the problems of learning English were available, its report did prompt discussions on the necessary changes to the curriculum. Indeed, some of the prescriptions proposed were seized upon by right-wing commentators. For instance, it was suggested (ibid., p. 513) that 'a system of monitoring should be introduced which will employ new instruments to assess a wider range of attainments than has been attempted in the past and allow new criteria to be established for the definition of literacy.' This chimed in with the newly established APU, as did more detailed recommendations for the control of reading and writing. Furthermore, the whole tone of the Report was towards exercising greater control over both teachers and the curriculum, which was in accordance with the new mood of political austerity.

Equally, however, parents were to be controlled and shown how to rear their children for healthy language development. In this respect, Bullock went further than previous committees on child-rearing and suggested that adequate parenting should begin with ante-natal care (ibid., p. 519):

> In ante-natal clinics the question of a child's language development should take its place alongside that of his physical and emotional growth as a matter of vital concern to expectant parents . . . Health and education authorities should cooperate to devise ways of providing expectant parents with advice and information on the language needs of young children.

This need to control parental activities both constrained and increased the role of the teacher. Teachers were expected to have more than mere academic or intellectual abilities – they were to develop social skills. One of the requirements of Bullock, which echoed Plowden's recommendations of eight years earlier, was that home visiting by teachers to the young child's parents was to be encouraged. The Bullock Committee also spelled out the implications of its recommendations for both the training and in-service education of teachers. Although the Report had claimed that reading standards had not declined – and that such a comparative methodological exercise was, in any case, impossible to attempt – the whole tenor of its recommendations was to suggest that the organization of schooling was far from well! This set the tone for public debate: the Bullock Report was not immediately implemented but formed the backbone for all subsequent curricular proposals and discussions.

What the Report did not consider at all was the question of differences between boys and girls in language acquisition. Again, neither 'boy' nor 'girl' (nor 'sex') was a category in the index of the Report. Of course, the impact of its recommendations on staffing was also not covered. The whole assumption was of traditional relations between boys and girls and men and women. Adequate parenting was really a synonym for adequate mothering: the active involvement of parents in language development would, inevitably, restrict the range of other activities open to mothers.

Although sex differences were not considered here, they were high on the political agenda in 1975 and the implications for education were raised. The Labour government, influenced by the Tory plans and by pressure from women within the Labour Party, early on put forward proposals for legislation to ban sex discrimination in public life. This legislation was to be wider than that proposed by the Tories and was to include attempts to limit sex discrimination in education. Whilst the Bill was being debated in Parliament, a group of HMIs investigated the nature and extent of sex discrimination in school curricula. Their findings were published in the summer before the Bill became law. Basically, their findings were that boys and girls were not given identical treatment, whether in single-sex or co-educational, primary or secondary schools. The HMIs were somewhat equivocal about whether this was a problem. They argued that 'this may indeed be to the advantage of both boys and girls', but added that 'some differences do militate against the career prospects or personal development of girls, for example, physical education.' Their evidence showed that differences between boys and girls occurred in three ways. First, in co-educational schools girls and boys were not necessarily taught together. Some subjects were provided for both boys and girls but taught separately – the best example being physical education and games – the justification being in terms of interest or preference. Second, all schools provided some special subjects for boys and some for girls. Girls were invariably provided with female courses such as home economics and needlework and boys with craftwork. Third, co-educational schools tended to provide more special sex-based subjects than single-sex schools (DES, 1975b, p. 14): 'Child-care, child development, mothercare and homemaking are usually regarded as the province of girls. In general, girls in single-sex schools do not enjoy as wide a variety of these courses as do their contemporaries of either sex.' The HMIs tried to explain why such sex-typing of the curriculum might be occurring. They argued (ibid., p. 20) that 'educational establishments do not exist in isolation from the community and will continue to take some account of tradition and custom (which are themselves changing) both in the family and the labour market.' In other words, they justified the ways in which schools continued to train girls for their roles in the home, as wives and mothers, and prepared boys only for the labour market. Margaret Drabble, writing in *The Times* (1975) around the same time, pointed out satirically how curious this tradition of courses was. She asked, 'Men eat too, so why aren't boys taught to cook?' She went on:

> There is no need at all, in the present state of society, to teach girls to cook and to sew. It is boys who should be taught these things. The familiar equation of the crafts of woodwork or metalwork and cookery is complete nonsense . . . but nobody seems to notice that woodwork is a highly irrelevant activity, whereas after all, we all eat . . . The pressure of history is so strong that men cannot boil eggs, cannot sew on buttons and do need to be taught these things. Let them be taught, then.

The HMIs were not entirely complacent about the state of affairs: their argument for changes, however, was not based upon evidence like Drabble's about the actual, current activities of men and women but on the waste of public money that a traditional course of action would incur (DES, 1975b, p. 24):

> It may be that society can justify the striking differences that exist between the subjects studied by boys and girls in secondary schools, but it is more likely that a society that needs to develop to the full the talents and skills of all its people will find the discrepancies disturbing . . . If all secondary schools were to carry out an analysis of both content and organisation of the curriculum . . . that would be one step towards eradicating prejudices about the roles of men and women which frustrate individual development and cause a wastage of talent a country can ill afford.

The Sex Discrimination Act, 1975, which came into force only four months after the HMIs had put forward these suggestions, did not require schools to analyse their curricula to ensure that girls were not discriminated against. It merely made illegal any discrimination in admission to co-educational schools (and allowed single-sex schools to continue) and in the nature of courses offered to pupils. Enforcement of these provisions was very weak, consisting of a complaints procedure to the LEA, the Secretary of State for Education and ultimately the county courts, or the use of the Equal Opportunities Commission (EOC) to monitor the work of schools.

The legal procedures for education were different from those for the other public issues covered, except for the role of the EOC. In part this was because the DES wanted to maintain control of the curriculum. Indeed, in the three years of the EOC's existence, there have been frequent quarrels with the DES over its legal powers. The EOC has therefore done little to monitor the work of schools or to follow up individual complaints. In the summer of 1976, it took up the complaints about sex discrimination in admissions to secondary schools in the Tameside LEA but took over a year to publish its findings. A year later, it agreed to support a girl's complaint about refusal to admit her to a craft class, but later withdrew its financial support. The Tameside report was to uphold the LEA's actions. The complaint was that more boys than girls had been provided with grammar school places as a result of the High Court's decision to allow Tameside to retain selection for secondary places for the 1976–7 academic session. The EOC did not find this to be the case. Although more boys than girls were provided with selective places, this was justified by reference to the fact that one of the schools was a single-sex (boys') school and not subject to the requirements of the Act (EOC, 1977a, p. 2):

> The Commission concludes that the evidence obtained in the course of its investigation does not establish the existence of any acts of unlawful sex discrimination by the Metropolitan Borough of Tameside in relation to the subject matter of the investigation . . .

Given that this is the one educational investigation (and indeed one of the very few EOC investigations) carried out it did not augur well for statutory changes to the curriculum or the organization of schooling. The Sex Discrimination Act, hedged round with a multitude of exceptions, etc., has not done much to modify the curriculum directly. Although sex differences in the curriculum have barely been tampered with, the curriculum itself was under heavy fire from 1976, and some changes have had implications for the future education of girls.

The Great Debate on Education

By 1976 both the economic climate and the new educational mood of control had become sufficiently in the public eye for them to head the political agenda. Standards in education could no longer be ignored since, apparently, their inadequacies were contributing to the economic ills that had befallen the country. As mentioned in the previous chapter, the Prime Minister himself saw fit to launch, in October 1976, the Great Debate on Education, the aims of which were twofold. One, as already shown, was to discuss the question of control of education and the other was to consider what the content of school curricula should be. Inevitably the two were closely entwined, especially since the tying of education to the economy entailed curricular changes. In fact, the main topics of discussion in the six formal debates organized in February and March 1977 were curricular topics. These were the compulsory school curriculum (for five- to sixteen-year-olds), assessment of standards, the education and training of teachers and school and working life. The DES even set the parameters for debate *within* each topic, publishing agenda and background data before the discussions were held. The DES therefore tried to focus the debate on what it deemed to be the essentials of each problem. With regard to the school curriculum, it argued that (DES, 1976, p. 4):

> In addition to establishing basic skills, the curriculum should enable children, as part of their essential general education, to understand the society of which they are a part, including the economics of everyday life and the role of industry and commerce in sustaining our standard of living.

Thus, the DES established from the outset the view that education should be intimately related to the economy in terms of both finance and also the role of industry. This general point led the DES to raise as the major issue whether there should be either a common curriculum or a common core to the curriculum (ibid., p. 3):

> The two terms are not wholly interchangeable: a common curriculum may imply maintaining the same educational pattern for all pupils with little choice; but a common core most often suggests an irreducible minimum essential to the education of all children . . . Some people use the term . . . to cover a small number of what they see as priority areas, for example, English and Mathematics . . .

But the DES was rather equivocal about this necessity and argued also for diversity to fit children's varied needs. Thus it ended up by arguing that (ibid., p. 5):

> Defining the essential needs that the curriculum has to satisfy is a necessary prelude to achieving that common guarantee of quality . . . The short list should be short because we are not talking about the whole of education, we are talking about the *basic* educational right of the country.

The desire was, therefore, for a very limited *core* to the curriculum. In discussing assessment of standards, the DES considered both what standards should be reviewed and what methods should be used. Its main concern was with basic skills and with the performance of children in relation to them. Three methods were raised: systematic individual assessment and observation; public examination; and assessment by sampling of the performance of the education system. For all, new procedures were suggested, such as a new public examination system and whether that should test the whole range of basic skills. The roles of the APU, HMIs and local advisers were re-emphasized as crucial. Thus the emphasis was on new methods of control. These were also behind the suggestions for the education and training of teachers. Here it was suggested (ibid., p. 12) that teachers themselves be trained to 'acquire a good understanding of the means by which a society makes its living and of the circumstances in which pupils will spend their working lives.' Teachers therefore were to learn new 'professional' skills. This same notion was behind the agenda for school and working life, which stressed that education should give children skills for the world of work. Specifically it was argued (ibid., p. 16) that:

> Children growing up in an industrial society need to understand it and to appreciate the dependence of our living standards on the creation and production of goods and services. Those engaged in industry are often critical of the schools on the grounds that basic skills have been neglected and that insufficient pupils pursue science and maths . . .

In this section basic skills again were deemed to be important and, in particular, were stressed as being necessary for industry. Indeed, the whole agenda focused on the relation between education and *industry*, rather than on the economy as a whole or the differentiated nature of work.

As both Hopkins (1978) and Devlin and Warnock (1977) have described, the regional conferences focused narrowly on the topics as chosen and defined by the DES. Indeed, there was little time for anything else: each debate lasted only a day! The question of whether boys and girls should be provided with the same educational fare was barely raised and yet education was to be tied to the world of work. Hitherto girls had been prepared, primarily, for the home and only as a second resort for the world of work (see chs. 5–7).

The Great Debate on Education did not really deserve its name. It was really neither great nor a debate. The only by-product in terms of public discussion was a series of late-night television programmes to raise further the issues of the regional conferences. Little was made of the debate in terms of policy change. Many of the central issues were deferred for further official review. For example, on the question of public examinations, as a result of the Schools Council report on common examinations, in July 1976 a departmental Committee of Enquiry was set up to investigate the matter again. As we have seen from the previous chapter, the question of control was deferred until the Taylor Committee reported.

The major outcome of the debate was a Green Paper entitled *Education in Schools: a Consultative Document* (DES, 1977a); this reiterated and expanded the issues of the regional conferences. Three new topics were added to the list: the transition between schools; the special needs of minority groups; and the school and the community. The major assumptions of the proposed curriculum were repeated, namely, that children should learn basic skills and be equipped for the transition to working life. As regards the secondary school curriculum, it was argued (ibid., para. 10.9): 'Young people need to be equipped with a basic understanding of the functioning of our democratic political system, of the mixed economy, and industrial activities, *especially manufacturing*, which create our national wealth' [my italics]. This time, the economy had been narrowed to the manufacturing sector only. Yet the curriculum was to cope with a wider scope than hitherto – a multicultural emphasis and the sexual division of labour. For the latter, it was argued that children should not be given 'sexual stereotypes' but provided with opportunities for personal development. However, the emphasis was placed more on imbuing boys with knowledge of the family than girls with the world of work (ibid., para. 10.10): 'Both sexes should learn how to cope with domestic tasks and parenthood.' The world of work was never far from the top of the agenda. It was the basis for the recommendations about school and working life. For instance, industry and commerce (local firms especially) should be involved in curriculum planning. On the other hand, schoolchildren as part of their school courses should have work experience and observation of *productive industry* [my italics]. Work experience had of course been initiated under a Tory government and the legal barriers to its possibilities removed by the Education (Work Experience) Act of 1973, which lifted employment restrictions for fifteen- and sixteen-year-olds. The type of experience envisaged in the Green Paper was to be mainly of manufacturing rather than the service industries.

The other emphasis of the Green Paper was on monitoring and control. The need for assessments both within and between schools was again raised. Equally, teachers were to be given more training and graduate entry was to become a minimum condition. The government also claimed (ibid., p. 13) to want to 'improve staffing standards as soon as economic conditions allow'. This was but a pious hope and was never implemented!

The two new topics in the Green Paper – school and community, and the special needs of minority groups – were barely discussed publicly pending first the Taylor Report and second the Warnock Report on special education and the handicapped. The only issue that was officially acted upon was the arrangements for the curriculum. The rest remained mere policy statements. For the former, a circular (14/77) was issued to LEAs in November 1977, requesting them to provide the DES with information about a variety of aspects of curricular arrangements. The question of whether LEAs provided a core curriculum was asked and, in addition, information was sought on the balance and breadth of the curriculum, the skills taught, the subjects (such as English, maths, science, modern languages and religious education) provided, the specific preparation for working life, especially in terms of links with industry and trade unions, or work experience and observation given. Questions were also asked about school records and assessments. What was excluded was information on the sex differences in the curriculum – perhaps because this was now supposed to be illegal. The plan was that the government would be able, from the replies, to assess future needs. In a government publication dated September 1978 and entitled *Progress in Education: a Report on Recent Initiatives* (1978a, p. 1), it was stated that: 'On the basis of (LEA) replies, and following further consultation, the Government will seek to establish with their partners national needs in respect of the curriculum. The radically reformed Schools Council will be well set to service these.' By the end of the Labour term of office (April 1979), no new national needs had been pronounced upon.

The question of public examinations remained equally in abeyance. The Waddell Committee reported in 1978 (DES, 1978b, p. i) and

> advised that it would be possible without harmful educational consequences to introduce a common system of examinations at 16-plus for all the candidates for whom O-level and CSE

examinations are now intended, and to award certificates all with the same title and with the grades on a single scale.

The government, however, did not act upon this recommendation and continued to await the Schools Council response on the question of a new system of 'O' and 'A' levels. The Green Paper had mooted the idea of a return to a grouped certificate, like the old Matriculation or School Certificate. This was still being argued when a general election was announced. Again, the question of special educational needs and the Warnock Committee's recommendation of integration were not acted upon.

The Great Debate on Education occupied educational party politics for over two years. There was much rhetoric but no policy action. What was more important than policy changes was the fact that a new ideological perspective was being produced and reinforced throughout this period. It became absolutely clear that the curriculum had to be more closely monitored and that it had to provide basic skills and people trained for manufacturing industry. It may have been unnecessary to enforce this ideology. The LEAs may have felt under sufficient pressure – both political and economic – to ring the changes without legal harassment. For many of them it probably chimed in with their ideological stance. The Labour government clearly adopted a right-wing educational ideology during this economic recession. To some extent, this was under pressure from both the Tories and right-wing interest groups. Hall (1979, p. 19) argued that 'the Right has won territory without having to win power.'

Unemployment and education

The impact of this new ideology was felt as much in the non-compulsory aspects of schooling as with compulsory education. It is particularly evident in further and higher education; since nursery provision has been reduced, there is little to show for the ideology except as discussed in the previous chapter. The question of provisions for sixteen- to nineteen-year-olds loomed large on Labour's educational agenda and yet this was not raised within the context of the Great Debate. Initially, major new provision for this age group was made outside the government's educational sphere: where it was covered by the DES it remained largely locally or regionally based. One of the first actions of the Labour government was the setting up of the Manpower Services Commission, a quango with ultimate responsibility to the Department of Employment. It was concerned with monitoring the effectiveness of the labour market and the supply of jobs. A separate unit, the Training Services Agency, was established to review and finance new job-training ventures. The TSA soon became a unit within the MSC where both jobs and training were monitored. An early venture of the MSC was the Job Creation Programme, which provided opportunities for jobs and training for young unemployed people (aged sixteen to twenty-four). Some of the training courses were run in further education colleges, but much of the control rested not with the LEAs but with the MSC and its appointed agents.

In 1976 the DES, concerned about the rising rates of unemployment amongst school-leavers, decided to initiate a number of joint schemes with the TSA and the Industrial Training Boards, the latter of which had been set up in 1964 as autonomous bodies with responsibilities for specific types of industrial training (see ch. 7). The new schemes were to pilot a range of different types of vocational preparation for unemployed school-leavers, based mainly in colleges of further education. At the outset it was recognized that the teachers would themselves require vocational preparation, but these needs were to be evaluated by the pilot schemes. Only a year later, the MSC's evaluative committee (Manpower Services Commission, 1977) produced a comprehensive review of the workings of its schemes for young people (see ch. 8). The DES and LEAs were represented on the Holland Committee. The Report recommended a number of new approaches to the problems of unemployed young people. In particular, it suggested special schemes for sixteen- to eighteen-year-olds, separate from those for young people in their twenties. The Youth Opportunities Programme was to provide either work preparation or work experience for unemployed school-leavers of over six weeks' duration. The work-preparation schemes were to be held in colleges of further education, and LEAs would be reimbursed by the MSC 80 per cent of their expenses. The plan was to make available almost a quarter of a million individual opportunities. The schemes would be determined locally. The YOP scheme was approved by the government and came into effect in 1978, replacing the JCP. In detailing 'the contribution of the education service' in 1977 (circular 10/77), the DES argued that the priority local schemes should comprise:

(i) more vocationally oriented courses, especially for women;
(ii) improved provision for the disabled and handicapped;
(iii) improved provision for ethnic minority groups;
(iv) three day per week courses for those in receipt of supplementary benefits;
(v) courses for those deficient in social skills, especially literacy and numeracy.

Thus the notion of certain basic skills was once again raised, now with respect to those who had not benefited from the compulsory education system. Interestingly, the DES had become concerned about the disadvantages women had experienced in compulsory schooling and their particular lack of vocational preparation. However, no changes were mooted for the compulsory curriculum. Over a year later, in the EOC's second annual report, the extent of female disadvantage in the Job Creation Programme was clearly demonstrated. Of the four youth unemployment relief schemes for sixteen- to eighteen-year-olds, girls constituted the following proportions (EOC, 1978, p. 70):

(i)	Youth Employment Subsidy	41 %
(ii)	Community industry	46 %
(iii)	Work experience	60 %
(iv)	Job Creation Programme	23 %

Yet throughout the period 1974–6 girls constituted 47 per cent of the unemployed school-leavers. Since the YOP courses were to be locally determined there was no guarantee that girls would fare any better than they had under JCP. One set of programmes – Training Opportunities (TOPS) – devised by the TSA in its early years, did appeal to women. However, by 1977 women had not constituted 50 per cent of the recipients, although their growth rate was far more rapid than that for men. In 1971, according to the EOC (1978b, p. 68), women represented 7.7 per cent and by 1976 this had risen to 44.5 per cent. Most of the increase was in colleges, rather than residential training colleges or skill centres, 'where they follow traditionally "female" courses in typing and other office skills' (ibid.). Women, therefore, were not guaranteed improved educational opportunities through either the DES's or the MSC's new initiatives. Before proceeding to the promised White Paper on sixteen- to eighteen-year-olds, the DES produced yet another consultative paper entitled *16-18: Education and Training for 16 to 18-Year-Olds* (DES, 1979). This was a slender document but meant to parallel the discussions on the compulsory curriculum. The DES was very open-minded about provisions for this age group and merely set out wide parameters for debate. The main emphasis was again on the relationship between education and industry and the extent to which the Industrial Training Boards could be involved in future provisions. But the DES also put forward the view that this age group had heterogeneous needs. Nevertheless, it did not mention any patterning to those needs, such as extended and improved educational opportunities for women.

By the end of the Labour period of office and therefore almost the end of the decade, a new ideology of the role of education had been promulgated. Education was no longer to be used broadly and for social and moral ends. It was to be seen as narrowly specific – fitting children to the requirements of the economy and in particular to those of manufacturing or productive industry. To achieve that objective, education was to be extended upwards through the age ranges and the curriculum made more specific. Teachers, too, were to be more regulated to ensure that they carried out the prevailing ideology. These controls operated not only through transformed systems of training but also through the curriculum provided. Public expenditure cuts increasingly affected the provision of schooling, especially through the limitation of resources for education. By 1979 many LEAs were imposing new restrictions on the curriculum through implementing charges for aspects of courses such as swimming and, more important, for school tools, for instance, paper, pencils and textbooks. The extent of these changes was never documented on a national basis but incidents were revealed through reports of increasing amounts of resistance to local schools policy.

This return to 'basics' heralded, too, a renewal of the emphasis on the sexual division of labour. The pious wish that girls would be treated as well as boys throughout their schooldays and that the emphasis on the family as opposed to work activities would be eradicated through such provisions as the Sex Discrimination Act became a receding possibility. Curiously, the tying of the curriculum more closely to the needs of the economy did not extend specifically to girls. No account was taken in the debates or policy documents of the changed and changing labour market conditions for women. Yet the two decades 1960–79 witnessed the most momentous transformation in women's paid employment. In particular, mothers have re-entered or remained in the labour force (Tizard *et al.*, 1976). The official figure for mothers with preschool children in employment is now over 30 per cent (Fonda and Moss, 1976). The ideology of motherhood and its translation into the school curriculum (as a requirement that girls learn about home duties rather than employment) is clearly no longer relevant to the economic realities. Equally, the reduction in opportunities for female teachers will cut off one of the main traditional avenues of employment for women and especially mothers. This change, in any event, has not been commensurate with the requirements for the practice of teachers – that they adopt a familial approach to the children in their care. This prescription has not only been evident in the instance illustrated here (the William Tyndale dispute) but also in the general rules governing teacher employment. It is, for example, written into the Burnham agreements on teachers' salaries and conditions of employment. Elizabeth Richardson (1973, p. 218) has argued:

> the Burnham Committee . . . in successive reports has stipulated that if, in a mixed school, the deputy head is a man, one woman on the staff may carry the title of and responsibility of 'senior mistress', and, conversely, that if the deputy head is a woman, then one man on the staff may carry the title of and responsibility of 'senior master'. The unconscious assumption underlying this stipulation appears to be that a head, whether man or woman, must ensure that the masculine and feminine aspects of his or her leadership are symbolized by the two most senior members of the staff. It seems to follow from this that a headmaster is not to be allowed his own feminine side or a headmistress her own masculine side, although all human beings are to some extent bi-sexual.

Officially, then, patriarchal authority is still to be exercised within schools. And, as is now well established, children learn as much through this hidden curriculum as through the official curriculum of courses. So children are still being taught through the sexual division of labour in teaching about the division of responsibilities in adult life. Yet they are being taught this as much by employed wives or mothers as by their own mothers, and by women who are highly trained and now considered professional, rather than motherly.

10

conclusions

How parents should care for their children, what kinds of teachers should stand in place of parents in the classroom and what subjects they should teach have been the central concerns of this book. I have looked at how the State has ordered familial relations with and within schools and the official reasons that have been given. The assumptions behind this formulation are that the State uses the 'family-education couple' to maintain and reinforce both class and sexual divisions and that these divisions are necessary for the reproduction of the conditions of the capitalist economy. Space has not allowed me to demonstrate the ways in which changes in State ideology have been predicated upon changes in the conditions of forces of production. I have stuck rigidly to the work of the State and merely asserted the connection between the economy and State ideology for changes in either parental relationships with schools or schools' treatment of children and their teachers. I have not been able to consider, again because of space, some of the contradictions between the needs for capital accumulation and the organization of the education system, except that I have made much of the inflexibility in the notion of the family and especially women's position within it. In particular, I have tried to demonstrate the persistence of the idea that women primarily are to be wives and mothers but that they may require special training adequately to pursue these tasks. At times of economic recession or labour shortage, however, women may be required to participate in the labour force, although on the whole their labour is related to, or an extension of, their domestic skills. This is shown most clearly in the employment of women teachers. Their involvement in teaching has been based upon the assumption that caring for children, especially young ones, is a feminine attribute: moreover, women teachers, especially those who have married, are best equipped to impart knowledge about wifehood, motherhood and domesticity. Nevertheless, these ideologies have not been applied in any straightforward way to the organization of education. In some instances, they are confounded with other ideologies about schooling.

The presentation in chronological order of the two themes in the book – family responsibilities for schooling and the familial ambiance within education – was chosen deliberately. Since the issues that I wanted to examine appeared complex, it seemed that the simplest organization of the material was into historical periods. The four periods chosen – early capitalism and the nineteenth century; the early twentieth century; the Second World War to 1970; and the current decade – are not entirely discrete. Nor do the two themes easily fit into them. But there are distinctive features that I will now highlight.

In Part I I showed how parental responsibilities for schoolchildren developed as children were gradually seen as needing to be moulded to the social and economic order and yet were also seen to be economically 'useful' to the State. These ideas were, however, applied in a variety of ways. In the nineteenth century, as argued in chapter 2, the family became an important unit to capitalism and, in particular, childhood was gradually recognized as a distinctive phase of personal development and separate from adulthood. But it was only in the last third of the century that the need for universal formal schooling was widely recognized. This need was not seen to be for training in specific economic skills but rather to ensure compliance with a particular socio-economic system. Hence, the schools that were established developed along class and sex divisions. The State was slow to recognize the need for formal schooling and its interventions in parent-child relationships only gradually developed. Certainly, not all families' child-rearing activities were explicitly regulated by the end of the century. Upper- and upper-middle-class families continued to rely on traditional forms of education – on the whole, these were home-based systems of tutoring, especially for girls. Middle-class schooling was enhanced and helped by State intervention; in particular, the funding and financing of such schools was regularized, a move of benefit to parents. Such parents, although after 1880 legally obliged to ensure that their children were educated, were not harassed into doing so. Rather, they were allowed a choice of schools, especially for older children, in the form of boarding schools for boys and mainly day schools for girls. Girls' education was more regulated than boys' in an effort to ensure a modicum of schooling for them. But this regulation had more to do with guaranteeing a supply of able teachers (as shown in ch. 5), than with defining the contours of schools' and parents' responsibilities.

Working-class families were dealt with more stringently, although initially the State abrogated responsibility to religious groups. The churches were not entirely successful at ensuring children's attendance at school, partly because of the attractions of employment and the income that parents derived from their children's labour and partly because they only had moral sanctions. But State intervention in schooling and the provision of secular instruction was the result not of humanitarianism but of working-class pressure, and the need to limit child unemployment rather than limit parental exploitation of children. The corollary of working-class schooling was, however, a limitation of parental rights over their children and an imposition of parental duties towards child-rearing. Indeed, by the end of the nineteenth century a complex system for ensuring school attendance had developed, including legal sanctions against parents for failure to do so. Children were still regarded as their parents' property, but parents had to conform to certain standards of child-rearing. To ensure that they did so, charges or fees for elementary schooling were eventually abolished. These elementary schools, however, were not provided to enhance children's intellectual development but as a method of social control – to demonstrate the rationality of the social and moral order and the place of both boys and girls within it.

Because caring for children came to be a female skill, from the 1860s women began to predominate in teaching, especially for the working class (see ch. 5). Pamela Horn (1976) has shown what a contradictory position the Victorian schoolmistress occupied. Certainly, she was not at all connected to the professional teachers for middle-class boys and her social position was even more anomalous than that of the Victorian governess (see Peterson, 1972). What Victorian schoolmasters and schoolmistresses had to teach was regulated by the State even before their schools came under State financial and administrative control. These early Codes of Regulations required that the sexual division of labour be taught and understood, although this was but a small part of the whole curriculum. Working-class girls learnt domestic subjects to equip them to be not only wives and mothers, but also domestic servants. Middle-class girls, by contrast, were taught the skills of household management rather than the practical domestic tasks. Needlework, however, was universally taught to girls as an important accomplishment, but by the end of the nineteenth century it was an almost insignificant part of the curriculum for middle-class girls. Schools for these girls were increasingly trying to emulate the academic fare of the boys' grammar and public schools. However, as I have demonstrated in Part II of the book, the specification of girls' domestic and maternal responsibilities and those of their teachers has been an overriding concern of the school system since its beginnings in the nineteenth century.

In the early twentieth century, as shown in Chapter 3, schooling became more specialized. Class differences in schools continued, but the State took over more responsibility both for types of school and for the length of schooling. In particular, various legal changes in the first two decades of the century gave middle-class schools State support through financial help from either local or central government. But schools for working- and middle-class children remained separate, although the distinction in types of attendance – day versus boarding – narrowed. More and more middle-class children attended day schools and the proportion of boys at boarding school declined. The schools continued to be distinguished in terms of their aims and parental access. Fees had been abolished only for working-class, elementary education: middle-class parents continued to pay to ensure their children's place at secondary schools. These latter schools increasingly supplied children with the qualifications for particular positions within the division of labour – professional and managerial posts. Working-class education was also extended but to ensure the more efficient use of manpower within the lower echelons of the division of labour. So economic skills, as well as the work ethic, were gradually included in the curricula of schools; the school-leaving age was raised, special vocational and trade schools were established and technical training courses invented. Job training was slowly being transferred from the work-place to the school system. This is best illustrated by the schemes proposed in the 1910s to make continuing education compulsory after the end of schooling, while adolescents were in employment. Tying education more clearly to the labour market and the efficient use of manpower raised other questions about the aims and nature of education. During this period, the State also became more concerned with the efficiency of schooling, as well as mere attendance. So a whole system of health and welfare provisions was set up to make sure that children not only received but benefited from their schooling. This inevitably affected parental responsibilities for children; for example, it required that children attend school adequately clothed, and fed and in good health. Mothering, therefore, became a more detailed activity during this period. Indeed, in other contexts, not illustrated in this book, the State sought to ensure that mothers were more effective – through the provision of infant and child welfare centres as well as special schools for mothers (Dyhouse, 1978). At the same time, as argued in chapter 6, mothers were progressively excluded from the educational labour market. The marriage bar, for instance, was more stringently applied in the early decades of the twentieth century, although it was never legally enforced. And women teachers, although they campaigned vigorously and vociferously, were not afforded equal pay with men – on the grounds that they did not have maternal responsibilities, whereas men were invariably assumed to be husbands and fathers. The curriculum increasingly reflected the ideology of motherhood: special courses in domestic science, as well as cookery and needlework, were developed along with hygiene and home management. These were linked with courses in domestic management and catering, taught in technical schools, which would provide girls with economically useful skills. By the Second World War, the education system was very different from that at the turn of the century. In particular, it provided children with skills for labour-force participation whilst, at the same time, pointing up economic differentiation between men and women. Motherhood, too, had become a skill to be taught and no longer merely seen as one of women's attributes.

The Second World War was an important watershed for the organization of education. The reproduction of class relations was considerably modified in the school system and parental responsibilities were more rigidly defined. In the first place, children's potential economic value had become an accepted tenet of schooling and, moreover, the new ideology was that children's abilities should be not merely trained but exploited. Hence, the length of schooling was extended for working-class children and its aims were brought more into line with those of middle-class children. State education became free universally, although middle-class parents were still entitled to opt out of the system and pay for their children's education, either in public schools or in schools only partly financed by the State. Class differences were by no means totally vitiated in the new system of schooling, since the arguments (and pressure brought to bear by teachers in the NUT and the Labour Party) for 'multilateral' schools did not influence the new organization. Secondary schools were distinguished by the pupils who were accepted for entry. Although pupils were ostensibly chosen on the grounds of ability, a clear correlation developed between social class and academic aptitude. Indeed, this correlation was the assumption behind the early rationales for tripartite systems of schooling. Yet the expressed reasons for tripartism were pupils' interests and aptitudes and the need to channel them into useful, economic pursuits. The now explicit ideology of individualism that lay behind secondary education and the principle of equality of educational opportunity was also applied to parental responsibilities with respect to schooling. This became apparent in the 1944 Education Act. Parental duties of ensuring children's school attendance were codified along with the principles of parental choice of school and 'parental wishes'. Moreover, since the health and welfare of schoolchildren were to be more closely organized and supervised, parental duties were further extended. These new conceptions of parental duties and rights were applied to other educational issues as schooling was extended and reformed in the 1950s and 1960s. In some instances, in order to ensure children's continuance at school, parents were helped with the costs of their education, for instance, through Educational Maintenance Allowances. Of course, this was certainly nothing like compensation for the loss of children's earnings. But education was extended, through the raising of the school-leaving age and provision of further and higher education, not to help parents specifically but to ensure the maintenance of the capitalist economy. The improvements to education occurred mainly in the provision of new science and technology curricula.

The curricula for boys and girls, however, did not entirely blend together. The principle of 'interests' was applied crudely to courses provided for boys and girls. It was assumed that the two sets of interests were not synonymous. The majority of girls, for example, would be naturally interested in a career in marriage first, whereas most boys would put work as a first priority. Hence girls should be provided with some courses in marriage and motherhood, but these should not predominate. Yet the job skills offered to girls related to their domestic and homely interests: boys' family and work obligations were regarded as two entirely separate spheres of interest. Domestic obligations in no way affected curricula for boys.

During this period, however, the campaigns of women teachers for the lifting of the marriage bar and the provision of equal pay were finally successful. In part, the ban on marriage was abolished because of wartime expediency but it provided the opportunity and the justification for encouraging the supply of married women teachers. The McNair Report and several later government-sponsored reports argued the efficacy of such teachers, especially for girls, particular girls' courses and the education of infants. But these arguments did not directly affect the resolution of the equal pay disputes. Here new principles of wage-bargaining comparability provided the rationale for including women teachers. And, indeed, this was a modest solution. Women teachers were certainly not afforded equal status, and continued to be treated differently from men and mainly placed in inferior positions in the teaching hierarchy. The justification was in terms of professional training and standing, and during this period attempts were made to improve teachers' professional status to attract men in order more adequately to teach the skills required by the economy.

By 1970 the education system had been transformed from its

origins a hundred years previously. The State was by now heavily involved in both its ordering and its regulation. Education was not only to reproduce the social and sexual division of labour but specifically to provide children with skills for participation in the capitalist economy. The form that the reproduction of social and sexual relations took had been changed. Schools were no longer entirely organized on class lines and different provisions made for boys and girls. The form had become more subtle and blurred. Class distinctions, for example, occurred within schools of the same type, depending on geographical area and type of teacher. Sex differences were taught as much through the hierarchical and patriarchal relations within school and by the expectations made of girls' and boys' progress through schooling as through specific issues. Parents' relationships with schools had altered. A greater emphasis was now being placed on individual parental involvement in, and with, schools. In particular, mothers' participation in the schooling process – rather than decision-making – was being fostered.

Contemporary issues in the way the State has used the 'family-education couple' have enhanced this involvement of parents in schools and yet, at the same time, set limits on the familial ambiance of schools. In Part III, I have examined the complexity of these processes. In summary, the State has seen the existing education system as one of the major causes of the current round of economic crises. Thus reforms of the education system have been manifold: most of them have involved modifications to the involvement of both parents and teachers in schooling. Parents' responsibilities have been crucially redefined. In fact, parents have been offered the semblance of greater rights over their children's education, on the premise that this would encourage them to press for improvements in educational standards and hence in the conditions for the reproduction of capitalism. So parents have been explicitly used to help solve the current crises in capitalism. In addition, mothers have been exhorted to help stem the rising tide of children's disaffection with school. Given that this kind of mothering has been deemed to be a major occupation, it has provided a rationale for the exclusion of such mothers from labour-force participation.

At the same time, teachers have been afforded a new role in the educational process. Attempts have been made to enhance their professional status, through a redefinition of their training requirements. The aim has been to make teaching a graduate profession – a far cry from the early origins of teacher training as apprenticeship. In this case, little attention has been paid to the need to involve women, and especially mothers, as teachers. In fact, the object seems to have been to try to discourage their participation. Moreover, their role in the reproduction of the sexual division of labour has been limited, in part because this problem has become tangential to the central purposes of education. Instead, the specification of at least a minimum *core* curriculum has become the overriding objective of educational discourse. This, it has been argued, will make a vital contribution to the maintenance and reproduction of the capitalist economy.

This analysis has relied mainly on evidence of the State's policy changes with regard to the 'family-education couple'. Some attention has been paid to the sources of changes. In particular, some changes have arguably derived from the struggles of certain groups within the education system. The struggles of groups of teachers have been especially influential in modifying State ordering of schooling. Perhaps the best examples cited – although they took about half a century to resolve – have been the demands of women teachers, especially in the NUT, for equal pay and equal treatment over marital status with men. Recent struggles within teaching have so far been less successful at providing a progressive transformation of schooling. Indeed, the results of the dispute at the William Tyndale Junior School in the ILEA are not a happy portent for the future, for they demonstrate the lengths to which at least one arm of the State will go in repressing resistance to its form of schooling. On the other hand, this dispute also illustrates how successful middle-class parental involvement in schooling can be. The teachers' sacking for indiscipline (although pupil indiscipline was the occasion for the dispute) resulted mainly from State support of such parental pressure. On the whole, however, the State's recent encouragement of both individual and collective parental involvement has resulted in reactionary measures in schooling – especially returns towards more traditional types of teaching. Curiously, the early parental struggles for State education provided the means for the State to supply universal mass education, albeit on class and sex lines. I have alluded to these struggles for educational provision and the reaction of the State to such demands, but they are dealt with far more fully by Brian Simon in his educational histories (1960, 1965 and 1974).

I have not been able to cover adequately all the origins of these educational policy developments. Indeed, I suspect that would require another book and one in which the frame of reference was very different. I have not really distinguished fully between the three major political parties – Liberal, Conservative and Labour – in their treatment of education and the family. This is because, although at critical junctures their ideologies may well be at odds with each other, on the whole they all have used the 'family-education couple' to sustain particular social and sexual divisions rather than transform the socio-economic system. The means by which they have maintained these relations have differed, but within a common set of ideological goals. The effects, in policy implementation, of these party political ideologies have been similar: for instance, although the Labour Party has been committed to comprehensive education for over thirty years, its efforts to achieve this when in office have merely resulted in minor modifications to the class composition of schooling. And indeed, as shown in chapter 8, most recently the Labour governments adopted what amounted to Tory ideology rather than continuing to pursue goals of equality. They pursued goals of economic efficiency.

I have relied on evidence about the law and legal changes as instances of policy, and to demonstrate social relationships and their ordering. This is an unusual use of the law and its interpretation, but it is being used increasingly in Marxian analyses of State policies (see D. McBarnet (1978) for a parallel analysis of criminal law). The argument is that the rule of law is not, as liberal commentators would have it, neutral but that it is used to sustain class relations. The legal changes cited in this book appear to have been predicated on the assumption that they would maintain both social and sexual relations and not that they would achieve any modification of the social order.

Finally, it may be asked, what is the future of 'the family-education couple' and the ways in which the State will use it? Moreover, what kinds of struggle will need to be engaged in to transform the socio-economic system? These questions are, inevitably, imponderable. But the evidence cited, particularly in chapters 8 and 9, would lead one to very pessimistic conclusions. The 'family-education couple' appears to be used more and more often by the State, and more explicitly, to maintain traditional relationships. Countless proposals, especially from the right, such as educational vouchers, parental participation and control of schools as well as additional courses in parentcraft and mothering, have been mooted recently. Although not of themselves necessarily reactionary, they have been suggested to return order to the educational and hence economic system. In fact, educational vouchers have been used by the left in the USA to achieve more educational equity for the poor (de la Noue, 1972), but here proposals are more limited (Maynard, 1975). Parental participation in educational decisions may be highly progressive, if it is used to include working-class parents in decision-making; and, indeed, it may be one of the main ways in which to achieve major changes in the educational system. When originally proposed in the 1960s, the rhetoric was a radical one (see David, 1975). Yet, currently, the pressure for such involvement derives from, and for, middle-class parents. Again, this is an issue in which to engage struggle. As far as curricular and teacher changes are concerned, the situation does not appear to be quite so bleak – and teachers are now frequently engaged in struggle over both courses and conditions of employment. The major problem, however, is how to achieve a more general and comprehensive transformation of the social and sexual division of labour through the 'family-education couple': how, especially, to bring about a situation in which all, regardless of class, sex or familial status (and also race), would be able to enjoy personal growth and development. From this analysis, such a revolution could only be achieved by concrete struggles within the education system and over the definitions of parenting and especially mothering for and in schooling.

Bibliography

Historical note In the nineteenth century, the government did not have one department responsible for education. The first central government department to 'superintend' education was set up in 1899. Previously, in 1839, the Committee of Council for Education had been set up to bear some responsibility. In 1853, the Department of Science and Art was founded, along with the Charity Commission. In 1856, the Education Department was given limited powers. In the twentieth century, the title of the central government department has been changed twice. In 1944, it became the Ministry of Education instead of the Board of Education. Twenty years later, in 1964, it became known as the Department of Education and Science (DES).

Adams, C. and Laurikietis, R. (1976), *The Gender Trap: a Closer Look at Sex Roles*, 3 vols, London, Virago.

Adams, M. (1976), *Single Blessedness*, London, Heinemann.

Adams, R. (1975), *A Woman's Place*, London, Chatto & Windus.

Adamson, J.W. (1930), *English Education 1789–1902*, 3 vols, Cambridge University Press.

Allen, S. *et al*. (eds) (1974), *Conditions of Illusion*, Leeds, Feminist Books.

Althusser, L. (1971), 'Ideology and Ideological State Apparatuses', in *Lenin and Philosophy and Other Essays*, London, New Left Books.

Anderson, M. (ed.) (1971), *Sociology of the Family*, Penguin.

Anderson, P. (1964), 'Origins of the Present Crisis', *New Left Review*, January–February.

Anderson, P. (1976), *Considerations on Western Marxism*, London, New Left Books.

Anderson, P. and Blackburn, R. (1965), *Towards Socialism*, London, Fontana.

Ardener, S. (ed.) (1978), *Defining Females: the Nature of Women in Society*, London, Croom Helm.

Aries, P. (1974), *Centuries of Childhood*, Penguin (orig. ed., 1962).
Arons, S. (1976), 'The Separation of School and State: Pierce Reconsidered', *Harvard Educational Review*, vol. 46, no. 1 (February).
Atherton, B.F. (1973). 'Coeducational and Single-Sex Schooling and the Happiness of Marriage', *Educational Research*, vol. 15, pp. 221–6.
Auld, R. (1976), *Report of the Inquiry into the William Tyndale Junior and Infants Schools*, London, Inner London Education Authority.
Bacon, W. (1978), *Public Accountability and the Schooling System: A Sociology of School Board Democracy*, London, Harper & Row.
Bagnall, N. (1974), *Parent Power*, London, Routledge & Kegan Paul.
Ball, C. and M. (1979), *Fit for Work? Youth, School and (Un)employment*, London, Writers & Readers Publishing Cooperative.
Bamford, T.W. (1967), *The Rise of the Public Schools*, London, Nelson.
Bane, M.J. (1976), *Here to Stay: American Families in the Twentieth Century*, New York, Basic Books.
Banks, J.A. (1954), *Prosperity and Parenthood*, London, Routledge & Kegan Paul.
Banks, J.A. and O. (1964), *Feminism and Family Planning: a Study in Victorian England*, Liverpool University Press.
Banks, O. (1955), *Parity and Prestige in English Secondary Education*, London, Routledge & Kegan Paul.
Banks, O. (1976), *The Sociology of Education*, London, Batsford.
Barker, D.L. (1978), 'The Regulation of Marriage: Repressive Benevolence?', in G. Littlejohn *et al.* (eds) (1978).
Barker, D.L. and Allen, S. (eds) (1976a), *Sexual Divisions and Society: Process and Change*, London, Tavistock.
Barker, D.L. and Allen, S. (eds) (1976b), *Dependence and Exploitation in Work and Marriage*, London, Longman.
Barker, R. (1972), *Education and Politics 1900–1950*, Oxford University Press.
Baron, G. and Howell, D.E. (1974), *The Government and Management of Schools*, London, Athlone Press.
Barrell, G.R. (1975), *Teachers and the Law*, London, Methuen.
Barrett, M. *et al.* (1979), *Ideology and Cultural Reproduction*, London, Croom Helm.
Baumrind, D. (1972). 'From Each According to her Ability', *School Review*, vol. 80, February.
Beechey, V. (1977), 'Some Notes on Female Wage Labour', *Capital and Class*, no. 3 (Autumn).
Beeton, Mrs I. (1861), *Beeton's Book of Household Management*, S.O. Beeton.
Benn, C. and Simon, B. (1972), *Half Way There*, Penguin.
Bennett, N. (1976), *Teaching Styles and Pupil Progress*, London, Open Books.
Benston, M. (1970), 'The Political Economy of Women's Liberation', in L. Tanner (ed), *Voices from Women's Liberation*, New York, Signet.
Benton, T. (1974), 'Education and Politics', in D. Holly (ed.) (1974).
Berg, L. (1968), *Risinghill: Death of a Comprehensive*, Penguin.
Berger, N. (1974), *Rights*, Penguin.
Bernard, J. (1971), *Women and the Public Interest*, Chicago, Aldine Atherton.
Bernstein, B. (1972), *Class, Codes and Control*, vol. 1, London, Routledge & Kegan Paul.
Bernstein, B. (1975), *Class, Codes and Control*, vol. 3, London, Routledge & Kegan Paul (2nd ed., 1977).
Best, G. (1973), *Mid-Victorian Britain 1850–1875*, London, Fontana.
Beveridge, W. (1942), *Social Insurance and Allied Services* (the Beveridge Report), Cmd 6404, London, HMSO.

Birmingham Women's Studies Group (1978), *Women Take Issue: Aspects of Women's Subordination*, Birmingham, Centre for Contemporary Cultural Studies, and Hutchinson.

Blackstone, T. (1971), *A Fair Start: the Provision of Preschool Education*, Allen Lane, the Penguin Press.

Blackstone, T. (1976a), 'The Limits of Legislating for Equality for Women', *New Community*, vol. 5, nos. 1-2, summer.

Blackstone, T. (1976b), 'The Education of Girls Today', in J. Mitchell and A. Oakley (eds) (1976).

Blackstone, T. (1979), 'Parental Investment in Education', *Educational Policy Bulletin*, vol. 7, no. 1 (spring), pp. 81–99.

Blackstone, T. and Fulton, O. (1975), 'Sex Discrimination among University Teachers: a British-American Comparison', *British Journal of Sociology*, vol. 26, no. 3, pp. 261–75.

Blaxall, M. and Reagan, B. (1976), *Women and the Workplace: the Implications of Occupational Segregation*, University of Chicago Press.

Board of Education (1904a), *Regulations for Secondary Schools*, Code 2128, London, HMSO.

Board of Education (1904b), *Report of the Inter-Departmental Committee on Physical Deterioration*, Cd 2175, London, HMSO.

Board of Education (1905a), *Reports on Children under Five Years of Age in Public Elementary Schools by Women Inspectors*, Cd 2726, London, HMSO.

Board of Education (1905b), *Code of Regulations for Public Elementary Schools*, Cd 2579, London, HMSO.

Board of Education (1908), *Report of the Consultative Committee upon the School Attendance of Children below the Age of Five*, Cd 4259, London, HMSO.

Board of Education (1917), *Juvenile Education in Relation to Employment*, London, HMSO.

Board of Education (1923), *Differentiation of the Curricula between the Sexes in Secondary Schools* (Hadow Report), London, HMSO.

Board of Education (1926), *The Education of the Adolescent* (Hadow Report), London, HMSO.

Board of Education (1931), *The Primary School* (Hadow Report), London, HMSO.

Board of Education (1933), *The Nursery School* (Hadow Report), London, HMSO.

Board of Education (1938), *Secondary Education* (Spens Report), London, HMSO.

Board of Education (1941), *Education after the War* ('Green Book'), London, HMSO.

Board of Education (1943a), *Educational Reconstruction* (White Paper), London, HMSO.

Board of Education (1943b), *The Public Schools and the General Education System* (Fleming Report), London, HMSO.

Board of Education (1944), *The Supply, Training and Recruitment of Teachers and Youth Leaders* (McNair Report), London, HMSO.

Borer, M.C. (1976), *Willingly to School*, London, Lutterworth Press.

Bott, E. (1957), *Family and Social Network*, London, Tavistock.

Bourdieu, P. (1971a), 'Systems of Education and Systems of Thought', in E. Hopper (ed.), *Readings in the Theory of Educational Systems*, London, Hutchinson.

Bourdieu, P. (1971b), 'Intellectual Field and Creative Project', in M.F.D. Young (ed.) (1971).
Bourdieu, P. (1973), 'Cultural Reproduction and Social Reproduction', in R. Brown (ed.) (1973).
Bourdieu, P. (1976), 'The School as a Conservative Force', in R. Dale *et al.* (eds) (1976).
Bourdieu, P. and Passeron, J.C. (1977), *Reproduction in Education, Society and Culture*, London, Sage.
Bowles, S. and Gintis, H. (1976), *Schooling in Capitalist America*, London, Routledge & Kegan Paul.
Boyson, R. (1975), *The Crisis in Education*, London, Woburn Press.
Braverman, H. (1974), *Labor and Monopoly Capital*, New York, Monthly Review Press.
Bremmer, M. (1976), 'Schoolgirl Mothers: Should Our Schools be Doing More?', *Sunday Times*, 21 November.
Bristol Women's Studies Group (1979), *Half the Sky: an Introduction to Women's Studies*, London, Virago.
Brittain, V. (1928), *Women's Work in Modern England*, London, Noel Douglas.
Bronfenbrenner, U. (1974), *Two Worlds of Childhood: US and USSR*, Penguin.
Brown, M. and Baldwin, S. (eds) (1977), *Year Book of Social Policy in Britain 1976*, London, Routledge & Kegan Paul.
Brown, M. and Baldwin, S. (eds) (1978), *Year Book of Social Policy in Britain 1977*, London, Routledge & Kegan Paul.
Brown, R. (ed.) (1973), *Knowledge, Education and Cultural Change*, London, Tavistock.
Bull, D. (ed.) (1972), *Family Poverty*, London, Duckworth.
Bull, D.G. (forthcoming), 'What Price "Free" Education?', *Poverty Research Series*, London, Child Poverty Action Group.
Burgess, T. and Pratt, J. (1970), *Policy and Practice: Colleges of Advanced Technology*, London, Allen Lane, the Penguin Press.
Burgess, T. and Pratt, J. (1974), *Polytechnics: a Report*, London, Pitman.
Burman, S. (ed.) (1979), *Fit Work for Women*, London, Croom Helm.
Burstall, S. and Douglas, M.A. (eds) (1911), *Public Schools for Girls*, London, Longman Green.
Burstyn, J. (1973), 'Education and Sex: the Medical Case against Higher Education for Women in England, 1870–1900', *Proceedings of the American Philosophical Society*, vol. 117, no. 2 (April), pp. 79–89.
Byrne, E. (1978), *Women and Education*, London, Tavistock.
Cadogan, M. and Craig, P. (1976), *You're a Brick, Angela!*, London, Gollancz.
Cagan, E. (1978), 'Individualism versus Collectivism: Strategies for Reform', *Harvard Education Review*, vol. 48, no. 2 (May).
Calder, A. (1969), *The People's War*, London, Cape.
Central Advisory Council for Education [CACE] (1947), *School and Life*, London, HMSO.
CACE (1954), *Early Leaving*, London, HMSO.
CACE (1959), *15 to 18* (Crowther Report), London, HMSO.
CACE (1963), *Half our Future* (Newsom Report), London, HMSO.
CACE (1967), *Children and their Primary Schools* (Plowden Report), London, HMSO.
Central Policy Review Staff (1978), *Day-Care for Children of Working Mothers*, London, HMSO.
Chapman, J.R. and Gates, M. (eds) (1977), *Women into Wives: the Legal and Economic Impact of Marriage*, Beverly Hills and London, Sage.

Chetwynd, J. and Hartnett, O. (eds) (1978), *The Sex-Role System*, London, Routledge & Kegan Paul.
Children's Rights Workshop (1976), *Sexism in Children's Books*, London, Writers and Readers Publishing Cooperative.
Chodorow, N. (1978), *The Reproduction of Mothering: Family Structure and Feminine Personality*, University of California Press.
Clark, A. (1968), *The Working Life of Women in the Seventeenth Century*, London, Frank Cass (orig. ed., 1919).
Cobbe, F.P. (1894), *Life of Frances Power Cobbe by Herself*, London, Bentley.
Cockburn, C. (1977), *The Local State: Management of Cities and People*, London, Pluto Press.
Comer, L. (1974), *Wedlocked Women*, Leeds, Feminist Books.
Committee on Child Health Services (1976), *Fit for the Future* (Court Report), Cmnd 6684, London, HMSO.
Committee on Higher Education (1963), *Higher Education* (Robbins Report), Cmnd 2154, London, HMSO.
Coote, A. and Gill, T. (1977), *Women's Rights: a Practical Guide*, 2nd ed., Penguin.
Cosin, B.R. *et al.* (eds) (1971), *School and Society: a Sociological Reader*, London, Routledge & Kegan Paul (2nd ed., 1977).
Cottle, T. (1976), *Barred from School: 2 Million Children!*, Washington, D.C., New Republic Book Co.
Coulson, M. *et al.* (1975), 'Women and the Class Struggle', *New Left Review*, 89.
Council for Scientific Policy (1968), *Enquiry into the Flow of Candidates in Science and Technology into Higher Education* (Dainton Report), Cmnd 3541, London, HMSO.
Counter Information Service (1977), *Crisis: Women under Attack*, CIS Anti-Report no. 15, London.
County of Avon Education Service (1977), 'External Influences and Pressures on Schools', Bristol, unpublished mimeograph.
Coussins, J. (1977), *The Equality Report*, London, NCCL.
Cowley, J. *et al.* (1977), *Community or Class Struggle*, London, Stage 7.
Cox, C.B. and Boyson, R. (eds) (1977), *Black Paper* no. 5, London, Temple Smith.
Cox, C.B. and Dyson, A.E. (eds) (1969), *Black Papers on Education*, nos 1, 2 and 3, London, *Critical Quarterly* Society.
Craft, M. (ed.) (1970), *Family, Class and Education*, London, Longman.
Craft, M. *et al.* (eds) (1972), *Linking Home and School*, 2nd ed., London, Longman.
Dale, R. (1979a), 'The Politicization of School Deviance: Reactions to William Tyndale', unpublished paper, Milton Keynes, the Open University.
Dale, R. (1979b), 'Parent Participation and Teacher Autonomy', unpublished paper, Milton Keynes, the Open University.
Dale, R. *et al.* (eds) (1976), *Schooling and Capitalism: a Sociological Reader*, London, Routledge & Kegan Paul.
Dale, R.R. (1969), *Mixed or Single-Sex School?*, vol. 1, London, Routledge & Kegan Paul.
Dale, R.R. (1971), *Mixed or Single-Sex School?*, vol. 2, London, Routledge & Kegan Paul.
Dale, R.R. (1974), *Mixed or Single-Sex School?*, vol. 3, London, Routledge & Kegan Paul.
David, M.E. (1975), *School Rule in the USA: Professionalism and Participation in School Budgeting*, Cambridge, Mass., Ballinger.
David, M.E. (1976), 'Size and Education: a Chimerical Relationship', *New*

Universities Quarterly, vol. 31, no. 7, winter.

David, M.E. (1977), *Reform, Reaction and Resources: the 3 Rs of Educational Planning*, Windsor, NFER Publishing Co.

David, M.E. (1978a), 'The Family-Education Couple: Towards an Analysis of the William Tyndale Dispute', in G. Littlejohn *et al.* (eds) (1978).

David, M.E. (1978b), 'Parents and Educational Politics in 1977', in M. Brown and S. Baldwin (eds) (1978).

David, M.E. (1978c), 'Women Caring for Preschoolers in the USA', *International Journal of Urban Regional Research*, vol. 2, no. 3.

David, M. and Lezine, I. (1975), *Early Child-Care in France*, London, Gordon & Breach.

Davidoff, L. (1973), *The Best Circles*, London, Croom Helm.

Davies, B. (1976), *Social Control and Education*, London, Methuen.

Davies, L. and Meighan, R. (1975), 'A Review of Schooling and Sex Roles with Particular Reference to the Experience of Girls in Secondary Schools', in R. Meighan and J. Doherty (eds) (1975), pp. 165–72.

Davies, M.L. (ed.) (1977), *Life as We Have Known It, by Cooperative Working Women*, London, Virago (orig. ed., 1931).

Davies, M.L. (ed.) (1978), *Maternity: Letters from Working Women*, London, Virago (orig. ed., 1915).

Davies, R. (1975), *Women and Work*, London, Arrow.

Davin, A. (1978), 'A Centre of Humanising Influence: the Schooling of Working Class Girls under the London School Board 1870–1902', work in progress.

Davin, A. (1979), 'Imperialism and Motherhood', *History Workshop*, no. 5, spring, pp. 9–65.

Deem, R. (1976), 'Professionalism, Unity and Militant Action: the Case of Teachers', *Sociological Review*, vol. 24, no. 1 (February), pp. 43–61.

Deem, R. (1978), *Women and Schooling*, London, Routledge & Kegan Paul.

Delamont, S. (1976), *Interaction in the Classroom*, London, Methuen.

Delamont, S. and Duffin, L. (eds) (1978), *The Nineteenth Century Woman: her Cultural and Physical World*, London, Croom Helm.

Dent, H.C. (1961), *The Educational System of England and Wales*, London, Hodder & Stoughton.

Department of Education and Science [DES] (1965), *The Organisation of Secondary Education*, circular 10/65.

DES (1966), *Study Group on Government of Colleges of Education* (Weaver Report), London, HMSO.

DES (1970), *Organisation of Secondary Education*, circular 10/70.

DES (1972a), *Education: a Framework for Expansion*, Cmnd 5174, London, HMSO.

DES (1972b), *Educational Priority*: vol. 1, *Problems and Policies*, by A.H. Halsey, London, HMSO.

DES (1972c), *Teacher Education and Training* (James Report), London, HMSO.

DES (1973), *Report on Education*, no. 78, July, London, HMSO.

DES (1974a), *Reorganisation of Secondary Education*, circular 4/74.

DES (1974b), *Educational Disadvantage and the Educational Needs of Immigrants* (White Paper), Cmnd 5720, London, HMSO.

DES (1974c), *School Building Programmes*, circular 10/74.

DES (1974d), *The Development of Higher Education in the Non-University Sector: Interim Arrangements for the Control of Advanced Courses*, circular 6/74.

DES (1975a), *Educational Priority*: vol. 3, *Curriculum Innovation in London's EPA's*, by J. Barnes, London, HMSO.

DES (1975b), *Curricular Differences for Boys and Girls*, Education Survey, no. 21, London, HMSO.
DES (1975c), *The Reorganisation of Higher Education in the Non-University Sector: The Further Education Regulations 1975*, circular 5/75.
DES (1976), *Educating Our Children: Four Subjects for Debate*, London, DES.
DES (1977a), *Education in Schools: a Consultative Document*, Cmnd 6869, London, HMSO.
DES (1977b), *Admission of Children to Schools of their Parents' Choice*, Consultation Paper, October, London, DES.
DES (1977c), *Ten Good Schools: a Secondary School Enquiry*, HMI series, no. 1, London, HMSO.
DES (1978a), *Progress in Education: a Report on Recent Initiatives*, London, HMSO.
DES (1978b), *School Examinations* (Waddell Report), London, HMSO.
DES (1979), *16-18: Education and Training for 16- to 18-Year-Olds: a Consultative Paper*, London, DES.
DES and Welsh Office (1977), *A New Partnership for our Schools* (Taylor Report), London, HMSO.
DES Committee of Enquiry (1973), *Adult Education: a Plan for Development* (Russell Report), London, HMSO.
DES Committee of Enquiry (1975), *A Language for Life* (Bullock Report), London, HMSO.
Department of Employment (1975), *Women and Work*, Manpower Paper no. 11, London, HMSO.
Department of Health and Social Security [DHSS] (1974a), *Report of the Committee on One-Parent Families* (Finer Report), Cmnd 5629-I, Appendix: 'The History of the Obligation to Maintain', by M. Finer and O. McGregor, London, HMSO.
DHSS (1974b), *The Family in Society: Dimensions of Parenthood*, London, HMSO.
DHSS (1974c), *The Family in Society: Preparation for Parenthood*, London, HMSO.
Devlin, T. and Warnock, M. (1977), *What Must We Teach?*, London, Temple Smith.
Donnison, J. (1977), *Midwives and Medical Men*, London, Heinemann.
Dore, R. (1976), *The Diploma Disease: Education, Qualification and Development*, London, Allen & Unwin.
Douglas, J.W.B. (1967), *The Home and the School*, London, Panther.
Douglas, J.W.B. *et al.* (1968), *All our Future*, London, Peter Davies.
Drabble, M. (1975), 'Men Eat Too, So Why Aren't Boys Taught to Cook?', *The Times*, 26 November.
Dyhouse, C. (1976), 'Social Darwinistic Ideas and the Development of Women's Education in England, 1870–1920', *History of Education*, vol. 5, no. 1, pp. 41–58.
Dyhouse, C. (1977), 'Good Wives and Little Mothers: Social Anxieties and the Schoolgirls' Curriculum, 1890–1920', *Oxford Review of Education*, vol. 3, no. 1.
Dyhouse, C. (1978), 'Working Class Mothers and Infant Mortality in England 1895–1914', *Journal of Social History*, vol. 12, no. 2.
Easton, B. (1978), 'Feminism and the Contemporary Family', *Socialist Review*, vol. 39.
Edholm, F. *et al.* (eds) (1977), Women's Issue of *Critique of Anthropology*, vol. 3, nos 9 and 10.

Edmonds, E.L. (1962), *The School Inspector*, London, Routledge & Kegan Paul.
Education (1972), 'Analysis of the James Report', 8 December, p. ii.
Education (1973), 'The Russell Report: a Summary', 30 March, pp. i–iv.
Education Commission (1861), *Report on the State of Popular Education in England* (Newcastle), London, Eyre & Spottiswoode for HMSO.
Edwards, B. (1974), *The Burston School Strike*, London, Lawrence & Wishart.
Elementary Education Acts (1888), *Report of the Commissioners* (Cross), C-5485, London, Eyre & Spottiswoode for HMSO.
Ellis, T. *et al.* (1976), *William Tyndale's: the Teachers' Story*, London, Writers and Readers Publishing Cooperative.
Engels, F. (1969), *The Condition of the Working Class in 1844*, London, Panther.
Engels, F. (1972), *The Origin of the Family, Private Property and the State*, New York, Pathfinder Press (orig. ed., 1884).
Equal Opportunities Commission [EOC] (1977a), *Report of the Formal Investigation into Equal Provision of Secondary Education as between the Sexes in the Area of the LEA of Tameside Metropolitan Borough 1976–77*, Manchester, EOC, December.
EOC (1977b), *First Annual Report*, Manchester, EOC.
EOC (1978a), *Second Annual Report*, Manchester, EOC.
EOC (1978b), 'I Want to Work but What About the Kids?', Manchester, EOC.
EOC (1979a), *Research Bulletin*, vol. 1, nos 1 and 2, Manchester, EOC.
EOC (1979b), *Third Annual Report*, Manchester, EOC.
Evans, E.J. (ed.) (1978), *Social Policy 1830–1914*, London, Routledge & Kegan Paul.
Expenditure Committee, House of Commons (Education and Arts Sub-committee) (1974), *Educational Maintenance Allowances in the 16–18 Years Age Group* (Third Report), London, HMSO.
Eyken, W. van der (1968), *The Pre-School Years*, Penguin.
Eyken, W. van der (1973), *Education, Child and Society 1900–1973: a Documentary History*, Penguin.
Fabian Society (1966), *Womanpower*, Young Fabian Pamphlet no. 11, London.
Fenwick, R.G. (1976), *The Comprehensive School, 1944–70*, London, Methuen.
Ferguson, S.M. and Fitzgerald, H. (1954), *Studies in the Social Services*, London, Longman, Green for HMSO.
Fine, B. and Harris, L. (1976), 'The State Expenditure Debate', *New Left Review*, 98.
Finer, M. and McGregor, O. (1974), *see* DHSS (1974a).
Finn, D. *et al.* (1977), 'Social Democracy, Education and the Crisis', in *On Ideology, Cultural Studies*, no. 10, Birmingham, Centre for Contemporary Cultural Studies, and Hutchinson.
Firestone, S. (1972), *The Dialectic of Sex*, St Albans, Paladin.
Fishel, A. and Pottker, J. (1977), *National Politics and Sex Discrimination in Education*, Lexington, Mass., D.C. Heath.
Fitzherbert, K. (1977), *Child-Care Services and The Teacher*, London, Temple Smi
Fleet, L. (1976), 'Some Margins of Compulsory Education', unpublished Ph.D. thesis, University of Bristol.
Floud, J., Halsey, A.H. and Anderson, C.A. (eds) (1961), *Education, Economy and Society*, New York, Free Press.
Flude, M. and Ahier, J. (eds) (1975), *Educability, Schools and Ideology*, London, Croom Helm.
Fonda, N. and Moss, P. (eds) (1976), *Mothers in Employment*, Uxbridge, Brunel University Management Programme and Thomas Coram Research Unit.
Foreman, A. (1977), *Femininity as Alienation: Women and the Family in*

Marxism and Psychoanalysis, London, Pluto Press.
Fowler, G. *et al.* (eds) (1973), *Decision-Making in Education*, London, Methuen.
Fransella, F. and Frost, K. (1977), *On Being a Woman*, London, Tavistock.
Friedan, B. (1965), *The Feminine Mystique*, Penguin.
Gardiner, D. (1929), *English Girlhood at School: a Study of Women's Education through Twelve Centuries to 1800*, Oxford University Press.
Gardiner, J. (1974), 'Women's Employment Since the Sixties', *Spare Rib*, no. 27 (September).
Gardiner, J. (1975), 'The Role of Domestic Labour', *New Left Review*, 89, pp. 47–58.
Gardiner, J. (1976), 'Political Economy of Domestic Labour in Capitalist Society', in D.L. Barker and S. Allen (eds) (1976b).
Gardiner, J. *et al.* (1975), 'Women's Domestic Labour', *Bulletin of the Conference of Socialist Economists*, vol. 4, no. 2, pp. 1–11.
Gartner, A. (ed.) (1973), *After Deschooling, What?*, New York, Harper & Row.
Gathorne-Hardy, J. (1972), *The Rise and Fall of the British Nanny*, London, Arrow.
Gathorne-Hardy, J. (1977), *The Public School Phenomenon*, London, Hodder & Stoughton.
Gavron, H. (1966), *The Captive Wife*, London, Routledge & Kegan Paul.
Geddes, D. (1979), 'What Will Happen to Grammar Schools?', *New Society*, vol. 49, no. 874, 5 July.
George, V. and Wilding, P. (1976), *Ideology and Social Welfare*, London, Routledge & Kegan Paul.
Gilbert, B. (1966), *The Evolution of National Insurance in Great Britain*, London, Michael Joseph.
Gilbert, B. (1970), *British Social Policy: 1914–1939*, London, Batsford.
Glennerster, H. (1971), 'Education and Inequality', in P. Townsend and N. Bosanquet (eds), *Labour and Inequality*, London, Fabian Society.
Glennerster, H. (1975), *Social Service Budgets and Social Policy*, London, Allen & Unwin.
Glennerster, H. and Wilson, G. (1971), *Paying for Private Schools*, London, Allen Lane, the Penguin Press.
Goodman, P. (1971), *Compulsory Miseducation*, Penguin.
Gordon, P. (1974), *The Victorian School Manager: a Study in the Management of Education*, London, Woburn Press.
Gosden, P.J.H. (1966), *The Development of Educational Administration in England and Wales*, Oxford, Basil Blackwell.
Gosden, P.J.H. (1972), *The Evolution of a Profession: a Study of the Contribution of Teacher Associations to the Development of School Teaching as a Professional Occupation*, Oxford, Basil Blackwell.
Gosden, P.J.H. (1976), *Education in the Second World War: a Study in Policy and Administration*, London, Methuen.
Gough, I. (1972), 'Marx's Theory of Productive and Unproductive Labour', *New Left Review*, 76.
Gough, I. (1979), *The Political Economy of the Welfare State*, London, Macmillan.
Gramsci, A. (1971), *Selections from the Prison Notebooks*, London, Lawrence & Wishart.
Graves, J.T.R. (1943), *Policy and Progress in Secondary Education 1902–1942*, London, Nelson.
Green, M. (1976), *Goodbye Father*, London, Routledge & Kegan Paul.
Greer, G. (1971), *The Female Eunuch*, St Albans, Paladin.

Gretton, J. and Jackson, M. (1976), *Collapse of a School or a System?*, London, Allen & Unwin.
Griffith, J.A.G. (1966), *Central Departments and Local Authorities*, London, Allen & Unwin.
Griffith, J.A.G. (1976), 'The Tameside Opinion', *New Statesman*, 29 October.
Griffith, J.A.G. (1977), *The Politics of the Judiciary*, London, Fontana.
Grubb, W.N. and Lazerson, M. (1977), 'Child-Care, Government Financing and the Public Schools: Lessons from the California Children's Centers', *School Review*, 86, pp. 5–37.
Haigh, G. (1974), *The School and the Parent*, London, Pitman.
Halevy, E. (1929), *A History of the British People 1895–1905*, London, Benn.
Hall, C. (1974), 'The History of the Housewife', *Spare Rib*, no. 26.
Hall, C. (1974), 'The Early Formation of Victorian Domestic Ideology', in S. Burman (ed.) (1979).
Hall, S. (1979), 'The Great Moving Right Show', *Marxism Today*, vol. 23, no. 1, pp. 14–21.
Halsey, A.H. (1977), 'Whatever Happened to Positive Discrimination?', *The Times Educational Supplement*, 21 January.
Hamilton, R. (1978), *The Liberation of Women*, London, Allen & Unwin.
Hammersley, M. and Woods, P. (eds) (1976), *The Process of Schooling*, London, Routledge & Kegan Paul.
Hargreaves, D. (1967), *Social Relations in a Secondary School*, London, Routledge & Kegan Paul.
Harris, C. (1969), *The Family*, London, Allen & Unwin.
Hewitt, M. (1958), *Wives and Mothers in Victorian Industry*, London, Barrie & Rockliffe.
Hobsbawm, E.J. (1964), *Labouring Men*, London, Weidenfeld & Nicolson.
Holcombe, L. (1973), *Victorian Ladies at Work 1850–1914*, Newton Abbot, David & Charles.
Holloway, J. and Picciotto, S. (eds) (1978), *State and Capital: a Marxist Debate*, London, Edward Arnold.
Holly, D. (ed.) (1974), *Education or Domination?*, London, Arrow.
Honey, J. de S. (1977), *Tom Brown's Universe: the Development of the Victorian Public School*, London, Millington Books.
Hopkins, A. (1978), *The School Debate*, Penguin.
Horn, P. (1976), 'Above their Class', *The Times Educational Supplement*, 6 August.
Horn, P. (1978), *Education in Rural England 1800–1914*, Dublin, Gill & Macmillan.
Howe, L. (1954), *A Galaxy of Governesses*, London, Verschoyle.
Hoyle, E. (1969), *The Role of the Teacher*, London, Routledge & Kegan Paul.
Huber, J. (ed.) (1973), *Changing Women in a Changing Society*, University of Chicago Press.
Hunt, A. (1978), *The Elderly at Home* (Government Social Survey), London, HMSO.
Hurt, J.S. (1971), *Education in Evolution: Church, State, Society and Popular Education 1800–1870*, London, R. Hart-Davis.
Hussain, A. (1976), 'The Economy and the Educational System in Capitalistic Societies', *Economy and Society*, vol. 5, no. 4, pp. 413–34.
Illich, I. (1972), *Deschooling Society*, London, Calder & Boyars.
Inter-Departmental Committee on Medical Inspection and Feeding of Children Attending Public Elementary Schools (1905), *Report*, Cd 2784, Wyman for HMSO.

Jackson, B. (1962), *Streaming: an Education System in Miniature*, London, Routledge & Kegan Paul.

Jackson, B. and S. (1979), *Childminder*, London, Routledge & Kegan Paul.

Jackson, B. and Marsden, D. (1966), *Education and the Working Class*, Penguin.

Jackson, J.A. (ed.) (1971), *Professions and Professionalization*, Cambridge University Press.

James, Lord (1973), 'Teacher Education and Training', in K. Jones (ed.) (1973).

Janeway, E. (1971), *Man's World, Woman's Place*, London, Michael Joseph.

Jencks, C. *et al.* (1975), *Inequality: a Reassessment of the Effects of Family and Schooling in America*, Penguin.

Joffe, C.E. (1977), *Friendly Intruders: Childcare Professionals and Family Life*, University of California Press.

Johnson, R. (1970), 'Education and Social Control in Early Victorian England', *Past and Present*, 49, pp. 96–119.

Johnson, T. (1972), *Professions and Power*, London, Macmillan.

Joll, C. (1977), 'Teachers' Pay', *Women in Education Newsletter*, no. 10, spring.

Jones, Karen (1977), 'Women's Education', Course E352, S5, Milton Keynes, Open University Press.

Jones, Kathleen (ed.) (1973), *Year Book of Social Policy in Britain 1972*, London, Routledge & Kegan Paul.

Judd, J. (1977), 'A Woman's Place is Less and Less in Teaching', *The Times Higher Educational Supplement*, 19 August.

Judge, H. (1974), *School Is Not Yet Dead*, London, Longman.

Kalton, G. (1966), *The Public Schools: a Factual Survey*, London, Longman.

Kamm, J. (1958), *How Different from Us: a Biography of Miss Buss and Miss Beale*, London, Bodley Head.

Kamm, J. (1965), *Hope Deferred: Girls' Education in English History*, London, Methuen.

Kamm, J. (1966), *Rapiers and Battleaxes: the Women's Movement and its Aftermath*, London, Allen & Unwin.

Kamm, J. (1971), *Indicative Past: the Girls' Public Day School Trust*, London, Bodley Head.

Katz, M. (1973), *Class, Bureaucracy and the Schools*, Boston, Little, Brown.

Keddie, N. (1974), *Tinker, Tailor: the Myth of Cultural Deprivation*, Penguin.

Kelly, A. (1974), 'Science for Men Only?', *New Scientist*, 29 August.

Kelly, A. (1976), 'Women in Science: a Bibliographical Review', *Durham Research Review*, vol. 36, spring.

Kelsall, R.K. and H.M. (1969), *The Schoolteacher in England and the United States*, Oxford, Pergamon.

King, R. (1971), 'Unequal Access in Education: Sex and Social Class', *Social and Economic Administration*, vol. 5, no. 3, pp. 167–75.

Kitteringham, J. (1975), 'Country Girls in Nineteenth-century England', in R. Samuel (ed.), *Village Life and Labour*, London, Routledge & Kegan Paul.

Kogan, M. (ed.) (1971), *The Politics of Education*, Penguin.

Kuhn, A. and Wolpe, A.M. (eds) (1978), *Feminism and Materialism*, London, Routledge & Kegan Paul.

Lacey, C. (1970), *Hightown Grammar*, Manchester University Press.

Laing, M. (ed.) (1971), *Woman on Woman*, London, Sidgwick & Jackson.

Lamb, F. and Pickthorn, H. (1968), *Locked up Daughters*, London, Hodder & Stoughton.

Lambart, A.M. (1976), 'The Sisterhood', in M. Hammersley and P. Woods (eds) (1976).

Lambert, R. (1966), *The State and Boarding Education*, London, Methuen.

Lambert, R. (1968a), *The Hothouse Society*, London, Weidenfeld & Nicolson.
Lambert, R. (1968b), *New Wine in Old Bottles?*, London, G. Bell.
Lambert, R. *et al.* (1975), *The Chance of a Lifetime?*, London, Weidenfeld & Nicolson.
Land, H. (1976), 'Women: Supporters or Supported?', in D.L. Barker and S. Allen (eds) (1976a).
Land, H. (1978), 'Who Cares for the Family?', *Journal of Social Policy*, vol. 7, no. 3.
Land, H. (1979), 'The Changing Place of Women in Europe', *Daedalus: Journal of American Academy of Arts and Sciences*, vol. 108, no. 2 (spring).
Lasch, C. (1977), *Haven in a Heartless World: the Family Besieged*, New York, Basic Books.
Laslett, P. (ed.) (1971), *Household and Family in Past Time*, Cambridge University Press.
Lawson, J. and Silver, H. (1973), *A Social History of Education in England*, London, Methuen.
Lawton, D. (1975), *Class, Culture and the Curriculum*, London, Routledge & Kegan Paul.
Lipshitz, S. (ed.) (1978), *Tearing the Veil: Essays on Femininity*, London, Routledge & Kegan Paul.
Littlejohn, G. *et al.* (eds) (1978), *Power and the State*, London, Croom Helm.
Lord President of the Council (1946), *Scientific Manpower: Report of a Special Committee* (Barlow Report), London, HMSO.
Lowndes, G.A.N. (1969), *The Silent Social Revolution: an Account of the Expansion of Public Education in England and Wales 1895–1965*, Oxford University Press (orig. ed., 1937).
McBarnet, D. (1978), 'Police and State: Arrest, Legality and the Law', in G. Littlejohn *et al.* (eds) (1978).
McClure, J.S. (1967), *Educational Documents for England and Wales 1815–1967*, London, Methuen.
McGeeney, P. (1969), *Parents Are Welcome*, London, Longman.
McGregor, O. (1955), 'The Social Position of Women in England 1850–1914: a Bibliography', *British Journal of Sociology*, vol. 6, no. 1.
McIntosh, M. (1978), 'The State and the Oppression of Women', in A. Kuhn and A.M. Wolpe (eds) (1978).
Mack, E.C. (1938), *Public Schools and British Opinion: 1780–1860*, London, Methuen.
Mack, J. (1979), 'Quality, not just Quantity, for London's Schools?', *New Society*, vol. 47, no. 857, 8 March.
Mackie, L. and Pattullo, P. (1977), *Women at Work*, London, Tavistock.
McRobbie, A. and Garber, J. (1976), 'Girls in Subcultures', in S. Hall and T. Jefferson (eds), *Resistance through Ritual: Youth Culture in Postwar Britain*, London, Hutchinson.
Mandel, E. (1975), *Late Capitalism*, London, New Left Books.
Manpower Services Commission (1977), *Young People and Work* (Holland Report) London, MSC.
Manzer, R. (1970), *Teachers and Politics*, Manchester University Press.
Marks, P. (1976), 'Femininity in the Classroom: an Account of Changing Attitudes', in J. Mitchell and A. Oakley (eds) (1976).
Marsden, D. (1969), *Mothers Alone*, Penguin.
Marsden, D. (1971), 'Politicians, Equality and Comprehensive Schools', in P. Townsend and N. Bosanquet (eds), *Labour and Inequality*, London, Fabian Society.

Marwick, A. (1965), *The Deluge: British Society and the First World War*, London, Bodley Head.
Marwick, A. (1968), *Britain in the Century of Total War*, London, Bodley Head.
Marwick, A. (1977), *Women at War: 1914–1918*, London, Fontana.
Marx, K. (1971), *Capital*, vol. 1, London, Allen & Unwin (orig. ed., 1889).
Mause, L. de (ed.) (1976), *The History of Childhood*, London, Souvenir Press.
Maynard, A. (1975), *Experiment with Choice in Education*, London, Institute of Economic Affairs.
Mayo, M. (ed.) (1977), *Women in the Community*, London, Routledge & Kegan Paul.
Meighan, R. and Doherty, J. (eds) (1975), *Education and Sex Roles, Educational Review*, vol. 27, no. 3 (June).
Midwinter, E. (1970), *Nineteenth Century Education*, London, Longman.
Midwinter, E. (1972), *Priority Education*, Penguin.
Miliband, R. (1973), *The State in Capitalist Society*, London, Quartet (orig. ed., 1969).
Miliband, R. (1977), *Marxism and Politics*, Oxford University Press.
Mill, J.S. and H.T. (ed. A. Rossi) (1970), *Essays on Sex Equality*, University of Chicago Press.
Millman, M. and Kanter, R.M. (eds) (1975), *Another Voice*, New York, Doubleday.
Ministry of Education (1945), *Higher Technological Education* (Percy Report), London, HMSO.
Ministry of Education (1950), *Report of the Working Party on the Supply of Women Teachers* (Roseveare Report), London, HMSO.
Ministry of Education (1956), *Technical Education*, Cmnd 9703, London, HMSO.
Ministry of Education (1957), *Report of the Working Party on EMAs* (Weaver Report), London, HMSO.
Ministry of Education (1958), *Secondary Education for All: a New Drive* (White Paper), London, HMSO.
Ministry of Education (1960), *Secondary School Examinations Other Than GCE* (Beloe Report), London, HMSO.
Ministry of Reconstruction (1919), *Report of the Women's Employment Committee*, Cd 9239, London, HMSO.
Mitchell, H. (1977), *The Hard Way up*, London, Virago (orig. ed., Faber & Faber, 1968).
Mitchell, J. (1971), *Women's Estate*, Penguin, esp. pp. 131–8.
Mitchell, J. and Oakley, A. (eds) (1976), *The Rights and Wrongs of Women*, Penguin.
Morgan, D. (1975), *Social Theory and the Family*, London, Routledge & Kegan Paul.
Moroney, R. (1978), *The Family and the State*, London, Longman.
Murphy, J. (1972), *The Education Act 1870: Text and Commentary*, Newton Abbot, David & Charles.
Musgrove, F. (1964), *Youth and the Social Order*, London, Routledge & Kegan Paul.
Musgrove, F. (1966), *Family, Education and Society*, London, Routledge & Kegan Paul.
Musgrove, F. (1971), *Patterns of Authority in English Education*, London, Routledge & Kegan Paul.
Nandy, L. and D. (1975), 'Towards True Equality for Women', *New Society*, 30 January.

Nandy, L. and D. (1976), 'Towards True Equality for Women', *New Community*, vol. 5, nos 1–2.
Neff, W.F. (1966), *Victorian Working Women: an Historical and Literary Study of Women in British Industry and Professions 1832–1850*, London, Frank Cass (orig. ed., 1929).
Neill, A.S. (1962), *Summerhill: a Radical Approach to Education*, London, Gollancz.
New Society (1977), 'Is Youth Unemployment Really the Problem?', vol. 24, no. 788, 10 November, pp. 287–9.
New Society (1978), *The World of Childhood*, vol. 46, nos 846–7, 21–28 December.
Newsom, J. (1948), *The Education of Girls*, London, Faber & Faber.
Newson, J. and E. (1977), *Perspectives on School at Seven Years Old*, London, Allen & Unwin.
Nicholson, J. (1977), *What Society Does to Girls*, London, Virago.
Noue, G. de la (ed.) (1972), *Educational Vouchers: Concepts and Controversies*, New York, Teachers College Press.
Oakley, A. (1972), *Sex, Gender and Society*, London, Temple Smith.
Oakley, A. (1974), *The Sociology of Housework*, London, Martin Robertson.
Oakley, A. (1977), *Housewife*, Penguin.
Oakley, A. (1979), 'The Failure of the Movement for Women's Equality', *New Society*, vol. 49, no. 881, 23 August, pp. 392–4.
Office of Population Censuses and Surveys [OPCS] (1975a), *Management Attitudes and Practices Towards Women at Work*, by A. Hunt, HMSO.
OPCS (1975b), *Fifth Form Girls: their Hopes for the Future*, by I. Rauta and A. Hunt, London, HMSO.
OPCS (1977), *Pre-school Children and the Need for Day-Care*, by M. Bone, London, HMSO.
Ollerenshaw, K. (1967), *The Girls' Schools*, London, Faber & Faber.
Packman, J. (1975), *The Child's Generation: Child Care Policy from Curtis to Houghton*, London and Oxford, Martin Robertson and Basil Blackwell.
Parker, J. (1975), *Social Policy and Citizenship*, London, Macmillan.
Parkinson, M. (1970), *The Labour Party and the Organisation of Secondary Education: 1918–1965*, London, Routledge & Kegan Paul.
Parry, N. and J. (1975), 'The Teacher and Professionalism: the Failure of an Occupational Strategy', in M. Flude and J. Ahier (eds) (1975).
Partington, G. (1976), *Women Teachers in the Twentieth Century*, Windsor, NFER Publishing Co.
Pedersen, J.S. (1975), 'Schoolmistresses and Headmistresses: Elites and Education in 19th Century England', *Journal of British Studies*, vol. 15, no. 7 (November), pp. 135–62.
Pedley, R. (1960), *The Comprehensive School*, Penguin.
Peterson, M.J. (1972), 'The Victorian Governess', in M. Vicinus (ed.) (1972).
Phillips, M. (1978), 'Family Policy: Years of Neglect', *New Society*, 8 June.
Pierotti, A.M. (1963), *The Story of the National Union of Women Teachers*, National Union of Women Teachers.
Pinchbeck, I. (1969), *Women Workers in the Industrial Revolution 1750–1850*, London, Frank Cass (orig. ed., 1930).
Pinchbeck, I. and Hewitt, M. (1969), *Children in English Society*: vol. 1, *From Tudor Times to the Eighteenth Century*, London, Routledge & Kegan Paul.
Pinchbeck, I. and Hewitt, M. (1973), *Children in English Society*: vol. 2, *From the Eighteenth Century to the Children Act 1948*, London, Routledge & Kegan Paul.

Piven, F.F. and Cloward, R. (1972), *Regulating the Poor*, New York, Pantheon.
Piven, F.F. and Cloward, R. (1978), *Poor People's Movements: How They Succeed: Why They Fail*, New York, Pantheon.
Political Economy of Women Group (1974), *On the Political Economy of Women*, Pamphlet no. 2, London, Conference of Socialist Economists.
Poster, M. (1978), *Critical Theory of the Family*, London, Pluto Press.
Poulantzas, N. (1973), *Political Power and Social Classes*, London, New Left Books.
Poulantzas, N. (1975), *Classes in Contemporary Capitalism*, London, New Left Books.
Pratt, J. *et al.* (1973), *Your Local Education*, Penguin.
Price, M. and Glenday, N. (1974), *Reluctant Revolutionaries*, London, Pitman.
Public Schools Commission (1864), *Revenues and Management of Certain Colleges and Schools* (Clarendon Report), London, Eyre & Spottiswoode for HMSO.
Public Schools Commission (1968), *First Report*, London, HMSO.
Public Schools Commission (1969), *Second Report*, London, HMSO.
Rapoport, R. and R. and Strelitz, Z. (1977), *Fathers, Mothers and Others*, London, Routledge & Kegan Paul.
Reddin, M. (1968), 'Educational Maintenance Allowances: Lost, Stolen or Strayed?', *Where*, November.
Reimer, E. (1973), *School Is Dead*, Penguin.
Rendel, M. *et al.* (1968), *Equality for Women*, Fabian Research Series no. 268, London, Fabian Society.
Rich, R.W. (1933), *The Training of Teachers in England and Wales in the Nineteenth Century*, Cambridge University Press.
Richardson, E. (1973), *The Teacher, the School and the Task of Management*, London, Heinemann.
Richmond, W.K. (1975), *Education and Schooling*, London, Methuen.
Riley, D. (1979), 'War in the Nursery', *Feminist Review*, vol. 1, no. 2.
Roach, J. (1971), *Public Examinations in England 1850–1960*, Cambridge University Press.
Robinson, P. (1977), *Education and Poverty*, London, Methuen.
Rogers, J. and Groombridge, B. (1976), *Right to Learn: the Case for Adult Equality*, London, Arrow.
Rosen, A. (1974), *Rise up Women*, London, Routledge & Kegan Paul.
Rosser, C. and Harris, C. (1968), *The Family and Social Change*, London, Routledge & Kegan Paul.
Rowbotham, S. (1972), *Women, Resistance and Revolution*, Penguin.
Rowbotham, S. (1973a), *Hidden from History*, London, Pluto Press.
Rowbotham, S. (1973b), *Woman's Consciousness: Man's World*, Penguin.
Royal Commission on Equal Pay, 1944–1946 (1946), *Report*, Cmd 6937, London, HMSO.
Royal Commission on Secondary Education (1895), *Report* (Bryce), C-7862, London, Eyre & Spottiswoode for HMSO.
Rubinstein, D. and Simon, B. (1969), *The Evolution of the Comprehensive School*, London, Routledge & Kegan Paul.
Rubinstein, D. and Stoneham, C. (eds) (1972), *Education for Democracy*, Penguin.
Russell, D. (1932), *In Defence of Children*, London, Hamilton.
Rutter, M. (1972), *Maternal Deprivation Reassessed*, Penguin.
Rutter, M. *et al.* (1979), *Fifteen Thousand Hours*, London, Open Books.
Rutter, M. and Madge, N. (1976), *Cycles of Disadvantage*, London, Heinemann.

Ryan, W. (1973), *Blaming the Victim*, New York, Vintage.
Sachs, A. and Wilson, J.H. (1978), *Sexism and the Law: a Study of Male Beliefs and Judicial Bias*, Oxford, Martin Robertson.
Sallis, J. (1978), *Current Practice in School Government* (A *Where* Survey), Cambridge, Advisory Centre for Education.
Saran, R. (1973), *Policy-Making in Secondary Education: a Case Study*, Oxford, the Clarendon Press.
Sarup, M. (1978), *Marxism and Education*, London, Routledge & Kegan Paul.
School without Walls (1978), *Lunatic Ideas: How Newspapers Treated Education in 1977*, London, Cornerhouse Bookshop.
Schools Council (1965), *Change and Response*, London, HMSO.
Schools Inquiry Commission [SIC] (1868), (Taunton), *Report*, London, Eyre & Spottiswoode for HMSO.
Searle, G. (1971), *The Quest for National Efficiency 1899–1914*, Oxford, Basil Blackwell.
Secombe, W. (1974), 'The Housewife and her Labour under Capitalism', *New Left Review*, 83, pp. 3–24.
Secombe, W. (1975), 'Domestic Labour: a Reply', *New Left Review*, 94.
Secondary Schools Examination Council (1939), *School Certificate Examinations*, London, HMSO.
Secondary Schools Examination Council (1943), *Curriculum and Examinations in Secondary Schools* (Norwood Report), London, HMSO.
Sharp, R. and Green, A. (1977), *Education and Social Control*, London, Routledge & Kegan Paul.
Sharpe, S. (1976), *Just Like a Girl: How Girls Learn to Be Women*, Penguin.
Shaw, J. (1976), 'Finishing School: Some Implications of Sex-Segregated Education', in D.L. Barker and S. Allen (eds) (1976a).
Shaw, J. (1977a), 'In Loco Parentis: a Relationship between Parents, State and Education', *Journal of Moral Education*, May.
Shaw, J. (1977b), 'Introduction: a Matter of Opinion', unpublished draft manuscript, University of Sussex.
Shepherd, A. (1971), 'Married Women Teachers: Role Perceptions and Career Patterns', *Educational Research*, vol. 13, pp. 191–7.
Shipman, M. (1972), *Childhood*, Windsor, NFER Publishing Co.
Shorter, E. (1976), *The Making of the Modern Family*, New York, Basic Books.
Silver, H. (1965), *The Concept of Popular Education*, London, MacGibbon & Kee.
Silver, H. (ed.) (1973), *Equal Opportunity in Education*, London, Methuen.
Silver, H. (1978a), 'Education and Social Policy', *New Society*, vol. 46, no. 843, 30 November.
Silver, H. (1978b), 'Education and Public Opinion', *New Society*, vol. 46, no. 844, 7 December.
Silver, P. and H. (1974), *The Education of the Poor: the History of a National School 1824–1974*, London, Routledge & Kegan Paul.
Simon, B. (1960), *Studies in the History of Education: 1780–1870*, London, Lawrence & Wishart.
Simon, B. (1965), *Studies in the History of Education: 1870–1920: Education and the Labour Movement*, London, Lawrence & Wishart.
Simon, B. (1974), *The Politics of Educational Reform: 1920–1940*, London, Lawrence & Wishart.
Simon, B. (1976), 'Contemporary Problems in Educational Theory', *Marxism Today*, June.
Simon, B. and Bradley, I. (eds) (1975), *The Victorian Public School*, Dublin,

Gill & Macmillan.
Simon, J. (1971), *The Social Origins of English Education*, London, Routledge & Kegan Paul.
Smith, T. (1972), *Anti-Politics*, London, Charles Knight.
Sofer, A. (1978), 'Educational Arguments in 1977', in M. Brown and S. Baldwin (eds) (1978).
Spring Rice, M. (1939), *Working-Class Wives*, Penguin.
Steinfels, M.O. (1973), *Who's Minding the Children? The History and Politics of Day Care in America*, New York, Simon & Schuster.
Stenton, D.M. (1957), *The English Woman in History*, London, Allen & Unwin.
Stern, V. and Wallis, S. (1977), *Caring for Under-fives in a Multiracial Society*, London, Commission for Racial Equality.
Stone, L. (1977), *The Family, Sex and Marriage in England 1500–1800*, London, Weidenfeld & Nicolson.
Strachey, R. (1978), *The Cause: a Short History of the Women's Movement in Great Britain*, London, Virago (orig. ed., 1928).
Sturt, M. (1967), *The Education of the People: a History of Primary Education in England and Wales in the Nineteenth Century*, London, Routledge & Kegan Paul.
Summerfield, P. (1977), 'Women Workers in Wartime', *Capital and Class*, no. 1 (Spring), pp. 27–42.
Sutherland, G. (1971), *Elementary Education in the Nineteenth Century*, London, Historical Association pamphlet.
Sutherland, G. (ed.) (1972), *Studies in the Growth of Nineteenth Century Government*, London, Routledge & Kegan Paul.
Sutherland, G. (1973), *Policy-Making in Elementary Education 1870–1895*, Oxford University Press.
Sutherland, G. (1975), 'Women's Long and Unfinished Battle for Equal Status', *The Times Higher Educational Supplement*, 10 October.
Sutherland, M.B. (1977), 'Educating Girls – "To repair the Ruins of our First Parents" ' (Galton Lecture, 1971), in W.H.G. Armytage and J. Peel (eds), *Perimeters of Social Repair*, London, Academic Press.
Szreter, R. (1964), 'The Origins of Full-time Compulsory Education at the Age of Five', *British Journal of Educational Studies*, vol. 13, no. 1.
Tawney, R.H. (1964), *Equality*, London, Allen & Unwin (orig. ed., 1931).
Taylor, G. and Saunders, J.B. (1976), *The Law of Education*, 8th ed., London, Butterworths.
Taylor, W. (1969), *Society and the Training of Teachers*, London, Faber & Faber.
Taylor, W. (1972), 'Family, School and Society', in M. Craft *et al.* (eds) (1972).
Thane, P. (1978), 'Women and the Poor Law in Victorian and Edwardian England', *History Workshop*, 6, autumn.
Thompson, E.P. (1963), *The Making of the English Working Class*, London, Gollancz.
Thompson, E.P. (1978a), 'The State versus its "Enemies" ', *New Society*, 19 October.
Thompson, E.P. (1978b), *The Poverty of Theory and Other Essays*, London, Merlin Press.
Titmuss, R.M. (1968), *Commitment to Welfare*, London, Allen & Unwin.
Titmuss, R.M. (1973), *Essays on the Welfare State*, London, Allen & Unwin (orig. ed., 1956).
Tizard, J., Moss, P. and Perry, J. (1976), *All our Children*, London, Temple Smith.

Tropp, A. (1957), *The Schoolteachers*, London, Heinemann.
TUC Working Party (1978), *The Under Fives*, London, TUC.
Turner, B. (1974), *Equality for Some*, London, Ward Lock.
Turner, B. (ed.) (1974), *Truancy*, London, Ward Lock Educational.
Tyack, D. (1976), 'Ways of Seeing: an Essay on the History of Compulsory Schooling', *Harvard Educational Review*, vol. 46, no. 3.
Vaizey, J. (1958), *The Costs of Education*, London, Allen & Unwin.
Vallance, E. (1974), 'Hiding the Hidden Curriculum: an Interpretation of the Language of Justification in Nineteenth-Century Educational Reform', *Curriculum Theory Network*, vol. 4, no. 1.
Vicinus, M. (ed.) (1972), *Suffer and Be Still*, Indiana University Press.
Vigne, T. (ed.) (1975), *Family History, Oral History*, vol. 3, no. 2 (autumn).
Wakeford, J. (1969), *The Cloistered Elite*, London, Macmillan.
Warwick, Countess of (ed.) (1898), *Progress in Women's Education in the British Empire*, London, Longman Green.
Watts, J. (1978), 'Caught between Money and Morality', *Observer*, 1 October p. 35.
Webb, B. (1915), 'English Teachers and their Professional Organisation', *New Statesman*, Special Supplement, pt 1, 25 September, pt 2, 2 October.
West, J. (1978), 'Women, Sex and Class', in A. Kuhn and A.M. Wolpe (eds) (1978).
West, J. (forthcoming), 'A Political Economy of the Family in Capitalism: Women, Reproduction and Wage Labour', in T. Nichols (ed.), *Capital and Labour*, London, Fontana.
Westergaard, J. and Little, A. (1965), *Educational Opportunity and Social Selection in England and Wales*, Paris, OECD.
Westergaard, J. and Resler, H. (1975), *Class in a Capitalist Society*, London, Heinemann.
Whitbread, N. (1972), *The Evolution of the Nursery-Infant School 1800–1970*, London, Routledge & Kegan Paul.
White, R. and Brockington, D. (1978), *In and Out of School: the ROSLA Community Education Project*, London, Routledge & Kegan Paul.
White Paper (1970), *The Reorganisation of Central Government*, Cmnd 4506, London, HMSO.
Wilby, P. (1977), 'Education and Equality', *New Statesman*, vol. 94, no. 2426, 16 September.
Williams, G. *et al.* (1974), *The Academic Labour Market*, Amsterdam, Elsevier Scientific.
Williams, R. (1961), *The Long Revolution*, Penguin.
Willis, P. (1977), *Learning to Labour: How Working Class Kids Get Working Class Jobs*, London, Saxon House.
Wilson, E. (1977), *Women and the Welfare State*, London, Tavistock.
Wilson, H. and Herbert, G.W. (1978), *Parents and Children in the Inner City*, London, Routledge & Kegan Paul.
Wober, M. (1971), *English Girls' Boarding Schools*, London, Allen Lane, the Penguin Press.
Wolff, J. (1977), 'Women's Studies and Sociology', *Sociology*, vol. 11, no. 1 (January), pp. 155–61.
Wolpe, A.M. (1975), 'The Official Ideology of Girls' Education', in M. Flude and J. Ahier (eds) (1975).
Wolpe, A.M. (1977), *Some Processes in Sexist Education*, London, Women's Research and Resources Centre.
Wolpe, A.M. (1978), 'Education and Employment: a Review of Women's

Position', unpublished paper, for EDC, Middlesex Polytechnic.
Women and Education (Manchester) (1977), 'The EOC and Education', no. 10, pp. 10–11.
Wright, E.O. (1976), 'Class Boundaries in Advanced Capitalist Societies', *New Left Review*, 98.
Wright, E.O. (1978), *Class, Crisis and the State*, London, New Left Books.
Wright, N. (1977), *Progress in Education*, London, Croom Helm.
Wright, P. (1976), 'The Birth of Child-Rearing as a Technical Field and its Importance as a Form of Social Control', paper read at BSA Annual Conference, Manchester, April.
Wynn, B. (1976), 'Domestic Subjects and the Sexual Division of Labour', Course E202, Units 14–15, Block III, Milton Keynes, Open University Press.
Wynn, M. (1971), *Family Policy*, Penguin.
Young, M. and Wilmott, P. (1957), *Family and Kinship in East London*, London, Routledge & Kegan Paul.
Young, M. and Wilmott, P. (1973), *The Symmetrical Family*, London, Routledge & Kegan Paul.
Young, M.F.D. (ed.) (1971), *Knowledge and Control*, London, Macmillan.
Young, M.F.D. and Whitty, G. (eds) (1977), *Society, State and Schooling*, Brighton, Falmer Press.
Yudkin, S. (1967), *0–5: a Report on the Care of Preschool Children*, London, National Society of Children's Nurseries.
Zaretzky, E. (1976), *Capitalism, the Family and Personal Life*, London, Pluto Press.
Zimmern, A. (1898), *The Renaissance of Girls' Education in England and Wales*, n.p., A.D. Innes.

Name index

Subject index

QUEEN MARY COLLEGE LIBRARY